ALBERUNI'S INDIA

ALBERUNI'S INDIA

Translated by

Edward C. Sachau

ABRIDGED EDITION

Edited with Introduction and Notes By

AINSLIE T. EMBREE

The Norton Library

W · W · NORTON & COMPANY · INC ·

NEW YORK

First published in the Norton Library 1971
by arrangement with the Asia Society

PUBLISHED SIMULTANEOUSLY IN
CANADA BY GEORGE J. MCLEOD LIMITED, TORONTO

SBN 393 00568 2

PRINTED IN THE UNITED STATES OF AMERICA

1 2 3 4 5 6 7 8 9 0

INTRODUCTION

Al Biruni, the author of the monumental study of India presented here in an abridged form, is a towering intellectual figure of the Islamic Middle Ages, one of the most splendid eras of human creativity.[1] Although not as well-known in the West as his famous contemporary, Avicenna, the breadth of his scholarship, his insight into the dynamics of society, and, above all, his scientific achievements, have given him a high place in the history of thought. For George Sarton, the historian of science, he was "one of the very greatest scientists of Islam, and, all considered, one of the greatest of all time."[2] He was the author of books on an astonishing range of subjects, including history, geography, physics, chemistry, and astronomy, but the one by which he became best known in modern times is his study of India, known from the title of the translation as *Alberuni's India.* Written early in the eleventh century, it remains one of the most penetrating accounts we have of Indian society. Not for over eight hundred years would any other writer examine India with such thoroughness and understanding, and even in modern times, with all the information now available and with all the new

[1] The pronunciation and transliteration of his name has been disputed by scholars. Most authorities spell it "Al-Bīrūnī," but E. C. Sachau, his translator, preferred "Alberuni." His full name, as transliterated by modern scholars, was Abū Raiḥān Muhammad ibn Aḥmad al-Bīrūnī. In this introduction diacritical marks are not used, except in quotations.

[2] George Sarton, *Introduction to the History of Science,* (Washington, Carnegie Institution, 1927) I, 407.

techniques of research, no one has produced a book at once so objective, so learned, and so compassionate. It is also unique as an historical document, for nothing else from the period remotely touches it in accuracy of observation and breadth of coverage of Hindu society.

Al Biruni was born in 973 A.D. in Khwarizm, near the modern Khiva in Soviet Central Asia. This region, which seems so remote now from the centers of civilization, was then in the mainstream of the great international culture that had grown up as a result of the Islamic conquests. Khwarizm had been part of the Ummayad Caliphate, the great Islamic empire centered on Damascus, but when Al Biruni was born it had long been under the control of the Samanids, a Persian dynasty. Under the Samanids, the Central Asian cities of Bukhara and Samarkand achieved their reputations as unrivalled centers of culture and wealth. Art, poetry, learning of all kinds, were patronized by the ruling classes, including the local rulers of Khwarizm, the Mamunids, who, when Al Biruni was a young man, became independent of the Samanid dynasty.

Little is known of Al Biruni's background or his early life, but he belonged to a social class that had access to the best learning of the time. "I was from my youth possessed with a real greed to acquire knowledge," [3] he wrote in later life. The study of languages was of special interest to him throughout his life. His mother tongue was Khwarizmi, but, as he put it, to try to use such an undeveloped language for scientific discussion would be like putting a giraffe in harness.[4] Nor did he regard Persian, which he knew well, as a suitable medium for scholarship—it was fitted for telling of the exploits of legendary heroes,[5] not for serious scientific discussion. For that only Arabic, the truly international language, would

[3] F. Krenkow, "Bērūnī and the Ms. Sultān Fātih No. 3386," in *Al-Bīrūnī Commemoration Volume,* Calcutta, Iran Society, 1951, p. 195.

[4] Quoted in Seyyed Hossein Nasr, *An Introduction to Islamic Cosmological Doctrines,* Cambridge, Mass., Belknap Press, 1964, p. 110.

[5] F. Krenkow, "Abu'r-Raihan Al-Beruni," *Islamic Culture,* Vol. VI (1932), p. 531.

suffice. Arabic was of value not only because the scientific works of the whole civilized world had been translated into it, but because it was, he insisted, a language that in itself enhanced and improved scientific thought.[6] This insight into the role of a language as something more than a mere medium of communication was characteristic of Al Biruni, the reflection of an approach to the world that we flatter ourselves by calling "modern" but which was very much a part of the intellectual life of his time.

Later in life he learned Sanskrit as the indispensable guide for penetrating Indian society. Apparently long before this he had become interested in India, but his critical approach to data had convinced him that the existing accounts in Arabic were worthless, "second hand information," he said, "which one has copied from the other, a farrago of materials never sifted by the sieve of critical examination."[7] This is perhaps somewhat misleading, for a very considerable amount of Indian learning had already reached the Arabic world. The astronomical works of Brahmagupta had introduced the Arabs to scientific astronomy in the middle of the eighth century, and in the ninth century Sanskrit books on medicine, astrology, and philosophy had been translated into Arabic. But in these early years, Al Biruni's intellectual allegiance was given to the ancient Greeks. He studied Greek, although he did not master it sufficiently to use Greek texts. What was available to him were careful translations in Arabic. For Al Biruni, the Greeks were the people above all others who had excelled in the spirit of inquiry, "promoting scientific things to their utmost degree and advancing them to perfection."[8]

The events that were changing the political structures of Central Asia at the end of the tenth century made their first direct impact on the intense scholarly life of Al Biruni in 995, when the local ruler of Khwarizm threw off his allegiance to

[6] Nasr, *Cosmological Doctrines,* p. 110.

[7] E. C. Sachau, editor and translator, *Alberuni's India,* London, Trübner, 1888, I, 6. Other references will be bracketed in the text.

[8] Quoted in Max Meyerhof, "On the Transmission of Greek and Indian Science to the Arabs," *Islamic Culture,* Vol. XI (1937), p. 27.

the Samanid dynasty. Al Biruni or his family must have been linked with the old power structure, for he apparently had to leave his native city and go to Jurjan in Persia. There he continued his work in mathematics and astronomy, but dynastic change lost him the patronage he needed for his studies, and he returned to Khwarizm in 1012. Another political change occurred in 1017 that profoundly altered the course of his life: the conquest of Khwarizm by one of the greatest figures of the age, Mahmud of Ghazna.

Mahmud of Ghazna (998–1030) was both product and creator of the ferment that transformed political institutions in Central Asia, Persia, and Northern India. He was a Turk, whose ancestors had served as soldiers and administrators in the Samanid dynasty in Persia until they established their own dynasty in the second half of the tenth century, in what is now Afghanistan. Their capital was at Ghazna, and it was from there that Mahmud set out on his wars of conquests that gave him a vast empire stretching from Lahore in North India to Samarkand in Central Asia to Ispahan in Persia. Mahmud lives in Indian history as a bloodthirsty fanatic, a destroyer of temples, and plunderer of their wealth, but in his own dominions he was a patron of art, literature, and science. He brought to his court and the university he established at Ghazna the greatest scholars and writers of the age.

Some of these scholars were slaves, although that word is misleading since it carries with it connotations derived from slavery in America and Europe. Slaves in the contemporary Islamic world were often men of talent, either captured in war or purchased, who served the state in high offices—the ancestors of the Ghaznavid dynasty had been slaves of the Samanids. Others of the galaxy of scholars and artists at Ghazna would have been attracted there by hope of royal patronage. Others would have been somewhere in between in status: not slaves in the technical sense, but neither had they gone of their own free will to Ghazna. They were caught up in Mahmud's net as he searched for talent in the cities he conquered. Al Biruni belonged to this last group. He was already a famous astronomer, mathematician, and philosopher when Khwarizm fell to Mahmud, who took him to Ghazna in 1017. It was not a question of his being led away as a captive; the ruler wanted his presence at his court, and his only hope for continuing his research and writing was to fit into Mahmud's entourage.

Information about Al Biruni's life in Ghazna is scanty and his references to Mahmud himself are veiled and ambiguous. It is the duty of kings, he said, "to free the minds of scholars from the daily anxiety for the necessities of life," but in the present times rulers do not behave in this fashion. (I,152) The reference must be to Mahmud, and Al Biruni's sense of having been ill treated by the great monarch. Yet Al Biruni never whines or complains. Instead, in a passage of great dignity he tells how he worked to gain as much knowledge and information as he could about India, but that it had never fallen to his lot "in my own doings and goings to be perfectly independent, nor to be invested with sufficient power to dispose and order as I thought best." (I, 24)

Al Biruni's "doings and goings" in the years he spent in Mahmud's entourage, from 1017 to the monarch's death in 1030, cannot be followed in much detail. These were the years when Mahmud was making almost yearly raids into the lands of the Indian kings, and it is reasonably certain that Al Biruni frequently accompanied him, probably as astronomer and astrologer. Unlike other chroniclers of the Turkish conquests in India, Al Biruni did not glory in the triumphs of the invaders or suggest that a higher civilization was bringing its benefits to a low one. His judgment of the effect of Mahmud's raids, all the more bitter because of its matter-of-fact statement, was that "Mahmud utterly ruined the prosperity of the country. . . . the Hindus became like atoms of dust scattered in all directions. . . . Their scattered remains cherish, of course, the most inveterate aversion towards all Muslims." (I, 22) It is to the credit of Al Biruni's compassion that he exaggerated the ultimate effects of Mahmud's raids, for Hindu civilization was by no means destroyed. The raids loom very large indeed in modern Indian historical writing, but they were scarcely mentioned in Hindu writings of the time. There is no reason, however, to doubt that he correctly reported the response of Hindus to the invaders, for added to the natural distaste of a conquered people for their conquerors was the peculiar repugnance that Hindus felt for foreigners. "They call them *mleccha*," he said, "impure, and forbid any connection with them . . . because thereby, they think, they would be polluted." (I, 20–21) They even, he went on, frighten their children with the Muslims,, saying they are of the devil's breed. But then, having said this, Al Biruni wryly points out that a depreciation of foreigners, for no other reason than that they are foreigners, "is common to all nations towards each other." (I, 20)

It was against this background that Al Biruni began his great study of Indian civilization, known in the English translation as *Alberuni's India.*[9] However restricted he felt by the conditions of his employment in Mahmud's entourage, he realized the opportunities that were afforded him by his new situation. Not only was he able to travel throughout North India and see Indian civilization at first hand, but many Indian scholars had been brought to Ghazna by Mahmud, just as had Al Biruni himself. Almost certainly contacts with these scholars were the source for much of his information, and from them he must have learned Sanskrit. As he points out in his opening pages, this was a difficult task, because of the immense vocabulary, with many names for the same object and numerous inflections. Another difficulty was that Sanskrit was known only to the educated upper classes, with the language of actual communication being what he called "a neglected vernacular." Al Biruni seems to have been the first Muslim to make a serious attempt to learn Sanskrit, nor did he have a successor until the time of Akbar, five hundred years later.

Indian works on astronomy and mathematics were available

[9] The usual transliteration of the Arabic title is *Kitāb fī tahqīq mā li'l-hind,* but it is often referred to simply as *Ta'rīkh al-hind,* "The History of India."

to Al Biruni in Arabic translations, as already noted, but he mistrusted them, and began to work from the Sanskrit originals. He went far beyond any of his predecessors in the study of works on religion, philosophy, and literature. As far as we know, he was the first Muslim to pay attention to the class of religious works known as the Puranas, vast compendiums of stories of the gods. He knew about the *Mahabharata,* with its account of the great war between the Kurus and the Pandavas, and he quotes frequently from the *Bhagavad Gita,* finding it, as have so many later foreigners, a guide to understanding Indian religion. While he apparently did not know the other great epic poem, Valmiki's *Ramayana,* he was familiar with its story.[10] But he was aware that despite all his labors, he had left much undone, for the Hindus, as he put it, "have a nearly boundless literature," large parts of which he could not study. Within his limitations of time and information, and in line with his special interests, he undertook to translate works on astronomy, including some which had already been translated, such as the basic texts of Brahmagupta, into Arabic.

What was Al Biruni's purpose in writing his study of Indian civilization, how did he justify it to himself, and perhaps to his patron, Mahmud, who, despite Al Biruni's veiled criticisms, gave him remarkable freedom to carry out his work? Perhaps the fundamental motivation was the one Al Biruni had said was the basis of all hard scholarly work: "to earn fame and favour." But given the kind of book he wrote, he clearly did not expect any kind of popular fame. He was a serious scholar, writing for other scholars. He summed up his aim in the last paragraph of his book: he would provide the essential facts for any Muslim who wanted to converse with Hindus, and to discuss with them questions of religion, science, or literature. This was to be achieved "on the very basis of their own civilization." (II, 246) This phrase is the clue to Al Biruni's method and intentions. The Hindus would speak for themselves, through their own literature. Al Biruni was aware how

[10] C. Bulke, S.J. "Alberuni and the Rāma-Kathā'" in *Al-Bīrūnī Commemoration Volume,* p. 78.

easy it was to misrepresent alien religions and philosophies by presenting them in forms that will appeal to one's own prejudices. He felt that Hinduism had been particularly misrepresented in this way, partly because its basic tenets were so different from those of Islam, partly because many of its features, such as idolatry, were so repugnant to Muslims, but also simply because it was so difficult to go to the original sources.

Al Biruni's desire to quote directly from Hindu sources involved a special problem in Muslim historiography. The principal duty of the historian was to show the truth of Islam: what value could there be, then, in studying the history of non-Muslim peoples? It was "a story of errors which could fulfill the great purpose of historiography, that is, to instruct, only in its negative aspect." [11] This meant that those aspects of non-Muslim civilization would have to be emphasized that demonstrated its shortcomings and evils. But such a procedure came in conflict with an equally strong commitment of the Muslim historian: to transmit the exact facts.[12] Al Biruni knew that he would be criticized for presenting the "utterly heathenish" views of the Hindus without any kind of polemical denunciation, but he was compelled to do so, he argued, if he was to be true to his vocation as an historian. (I, 7)

Al Biruni's methodology for the study of Indian civilization was grounded in his passionate concern for truth. Whether he is dealing with astronomy, medicine, geography, or religion, his guiding principle is his commitment to see them from within Indian civilization itself. This meant, first of all, a careful examination of the written documents of the tradition, and for this he had devoted his time and energy to a study of Sanskrit. But Al Biruni knew that knowledge of language in itself would not get him very far: beyond the barrier of language was the greater barrier of thought patterns and ways of looking at the world. Only a willingness to try to see the

[11] Franz Rosenthal, *A History of Muslim Historiography*, Leiden, E. J. Brill, 1968, p. 90.

[12] Ibid., p. 63.

world as the writers of the documents saw it would permit one to understand the implications of their ideas. But Al Biruni was far from accepting documentary evidence as reliable without tests for veracity and authenticity. Texts were corrupt because of careless copyists; the writers sometimes expressed personal animosities; or they might simply have been ignorant of the facts. So aside from documentary evidence, he placed great emphasis on discussion with learned men, noting that he had brought Hindu scholars from remote places to help him understand the texts he was reading. (I, 24) Checking one source against another, looking for different manuscript readings, studying the different uses of the same word depending on its context, he amassed the material that went into his *India*.

Material drawn from textual research bulks large in his book, but Al Biruni did not depend only on the library and the learning of other scholars. He was a scientist, and in his *India*, as in his other books, he made constant use of observation, measurement, and, within the limits of current knowledge, of experimentation. Travelling through the plains of North India, he was struck by the nature of soil, and concluded that the whole area "has once been a sea which by degrees has been filled by the alluvium of the streams." (I, 198) One gets a picture of the traveller seeing what everyone else had seen, but bringing to his own observations that trained intelligence and lively imagination that characterizes the scientific mind.

A combination of observation, wide reading, and imagination led him to express an idea that is curiously similar to Darwin's theory of natural section.[13] The idea occurs in the passage where Al Biruni is discussing the Great War of ancient India, and is apparently the result of his reflection on the cause of struggles in the world. Another idea in the same passage is reminiscent of Thomas Malthus.[14] While procrea-

[13] Jan L. Wilczynki, 'On the Presumed Darwinism of Alberuni Eight Hundred Years before Darwin," in *Isis*, Vol. 50 (1959), pp. 459–466.

[14] Joseph J. Spengler, "Alberuni: Eleventh Century Iranian Malthusian?" in *History of Political Economy*, vol. 3 (1971).

tion can increase indefinitely, the world's resources are limited. To remedy the situation, Providence sends messengers—war or famine—for "reducing the too great number."

Measurement was fundamental for Al Biruni's scientific method. "Counting is innate to man," he declared. "The measure of a thing becomes known by its being compared with another thing which belongs to the same species and is assumed as a unit by general consent."[15] India had a special meaning for him in this area of thought, for long before coming to India he had known of the debt that the Islamic civilization—and the world—owed to Indian mathematics, and, according to George Sarton, his account of Hindu numerals is the best we have from the medieval period.[16]

For Al Biruni the measurement of distances had more than utilitarian value: it was a fundamental way of expressing the truth. The knowledge that came with the study of geometry was of the harmony of nature itself, as shown in his belief that the number of the leaves of a flower followed the laws of geometry.[17] The determination of longitude was of special importance for Al Biruni, as he used it both for measuring distances between cities and for his calculations of the circumference of the earth. (I, 311–313) He had worked on the problem before coming to India, but had not been able to get exact results. Then in North India he found the proper conditions for his researches—"a mountain adjacent to a level-faced plain." He explained how, after first working out the mountain's height above sea-level, "I then imagined the sight line passing on its peak and connecting the earth with the sky, that is, the horizon. I found through my instrument that its horizon inclined from the Eastern and Western lines a little less than one-third and one-quarter degrees. I then ascertained the altitude of the mountain. . . ." From this data he worked out the circumference of the earth to be 24,778 miles, which

[15] *Alberuni's India,* I, 160. This passage is not included in the abridgement.

[16] Sarton, *History of Science,* I, 707.

[17] Nasr, *Islamic Cosmological Doctrines,* p. 127.

is very close to the true circumference.[18]

Another characteristic of Al Biruni's method of studying Indian civilization was through comparisons between Greek and Indian ideas. These comparisons, which bulk very large in *Alberuni's India,* assume that his readers will be familiar with Greek thought. The main purpose of the Greek analogies is to indicate that Hindu ideas, at first glance so strange and even ludicrous, resemble Greek thought. Thus he points out that Plato's *Phaedo* gives an account of transmigration very similar to the Hindu belief. Al Biruni's comparative method has another important function: through observing the Greek and Hindu systems, it will be seen, he argues, that though they have many similarities, the Greeks, unlike the Hindus, had philosophers who were able to distinguish scientific truth from superstition. The point that he is making here and elsewhere is that while Indian thought equals, and in some respect surpasses, that of the Greeks, there is a final lack of discrimination. The Greeks had men, like Socrates, who were willing to die for the truth, rather than to yield to the prejudices of the crowd. The Hindus, he said, had no men of this stamp, with the result that "the scientific theorems of the Hindus are in a state of utter confusion . . . always mixed up with the silly superstitions of the crowd." (I, 24–25)

Using these three methods, Al Biruni ranged widely in his analysis of Indian civilization: geography, chronology, medicine, literature, weights and measures, marriage customs, laws of inheritance. But overarching all these interests was his concern with astronomy, including what we would call astrology, and religion. There are not many chapters of the *India* where some reference is not made to one or the other, indicating that Al Biruni found in Indian civilization an intellectual orientation that conformed to his own temperament and interests.

Astrology has for so long been dismissed in the modern

[18] This translation and a discussion in detail of Al Biruni's work on geodesy is found in S. H. Barani, "Muslim Researches in Geodesy," *Al-Bīrūnī Commemoration Volume,* pp. 1–52.

world as superstition and quackery that it is difficult to take Al Biruni's interest in it seriously. There is no doubt, however, that not only did he believe in the influence of the stars and planets on human affairs, but much of his great reputation in the Islamic world rested on his astrological works, with his book, *Elements of Astrology*, remaining the standard text for centuries.[19] As the *India* and his other works make clear, he had a precise and detailed knowledge of what we would think of as a "scientific" view of the world. He had, for example, an intelligent appreciation of the argument that the world was heliocentric, not geocentric. (I, 276–277) He accepted the geocentric interpretation because it answered better to human psychological and spiritual needs, not because he was unaware of Greek and Indian speculations arguing for a heliocentric universe. Astrology was the science that, quite literally, defined man's place in the cosmos. It linked man's daily life, as well as the rise and fall of nations, in the Great Chain of Being that reached from earth through the heavens to God himself. A modern Islamic scholar has summed up what astrology meant for Al Biruni—and, by extension, for the Hindus:

> The acceptance of astrology by Al Biruni . . . is due to the unitive point of view of this very ancient form of wisdom. This perspective is based on the idea of the polarization of Pure Being into the qualities of the signs of the Zodiac which are the archetypes for all cosmic phenomena. These archetypes are "transmitted" by the intermediate planetary spheres whose last sphere, that of the Moon, synthesizes all the cosmic qualities and as the "cosmic memory" transmits these qualities to the terrestrial domain. The qualities found here on earth are themselves reflections of the heavenly archetypes which are the causes of all the diverse phenomena of Nature.[20]

[19] Nasr, *Islamic Cosmological Doctrines*, p. 165.
[20] Ibid., p. 165.

Al Biruni's attitude towards astrology explains to a considerable extent his fascination with Indian religion. To a Muslim, Hinduism and other religions of India were superstitions, marked by the most blatant idolatry. And yet, as he said in a remarkable passage, all heathenism, whether Indian or Greek, "is only a deviation from the truth." (I, 24) A deviation, not an utter falsehood. In the *India,* Islam for Al Biruni is always *the* truth; but he seems to hint here and elsewhere that heathenism has at least some broken light.[21] Furthermore, Al Biruni recognized that there was a great difference between the high tradition of Brahmanical Hinduism and the popular cults, and he was convinced that it was the beliefs of the educated and the scholarly, not the superstitions of the masses, that should be considered the true representation of Indian religion. It was such insight that led Arthur Jeffery, one of the leading modern students of Islam, to say that Al Biruni's contributions to scientific disciplines have tended to obscure the fact that "he stands unique in his age, and perhaps unique in the history of his faith, for his contributions to the study of Comparative Religion."[22] For Al Biruni, therefore, Hinduism was not, as it was for most Muslims, polytheistic, but it was strongly monistic, stressing the ultimate unity of all things. The soul, bound by ignorance to this world, is entangled in the endless cycle of transmigration, and seeks liberation. (1, 79)

Al Biruni seems to have come in contact mainly with the Vaishnavite sect of Hinduism, and the *Bhagavad Gita,* whose message he finds reminiscent of the Sufis of Islam, obviously appealed to him greatly. Al Biruni says little about his own religious beliefs, but his sympathetic treatment of devotional Hinduism supports the suggestion of the historian, Philip Hitti, that he was "a Shī'ite with agnostic leanings."[23] Al Biruni

[21] The best discussion of Al Biruni's treatment of religion is Arthur Jeffery, "Al-Bīrūnī's Contribution to Comparative Religion," in *Al-Bīrūnī Commemoration Volume,* pp. 125–160.

[22] Ibid., p. 125.

[23] Philip K. Hitti, *History of the Arabs,* London: Macmillan, 1963, p. 377.

has only a few rather uninformative references to Buddhism in India, although he believed that in ancient times it had spread to Iraq and Central Asia. Presumably his silence indicates that Buddhism had already ceased to be an important force in North India, the area he knew best.

Despite Al Biruni's unparalleled knowledge of Indian science, religion, and geography, his *India* exercised very little influence on the thinking of subsequent generations. As noted above, his works on astronomy and astrology were well known, particularly his major study on the subject, *al-Qānūn al-mas'ūdī*. The *India*, however, seems not to have been referred to as a source book for information about India until it was used about 1305 by the Persian historian Rashid al-Din in his famous history of the world.[24]

The selections from Al Biruni's study of Indian civilization presented here are from the translation by the great nineteenth-century German scholar, E. C. Sachau. Sachau tells in his original introduction how he began the long process of translation by first preparing an Arabic text in 1872 and then a German translation in 1885. Two years later he translated it again, this time into English. For a person to whom English was not his mother-tongue, to attempt to translate an Arabic work into English was, he commented, "an act of temerity, which . . . gravely affected my conscience to such a degree that I began to falter."[25] Not only was Al Biruni's Arabic style difficult, but he covered such a range of subjects that Sachau could never be sure that he had understood every passage. Succeeding generations of scholars have worked on the Arabic text of Al Biruni, and much more information about both Islamic and Indian civilization is now available, but Sachau's translation has stood the test of time. The accuracy of his translation has been accepted by scholars, and no one has undertaken the labor of preparing a fresh translation.

What is given here are selections from Sachau's translation,

[24] Karl Jahn, *Rashīd al-Dīn's History of India*, The Hague: Mouton, 1965, pp. ix–xiii.

[25] *Alberuni's India*, Preface I, xlviii; not included in abridgement.

not summaries. Sachau's work has been reduced in half, but his order remains. An attempt has been made to preserve intact all of the material relating directly to India. What has been omitted is mainly Sachau's philological notes, some repetitious portions, some of the many discussions of Greek philosophy, some astrological charts, and lists of technical terms that Al Biruni collected. What remains, it is hoped, will convey something of the drama and excitement engendered as one of the world's great minds met an ancient and alien civilization in a creative encounter.

This presentation of Al Biruni's great work was initiated by the Asian Literature Program of the Asia Society, New York. The Society and the Norton Library deserve the thanks of those who will make their first acquaintance, or renew an old one, with Al Biruni and his *India.*

NOTE: Because this book has been reproduced by a photographic process, the original page numbers are given. When pages are omitted, an indication of their contents is given in a brief summary. The text used in this abridgment is the original edition: E. C. Sachau, editor and translator, *Alberuni's India,* London, Trübner, 1888, 2 vols. A one-volume edition was issued by Kegan Paul in 1914, which was reprinted in Delhi by S. Chand and Co. in 1964. The two-volume edition was reprinted under the auspices of the Government of West Pakistan in 1962.

Ainslie T. Embree
Duke University

ALBÊRÛNÎ'S INDIA

AN

ACCURATE DESCRIPTION OF ALL CATEGORIES OF HINDŬ THOUGHT,

AS WELL THOSE WHICH ARE ADMISSIBLE AS THOSE WHICH MUST BE REJECTED.

COMPOSED BY

'ABÛ-ALRAIḤÂN MUḤAMMAD IBN 'AḤMAD

ALBÊRÛNÎ.

PREFACE.

IN THE NAME OF GOD, THE COMPASSIONATE, THE MERCIFUL. Page 2.

No one will deny that in questions of historic authenticity *hearsay* does not equal *eye-witness*; for in the latter the eye of the observer apprehends the substance of that which is observed, both in the time when and in the place where it exists, whilst hearsay has its peculiar drawbacks. But for these, it would even be preferable to eye-witness; for the object of eye-witness can only be *actual* momentary existence, whilst hearsay comprehends alike the present, the past, and the future, so as to apply in a certain sense both to that which *is* and to that which is *not* (*i.e.* which either has ceased to exist or has not yet come into existence). Written tradition is one of the species of hearsay—we might almost say, the most preferable. How could we know the history of nations but for the everlasting monuments of the pen?

1. On tradition, hearsay and eye-witness.
2. The different kinds of reporters.
3. Praise of truthfulness.

The tradition regarding an event which in itself does not contradict either logical or physical laws will invariably depend for its character as true or false upon the character of the reporters, who are influenced by the divergency of interests and all kinds of animosities and antipathies between the various nations. We must distinguish different classes of reporters.

One of them tells a lie, as intending to further an

interest of his own, either *by lauding* his family or nation, because he is one of them, or *by attacking* the family or nation on the opposite side, thinking that thereby he can gain his ends. In both cases he acts from motives of objectionable cupidity and animosity.

Another one tells a lie regarding a class of people whom he likes, as being under obligations to them, or whom he hates because something disagreeable has happened between them. Such a reporter is near akin to the first-mentioned one, as he too acts from motives of personal predilection and enmity.

Another tells a lie because he is of such a base nature as to aim thereby at some profit, or because he is such a coward as to be afraid of telling the truth.

Another tells a lie because it is his nature to lie, and he cannot do otherwise, which proceeds from the essential meanness of his character and the depravity of his innermost being.

Lastly, a man may tell a lie from ignorance, blindly following others who told him.

If, now, reporters of this kind become so numerous as to represent a certain body of tradition, or if in the course of time they even come to form a consecutive series of communities or nations, both the first reporter and his followers form the connecting links between the hearer and the inventor of the lie; and if the connecting links are eliminated, there remains the originator of the story, one of the various kinds of liars we have enumerated, as the only person with whom we have to deal.

That man only is praiseworthy who shrinks from a lie and always adheres to the truth, enjoying credit even among liars, not to mention others.

It has been said in the Koran, "*Speak the truth, even if it were against yourselves*" (Sûra, 4, 134); and the Messiah
Page 3. expresses himself in the Gospel to this effect: "*Do not mind the fury of kings in speaking the truth before them.*

They only possess your body, but they have no power over your soul" (*cf.* St. Matt. x. 18, 19, 28; St. Luke xii. 4). In these words the Messiah orders us to exercise *moral courage*. For what the crowd calls courage—bravely dashing into the fight or plunging into an abyss of destruction—is only a *species* of courage, whilst the *genus*, far above all *species*, is *to scorn death*, whether by word or deed.

Now as justice (*i.e.* being just) is a quality liked and coveted for its own self, for its intrinsic beauty, the same applies to *truthfulness*, except perhaps in the case of such people as never tasted how sweet it is, or know the truth, but deliberately shun it, like a notorious liar who once was asked if he had ever spoken the truth, and gave the answer, "If I were not afraid to speak the truth, I should say, no." A liar will avoid the path of justice; he will, as matter of preference, side with oppression and false witness, breach of confidence, fraudulent appropriation of the wealth of others, theft, and all the vices which serve to ruin the world and mankind.

I. On the defects of Muslim works on religious and philosophical doctrines. II. Exemplified with regard to the Hindus. Criticism of the book of Erânshahrî. III. Bêrûnî asked to write a book on the subject. IV. He states his method.

When I once called upon the master 'Abû-Sahl ʿAbd-Almunʿim Ibn ʿAlî Ibn Nûḥ At-tiflîsî, may God strengthen him! I found that he blamed the tendency of the author of a book on the Muʿtazila sect to misrepresent their theory. For, according to them, God is omniscient of himself, and this dogma that author had expressed in such a way as to say that *God has no knowledge* (like the knowledge of man), thereby misleading uneducated people to imagine that, according to the Muʿtazilites, *God is ignorant*. Praise be to God, who is far above all such and similar unworthy descriptions! Thereupon I pointed out to the master that precisely the same method is much in fashion among those who undertake the task of giving an account of religious and philosophical systems from which they slightly differ or to which they are entirely opposed. Such misrepresentation is easily detected in a report about dogmas comprehended within the frame of one single religion, because they are closely related and blended with each other. On the other hand, you would have great difficulty in detecting it in a report about entirely foreign systems of thought totally differing both in principle and details, for such a research is rather an out-of-the-way one, and there are few means of arriving at a thorough comprehension of it. The same tendency prevails throughout our whole literature on philosophical and religious sects. If such an author is not alive to the requirements of a strictly scientific method, he will procure some superficial information which will satisfy neither the adherents of the doctrine in question nor those who really know it. In such a case, if he be an honest character, he will simply retract and feel ashamed; but if he be so base as not to give due honour to truth, he will persist in litigious wrangling for his own original standing-point. If, on the contrary, an author has the right method, he will do his utmost to deduce the tenets of a sect from their legendary lore, things which people tell him, pleasant enough to listen to, but which he would never dream of taking for true or believing.

In order to illustrate the point of our conversation,
Page 4. one of those present referred to the religions and doctrines of the Hindus by way of an example. Thereupon I drew their attention to the fact that everything which exists on this subject in our literature is second-hand information which one has copied from the other, a farrago of materials never sifted by the sieve of critical examination. Of all authors of this class, I know only one who had proposed to himself to give a simple and exact report of the subject *sine irâ ac studio*, viz. 'Abû-alʿabbâs Alêrânshahrî. He himself did not believe in any of the then existing religions, but was the sole believer in a religion invented by himself, which he tried to propagate. He has given a very good account of the doctrines of the Jews and Christians as well as

of the contents of both the Thora and the Gospel. Besides, he furnishes us with a most excellent account of the Manichæans, and of obsolete religions of bygone times which are mentioned in their books. But when he came in his book to speak of the Hindus and the Buddhists, his arrow missed the mark, and in the latter part he went astray through hitting upon the book of *Zarḳân*, the contents of which he incorporated in his own work. That, however, which he has not taken from *Zarḳân*, he himself has heard from common people among Hindus and Buddhists.

At a subsequent period the master 'Abû-Sahl studied the books in question a second time, and when he found the matter exactly as I have here described it, he incited me to write down what I know about the Hindus as a help to those who want to discuss religious questions with them, and as a repertory of information to those who want to associate with them. In order to please him I have done so, and written this book on the doctrines of the Hindus, never making any unfounded imputations against those, our religious antagonists, and at the same time not considering it inconsistent with my duties as a Muslim to quote their own words at full length when I thought they would contribute to elucidate a subject. If the contents of these quotations happen to be utterly heathenish, and *the followers of the truth*, *i.e.* the Muslims, find them objectionable, we can only say that such is the belief of the Hindus, and that they themselves are best qualified to defend it.

This book is not a *polemical* one. I shall not produce the arguments of our antagonists in order to refute such of them as I believe to be in the wrong. My book is nothing but *a simple historic record of facts*. I shall place before the reader the theories of the Hindus exactly as they are, and I shall mention in connection with them similar theories of the Greeks in order to show the relationship existing between them. For the

Greek philosophers, although aiming at truth in the abstract, never in all questions of popular bearing rise much above the customary exoteric expressions and tenets both of their religion and law. Besides Greek ideas we shall only now and then mention those of the Ṣûfîs or of some one or other Christian sect, because in their notions regarding the transmigration of souls and the pantheistic doctrine of the unity of God with creation there is much in common between these systems.

I have already translated two books into Arabic, one about the *origines* and a description of all created beings, called *Sâṁkhya,* and another about the emancipation of the soul from the fetters of the body, called *Patañjali* (*Pâtañjala ?*). These two books contain most of the elements of the belief of the Hindus, but not all the single rules derived therefrom. I hope that the present book will enable the reader to dispense with these two earlier ones, and with other books of the same kind; that it will give a sufficient representation of the subject, and will enable him to make himself thoroughly acquainted with it—God willing!

TABLE OF CONTENTS.

CHAPTER L.

HOW MANY STAR-CYCLES THERE ARE BOTH IN A "KALPA" AND IN A "CATURYUGA."

CHAPTER LI.

AN EXPLANATION OF THE TERMS "ADHIMÂSA," "ÛNARÂTRA," AND THE "AHARGANAS," AS REPRESENTING DIFFERENT SUMS OF DAYS.

CHAPTER LII.

ON THE CALCULATION OF "AHARGANA" IN GENERAL, THAT IS, THE RESOLUTION OF YEARS AND MONTHS INTO DAYS, AND, VICE VERSÂ, THE COMPOSITION OF YEARS AND MONTHS OUT OF DAYS.

CHAPTER LIII.

ON THE AHARGANA, OR THE RESOLUTION OF YEARS INTO MONTHS, ACCORDING TO SPECIAL RULES WHICH ARE ADOPTED IN THE CALENDARS FOR CERTAIN DATES OR MOMENTS OF TIME.

CHAPTER LIV.

ON THE COMPUTATION OF THE MEAN PLACES OF THE PLANETS.

CHAPTER LV.

ON THE ORDER OF THE PLANETS, THEIR DISTANCES AND SIZES.

CHAPTER LVI.

ON THE STATIONS OF THE MOON.

CHAPTER LVII.

ON THE HELIACAL RISINGS OF THE STARS, AND ON THE CEREMONIES AND RITES WHICH THE HINDUS PRACTISE AT SUCH A MOMENT.

CHAPTER LVIII.

HOW EBB AND FLOW FOLLOW EACH OTHER IN THE OCEAN.

CHAPTER LIX.

ON THE SOLAR AND LUNAR ECLIPSES.

CHAPTER LX.

ON THE PARVAN.

CHAPTER LXI.

ON THE DOMINANTS OF THE DIFFERENT MEASURES OF TIME IN BOTH RELIGIOUS AND ASTRONOMICAL RELATIONS, AND ON CONNECTED SUBJECTS.

CHAPTER LXII.

ON THE SIXTY YEARS-SAMVATSARA, ALSO CALLED "SHASHṬYABDA." Page 8.

CHAPTER LXIII.

ON THAT WHICH ESPECIALLY CONCERNS THE BRAHMANS, AND WHAT THEY ARE OBLIGED TO DO DURING THEIR WHOLE LIFE.

CHAPTER LXIV.

ON THE RITES AND CUSTOMS WHICH THE OTHER CASTES, BESIDES THE BRAHMANS, PRACTISE DURING THEIR LIFETIME.

CHAPTER LXV.

ON THE SACRIFICES.

CHAPTER LXVI.

ON PILGRIMAGE AND THE VISITING OF SACRED PLACES.

CHAPTER LXVII.

ON ALMS, AND HOW A MAN MUST SPEND WHAT HE EARNS.

CHAPTER LXVIII.

ON WHAT IS ALLOWED AND FORBIDDEN IN EATING AND DRINKING.

CHAPTER LXIX.

ON MATRIMONY, THE MENSTRUAL COURSES, EMBRYOS, AND CHILDBED.

CHAPTER LXX.

ON LAWSUITS.

CHAPTER LXXI.

CHAPTER LXXII.

CHAPTER LXXIII.

CHAPTER LXXIV.

CHAPTER LXXV.

CHAPTER LXXVI.

CHAPTER LXXVII.

CHAPTER LXXVIII.

CHAPTER LXXIX.

CHAPTER LXXX.

CHAPTER I.

ON THE HINDUS IN GENERAL, AS AN INTRODUCTION TO OUR ACCOUNT OF THEM.

Page 9.

Description of the barriers which separate the Hindus from the Muslims and make it so particularly difficult for a Muslim to study any Indian subject.

BEFORE entering on our exposition, we must form an adequate idea of that which renders it so particularly difficult to penetrate to the essential nature of any Indian subject. The knowledge of these difficulties will either facilitate the progress of our work, or serve as an apology for any shortcomings of ours. For the reader must always bear in mind that the Hindus entirely differ from us in every respect, many a subject appearing intricate and obscure which would be perfectly clear if there were more connection between us. The barriers which separate Muslims and Hindus rest on different causes.

First reason: Difference of the language and its particular nature.

First, they differ from us in everything which other nations have in common. And here we first mention the language, although the difference of language also exists between other nations. If you want to conquer this difficulty (*i.e.* to learn Sanskrit), you will not find it easy, because the language is of an enormous range, both in words and inflections, something like the Arabic, calling one and the same thing by various names, both original and derived, and using one and the same word for a variety of subjects, which, in order to be properly understood, must be distinguished from each other by various qualifying epithets. For nobody could distinguish between the various meanings of a word unless he understands the context in which it occurs, and its relation both to the following and the preceding parts of the sentence. The Hindus, like other people, boast of this enormous range of their language, whilst in reality it is a defect.

Further, the language is divided into a neglected vernacular one, only in use among the common people, and a classical one, only in use among the upper and educated classes, which is much cultivated, and subject to the rules of grammatical inflection and etymology, and to all the niceties of grammar and rhetoric.

Besides, some of the sounds (consonants) of which the language is composed are neither identical with the sounds of Arabic and Persian, nor resemble them in any way. Our tongue and uvula could scarcely manage to correctly pronounce them, nor our ears in hearing to distinguish them from similar sounds, nor could we transliterate them with our characters. It is very difficult, therefore, to express an Indian word in our writing, for in order to fix the pronunciation we must change our orthographical points and signs, and must pronounce the case-endings either according to the common Arabic rules or according to special rules adapted for the purpose.

Add to this that the Indian scribes are careless, and do not take pains to produce correct and well-collated copies. In consequence, the highest results of the author's mental development are lost by their negligence, and his book becomes already in the first or second copy so full of faults, that the text appears as something entirely new, which neither a scholar nor one familiar with the subject, whether Hindu or Muslim, could any longer understand. It will sufficiently illustrate the matter if we tell the reader that we have sometimes written down a word from the mouth of Hindus, taking the greatest pains to fix its pronunciation, and that afterwards when we repeated it to them, they had great difficulty in recognising it.

As in other foreign tongues, so also in Sanskrit, two or three consonants may follow each other without an intervening vowel—consonants which in our Persian grammatical system are considered as having a *hidden* vowel. Since most Sanskrit words and names begin with such consonants without vowels, we find it very difficult to pronounce them.

Besides, the scientific books of the Hindus are composed in various favourite metres, by which they intend, considering that the books soon become corrupted by additions and omissions, to preserve them exactly as they are, in order to facilitate their being learned by heart, because they consider as canonical only that which is known by heart, not that which exists in writing. Now it is well known that in all metrical compositions there is much misty and constrained phraseology merely intended to fill up the metre and serving as a kind of patchwork, and this necessitates a certain amount of verbosity. This is also one of the reasons why a word has sometimes one meaning and sometimes another.

Page 10.

From all this it will appear that the metrical form of literary composition is one of the causes which make the study of Sanskrit literature so particularly difficult.

Second reason: Their religious prejudices.

Secondly, they totally differ from us in religion, as we believe in nothing in which they believe, and *vice versâ*. On the whole, there is very little disputing about theological topics among themselves; at the utmost, they fight with words, but they will never stake their soul or body or their property on religious controversy. On the contrary, all their fanaticism is directed against those who do not belong to them—against all foreigners. They call them *mleccha, i.e.*, impure, and forbid having any connection with them, be it by intermarriage or any other kind of relationship, or by sitting, eating, and drinking with them, because thereby, they think, they would be polluted. They consider as impure anything which touches the fire and the water of a foreigner; and no household can exist without these two elements. Besides, they never desire that a thing which once has been polluted should be purified and thus recovered, as, under ordinary circumstances, if anybody or anything has become unclean, he or it would strive to regain the state of purity. They are not allowed to receive anybody who does not belong to them, even if he wished it, or was inclined to their religion. This, too, renders any connection with them quite impossible, and constitutes the widest gulf between us and them.

Third reason: The radical difference of their manners and customs.

In the third place, in all manners and usages they differ from us to such a degree as to frighten their children with us, with our dress, and our ways and customs, and as to declare us to be devil's breed, and our doings as the very opposite of all that is good and proper. By the bye, we must confess, in order to be just, that a similar depreciation of foreigners not only prevails among us and the Hindus, but is common to all nations towards each other. I recollect a Hindu who wreaked his vengeance on us for the following reason:—

Some Hindu king had perished at the hand of an enemy of his who had marched against him from our country. After his death there was born a child to him, which succeeded him, by the name of Sagara. On coming of age, the young man asked his mother about his father, and then she told him what had happened. Now he was inflamed with hatred, marched out of his country into the country of the enemy, and plentifully satiated his thirst of vengeance upon them. After having become tired of slaughtering, he compelled the survivors to dress in our dress, which was meant as an ignominious punishment for them. When I heard of it, I felt thankful that he was gracious enough not to compel us to Indianise ourselves and to adopt Hindu dress and manners.

Fourth reason: Aversion of the Buddhists towards the countries of the West, whence they had been expelled. First inroads of the Muslims into India.

Another circumstance which increased the already existing antagonism between Hindus and foreigners is that the so-called Shamaniyya (Buddhists), though they cordially hate the Brahmans, still are nearer akin to them than to others. In former times, Khurâsân, Persis, 'Irâk, Mosul, the country up to the frontier of Syria, was Buddhistic, but then Zarathustra went forth from Âdharbaijân and preached Magism in Balkh (Baktra). His doctrine came into favour with King Gushtasp, and his son Isfendiyâd spread the new faith both in east and west, both by force and by treaties. He founded fire-temples through his whole empire, from the frontiers of China to those of the Greek empire. Page 11. The succeeding kings made their religion (*i.e.* Zoroastrianism) the obligatory state-religion for Persis and 'Irâk. In consequence, the Buddhists were banished from those countries, and had to emigrate to the countries east of Balkh. There are some Magians up to the present time in India, where they are called *Maga*. From that time dates their aversion towards the countries of Khurâsân. But then came Islam; the Persian empire perished, and the repugnance of the Hindus against foreigners increased more and more when the Muslims began to make their inroads into their country; for Muhammad Ibn Elkâsim Ibn Elmunabbih entered Sindh from the side of Sijistân (Sakastene) and conquered the cities of Bahmanwâ and Mûlasthâna, the former of which he called *Al-manṣûra*, the latter *Al-ma'mûra*. He entered India proper, and penetrated even as far as Kanauj, marched through the country of Gandhâra, and on his way back, through the confines of Kashmîr, sometimes fighting sword in hand, sometimes gaining his ends by treaties, leaving to the people their ancient belief, except in the case of those who wanted to become Muslims. All these events planted a deeply rooted hatred in their hearts.

Muhammadan conquest of the country by Maḥmûd.

Now in the following times no Muslim conqueror passed beyond the frontier of Kâbul and the river Sindh until the days of the Turks, when they seized the power in Ghazna under the Sâmânî dynasty, and the supreme power fell to the lot of Nâṣir-addaula Sabuktagîn. This prince chose the holy war as his calling, and therefore called himself *Al-ghâzî* (i.e. *warring on the road of Allah*). In the interest of his successors he constructed, in order to weaken the Indian frontier, those roads on which afterwards his son Yamîn-addaula Maḥmûd marched into India during a period of thirty years and more. God be merciful to both father and son! Maḥmûd utterly ruined the prosperity of the country, and performed there wonderful exploits, by which the Hindus became like atoms of dust scattered in all directions, and like a tale of old in the mouth of the people. Their scattered remains cherish, of course, the most inveterate aversion towards all Muslims. This is the reason, too, why Hindu sciences have retired far away from those parts of the country conquered by us, and have fled to places which our hand cannot yet reach, to Kashmîr, Benares, and other places. And there the antagonism between them and all foreigners receives more and more nourishment both from political and religious sources.

Fifth reason: The self-conceit of the Hindus, and their depreciation of anything foreign.

In the fifth place, there are other causes, the mentioning of which sounds like a satire—peculiarities of their national character, deeply rooted in them, but manifest to everybody. We can only say, folly is an illness for which there is no medicine, and the Hindus believe that there is no country but theirs, no nation like theirs, no kings like theirs, no religion like theirs, no science like theirs. They are haughty, foolishly vain, self-conceited, and stolid. They are by nature niggardly in communicating that which they know, and they take the greatest possible care to withhold it from men of another caste among their own people, still much more, of course from any foreigner. According to their belief, there is no other country on earth but theirs, no other race of man but theirs, and no created beings besides them have any knowledge or science whatsoever. Their haughtiness is such that, if you tell them of any science or scholar in Khurâsân and Persis, they will think you to be both an ignoramus and a liar. If they travelled and mixed with other nations, they would soon change their mind, for their ancestors were not as narrow-minded as the present generation is. One of their scholars, Varâhamihira, in a passage where he calls on the people to honour the Brahmans, says: "*The Greeks, though impure, must be honoured, since they were trained in sciences, and therein excelled others. What, then, are we to say of a Brahman, if he combines with his* Page 12. *purity the height of science?*" In former times, the Hindus used to acknowledge that the progress of science due to the Greeks is much more important than that which is due to themselves. But from this passage of Varâhamihira alone you see what a self-lauding man he is, whilst he gives himself airs as doing justice to others. At first I stood to their astronomers in the relation of a pupil to his master, being a stranger among them and not acquainted with their peculiar national and traditional methods of science. On having made some progress, I began to show them the elements on which this science rests, to point out to them some rules of logical deduction and the scientific methods of all mathematics, and then they flocked together round me from all parts, wondering, and most eager to learn from me, asking me at the same time from what Hindu master I had learnt those things, whilst in reality I showed them what they were worth, and thought myself a great deal superior to them, disdaining to be put on a level with them. They almost thought me to be a sorcerer, and when speaking of me to their leading men in their native tongue, they spoke of me as *the sea* or as *the water which is so acid that vinegar in comparison is sweet.*

Personal relations of the author.

Now such is the state of things in India. I have found it very hard to work my way into the subject, although I have a great liking for it, in which respect I stand quite alone in my time, and although I do not spare either trouble or money in collecting Sanskrit books from places where I supposed they were likely to be found, and in procuring for myself, even from very remote places, Hindu scholars who understand them and are able to teach me. What scholar, however, has the same favourable opportunities of studying this subject as I have? That would be only the case with one to whom the grace of God accords, what it did not accord to me, a perfectly free disposal of his own doings and goings; for it has never fallen to my lot in my own doings and goings to be perfectly independent, nor to be invested with sufficient power to dispose and to order as I thought best. However, I thank God for that which he has bestowed upon me, and which must be considered as sufficient for the purpose.

The author declares his intention of comparing Greek theories, because of their being near akin, and of their strictly scientific character as contrasted with those of the Hindus.

The heathen Greeks, before the rise of Christianity, held much the same opinions as the Hindus; their educated classes thought much the same as those of the Hindus; their common people held the same idolatrous views as those of the Hindus. Therefore I like to confront the theories of the one nation with those of the other simply on account of their close relationship, not in order to correct them. For that which is not *the truth* (*i.e.* the true belief or monotheism) does not admit of any correction, and all heathenism, whether Greek or Indian, is in its pith and marrow one and the same belief, because it is only a deviation *from the truth.* The Greeks, however, had philosophers who, living in their country, discovered and worked out for them the elements of science, not of popular superstition, for it is the object of the upper classes to be guided by the results of science, whilst the common crowd will always be inclined to plunge into wrong-headed wrangling, as long as they are not kept down by fear of punishment. Think of Socrates when he opposed the crowd of his nation as to their idolatry and did not want to call the stars gods! At once eleven of the twelve judges of the Athenians agreed on a sentence of death, and Socrates died faithful to the truth.

The Hindus had no men of this stamp both capable and willing to bring sciences to a classical perfection. Therefore you mostly find that even the so-called scientific theorems of the Hindus are in a state of utter confusion, devoid of any logical order, and in the last instance always mixed up with the silly notions of the crowd, *e.g.* immense numbers, enormous spaces of time, and all kinds of religious dogmas, which the vulgar belief does not admit of being called into question. Therefore it is a prevailing practice among the Hindus *jurare in verba magistri;* and I can only compare their mathematical and astronomical literature, as far as I know it, to a mixture of pearl shells and sour dates, or of pearls Page 13. and dung, or of costly crystals and common pebbles. Both kinds of things are equal in their eyes, since they cannot raise themselves to the methods of a strictly scientific deduction.

The author's method.

In most parts of my work I simply relate without criticising, unless there be a special reason for doing so. I mention the necessary Sanskrit names and technical terms once where the context of our explanation demands it. If the word is an *original* one, the meaning of which can be rendered in Arabic, I only use the corresponding Arabic word; if, however, the Sanskrit word be more practical, we keep this, trying to transliterate it as accurately as possible. If the word is a secondary or *derived* one, but in general use, we also keep it, though there be a corresponding term in Arabic, but before using it we explain its signification. In this way we have tried to facilitate the understanding of the terminology.

Lastly, we observe that we cannot always in our discussions strictly adhere to the geometrical method, only referring to that which precedes and never to that which follows, as we must sometimes introduce in a chapter an unknown factor, the explanation of which can only be given in a later part of the book, God helping us!

CHAPTER II.

ON THE BELIEF OF THE HINDUS IN GOD.

The nature of God.

THE belief of educated and uneducated people differs in every nation; for the former strive to conceive abstract ideas and to define general principles, whilst the latter do not pass beyond the apprehension of the senses, and are content with derived rules, without caring for details, especially in questions of religion and law, regarding which opinions and interests are divided.

The Hindus believe with regard to God that he is one, eternal, without beginning and end, acting by free-will, almighty, all-wise, living, giving life, ruling, preserving; one who in his sovereignty is unique, beyond all likeness and unlikeness, and that he does not resemble anything nor does anything resemble him. In order to illustrate this we shall produce some extracts from their literature, lest the reader should think that our account is nothing but hearsay.

Quotation from Patañjali.

In the book of Patañjali the pupil asks:

"Who is the worshipped one, by the worship of whom blessing is obtained?"

The master says:

"It is he who, being eternal and unique, does not for his part stand in need of any human action for which he might give as a recompense either a blissful repose, which is hoped and longed for, or a troubled existence, which is feared and dreaded. He is unattainable to thought, being sublime beyond all unlikeness which is abhorrent and all likeness which is sympathetic. He by his essence knows from all eternity. *Knowledge,* in the human sense of the term, has as its object that which was *unknown* before, whilst *not knowing* does not at any time or in any condition apply to God."

Further the pupil speaks:

"Do you attribute to him other qualities besides those you have mentioned?"

The master says:

"He is height, absolute in the idea, not in *space,* for he is sublime beyond all existence *in any space.* He is the pure absolute good, longed for by every created being. He is the knowledge free from the defilement of forgetfulness and not-knowing."

The pupil speaks:

"Do you attribute to him speech or not?"

The master says:

"As he knows, he no doubt also speaks."

The pupil asks:

"If he *speaks* because he *knows,* what, then, is the difference between him and the *knowing* sages who have *spoken* of their *knowing?*"

The master says:

Page 14. "The difference between them is time, for they have learned in time and spoken in time, after having been not-knowing and not-speaking. By speech they have transferred their knowledge to others. Therefore their speaking and acquiring knowledge take place in time. And as divine matters have no connection with time, God is *knowing, speaking* from eternity. It was he who spoke to Brahman, and to others of the first beings in different ways. On the one he bestowed a book; for the other he opened a door, a means of communicating with him; a third one he inspired so that he obtained by cogitation what God bestowed upon him."

The pupil asks:

"Whence has he this knowing?"

The master answers:

"His knowing is the same from all eternity, for ever and ever. As he has never been not-knowing, he is *knowing* of himself, having never acquired any knowledge which he did not possess before. He speaks in the Veda which he sent down upon Brahman:

"'*Praise and celebrate him who has spoken the Veda, and was before the Veda.*'"

The pupil asks:

"How do you worship him to whom the perception of the senses cannot attain?"

The master says:

"His name proves his existence, for where there is a report there must be something to which it refers, and where there is a name there must be something which is named. He is hidden to the senses and unperceivable by them. However, the soul perceives him, and thought comprehends his qualities. This meditation is identical with worshipping him exclusively, and by practising it uninterruptedly beatitude is obtained."

In this way the Hindus express themselves in this very famous book.

The following passage is taken from the book *Gîtâ*, a part of the book *Bhârata*, from the conversation between Vâsudeva and Arjuna:— Quotation from the book *Gîtâ*.

"I am the universe, without a beginning by being born, or without an end by dying. I do not aim by whatever I do at any recompense. I do not specially belong to one class of beings to the exclusion of others, as if I were the friend of one and the enemy of others. I have given to each one in my creation what is sufficient for him in all his functions. Therefore whoever knows me in this capacity, and tries to become similar to me by keeping desire apart from his action, his fetters will be loosened, and he will easily be saved and freed."

This passage reminds one of the definition of philosophy as *the striving to become as much as possible similar to God.*

Further, Vâsudeva speaks in the same book :—

"It is desire which causes most men to take refuge with God for their wants. But if you examine their case closely, you will find that they are very far from having an accurate knowledge of him; for God is not apparent to every one, so that he might perceive him with his senses. Therefore they do not know him. Some of them do not pass beyond what their senses perceive; some pass beyond this, but stop at the knowledge of the *laws of nature,* without learning that above them there is one who did not give birth nor was born, the essence of whose being has not been comprehended by the knowledge of any one, while *his* knowledge comprehends everything."

On the notions of the action and the agent.

The Hindus differ among themselves as to the definition of what is *action.* Some who make God the source of action consider him as the universal cause; for as the existence of the *agents* derives from him, he is the cause of their action, and in consequence it is his own action coming into existence through their intermediation. Others do not derive action from God, but from other sources, considering them as the *particular causes* which in the last instance—according to external observation—produce the action in question.

Quotation from the book *Sâṁkhya.*

In the book *Sâṁkhya* the devotee speaks: "Has there been a difference of opinion about *action* and the *agent,* or not?"

The sage speaks: "Some people say that the soul is not alive and the matter not living; that God, who is self-sufficing, is he who unites them and separates them from each other; that therefore in reality he himself is the *agent. Action* proceeds from him in such a way that he causes both the soul and the matter to move, like as that which is living and powerful moves that which is dead and weak.

Page 15.

"Others say that the union of *action* and the *agent* is effected by nature, and that such is the usual process in everything that increases and decreases.

"Others say the agent is the soul, because in the Véda it is said, 'Every being comes from Purusha.' According to others, the agent is time, for the world is tied to time as a sheep is tied to a strong cord, so that its motion depends upon whether the cord is drawn tight or slackened. Still others say that action is nothing but a recompense for something which has been done before.

"All these opinions are wrong. The truth is, that action entirely belongs to matter, for matter binds the soul, causes it to wander about in different shapes, and then sets it free. Therefore matter is the agent, all that belongs to matter helps it to accomplish action. But the soul is not an agent, because it is devoid of the different faculties."

Philosophical and vulgar notions about the nature of God.

This is what educated people believe about God. They call him *îśvara, i.e.* self-sufficing, beneficent, who gives without receiving. They consider the unity of God as absolute, but that everything beside God which may appear as a unity is really a plurality of things. The existence of God they consider as a real existence, because everything that exists exists through him. It is not impossible to think that the existing beings are *not* and that he *is*, but it is impossible to think that he *is not* and that they *are*.

If we now pass from the ideas of the educated people among the Hindus to those of the common people, we must first state that they present a great variety. Some of them are simply abominable, but similar errors also occur in other religions. Nay, even in Islam we must decidedly disapprove, *e.g.* of the anthropomorphic doctrines, the teachings of the Jabriyya sect, the prohibition of the discussion of religious topics, and such like. Every religious sentence destined for the people at large must be carefully worded, as the following example shows. Some Hindu scholar calls God *a point*, meaning to say thereby that the qualities of bodies do not apply to him. Now some uneducated man reads this and imagines, God is as small as *a point*, and he does not find out what the word *point* in this sentence was really intended to express. He will not even stop with this offensive comparison, but will describe God as much larger, and will say, "He is twelve fingers long and ten fingers broad." Praise be to God, who is far above measure and number! Further, if an uneducated man hears what we have mentioned, that God comprehends the universe so that nothing is concealed from him, he will at once imagine that this comprehending is effected by means of eyesight; that eyesight is only possible by means of an eye, and that two eyes are better than only one; and in consequence he will describe God as having a thousand eyes, meaning to describe his omniscience.

Similar hideous fictions are sometimes met with among the Hindus, especially among those castes who are not allowed to occupy themselves with science, of whom we shall speak hereafter.

CHAPTER III.

ON THE HINDU BELIEF AS TO CREATED THINGS, BOTH "INTELLIGIBILIA" AND "SENSIBILIA."

ON this subject the ancient Greeks held nearly the same views as the Hindus, at all events in those times before philosophy rose high among them under the care of the seven so-called *pillars of wisdom*, viz. Solon of Athens, Bias of Priene, Periander of Corinth, Thales of Miletus, Chilon of Lacedæmon, Pittacus of Lesbos, and Cleobulus of Lindos, and their successors. Some of them thought that all things are *one*, and this *one* thing is according to some *τὸ λανθάνειν*, according to others *ἡ δύναμις*; that *e.g.* man has only this prerogative before a stone and the inanimate world, that he is by one degree nearer than they to the *First Cause*. But this he would not be anything better than they.

Notions of the Greeks and the Ṣûfî philosophers as to the *First Cause*.

Page 16.

Others think that only *the First Cause* has real existence, because it alone is self-sufficing, whilst everything else absolutely requires it; that a thing which for its existence stands in need of something else has only a dream-life, no real life, and that reality is only that *one* and *first* being (*the First Cause*).

This is also the theory of the *Ṣûfîs*, i.e. *the sages*, for *ṣûf* means in Greek *wisdom* (*σοφία*). Therefore a philosopher is called *pailâsôpâ* (*φιλόσοφος*), *i.e.* loving wisdom. When in Islam persons adopted something like the doctrines of these *philosophers*, they also adopted their name; but some people did not understand the meaning of the word, and erroneously combined it with

Origin of the word Ṣûfî.

the Arabic word *ṣuffa*, as if the *Ṣûfî* (=φιλόσοφοι) were identical with the so-called *'Ahl-aṣṣuffa* among the companions of Muḥammad. In later times the word was corrupted by misspelling, so that finally it was taken for a derivation from *ṣûf*, i.e. *the wool of goats*. Abû-alfatḥ Albustî made a laudable effort to avoid this mistake when he said, "From olden times people have differed as to the meaning of the word *ṣûfî*, and have thought it a derivative from *ṣûf*, *i.e.* wool. I, for my part, understand by the word a youth who is *ṣâfî*, *i.e.* pure. This *ṣâfî* has become *ṣûfî*, and in this form the name of a class of thinkers, the *Ṣûfî*."

Further, the same Greeks think that the existing world is only *one* thing; that the First Cause appears in it under various shapes; that the power of the First Cause is inherent in the parts of the world under different circumstances, which cause a certain difference of the things of the world notwithstanding their original unity.

Others thought that he who turns with his whole being towards the First Cause, striving to become as much as possible similar to *it*, will become united with *it* after having passed the intermediate stages, and stripped of all appendages and impediments. Similar views are also held by the *Ṣûfî*, because of the similarity of the dogma.

As to the souls and spirits, the Greeks think that they exist by themselves before they enter bodies; that they exist in certain numbers and groups, which stand in various relations to each other, knowing each other and not knowing; that they, whilst staying in bodies, earn by the actions of their free-will that lot which awaits them after their separation from the bodies, *i.e.* the faculty of ruling the world in various ways. Therefore they called them gods, built temples in their names and offered them sacrifices; as Galenus says in his book called προτρεπτικὸς εἰς τὰς τέχνας: "Excel-

Galenus.

lent men have obtained the honour of being reckoned among the deified beings only for the noble spirit in which they cultivated the arts, not for their prowess in wrestling and discus-throwing. *E.g.* Asclepius and Dionysos, whether they were originally human beings in bygone times and afterwards deified, or were divine beings from the very beginning, deserved in any case the greatest of honours, because the one taught man- Page 17.
kind the science of medicine, the other the art of the cultivation of the vine."

Galenus says in his commentary on the aphorisms of Hippocrates: "As regards the offerings to Asclepius, we have never heard that anybody offered him a goat, because the weaving of goat's-hair is not easy, and much goat's-meat produces epilepsy, since the humours of the goats are bad. People only offer him a cock, as also Hippocrates has done. For this divine man acquired for mankind the art of medicine, which is much superior to that which Dionysos and Demeter have invented, *i.e.* the wine and the cereals whence bread is prepared. Therefore cereals are called by the name of Demeter and the vine is called by the name of Dionysos."

Plato says in his *Timæus:* "The θεοί whom the Plato.
barbarians call *gods,* because of their not dying, are the δαίμονες, whilst they call *the* god *the first god.*"

Further he says: "God spoke to the gods, 'You are not of yourselves exempt from destruction. Only you will not perish by death. You have obtained from my will at the time when I created you, the firmest covenant.'"

In another passage of the same book he says: "God is in the single number; there are no gods in the plural number."

These quotations prove that the Greeks call in general *god* everything that is glorious and noble, and the like usage exists among many nations. They go even so far as to call *gods* the mountains, the seas, &c. Secondly, they apply the term *god* in a special sense to the *First Cause*, to the angels, and to their souls. According to a third usage, Plato calls gods the *Sekînât* (= *Μοῦσαι*). But on this subject the terms of the interpreters are not perfectly clear; in consequence of which we only know the name, but not what it means. Johannes Grammaticus says in his refutation of Proclus: "The Greeks gave the name of gods to the visible bodies in heaven, as many barbarians do. Afterwards, when they came to philosophise on the abstract ideas of the world of thought, they called these by the name of gods."

Johannes Grammaticus.

Hence we must necessarily infer that being deified means something like the state of angels, according to our notions. This Galenus says in clear words in the same book: "If it is true that Asclepius was a man in bygone times, and that then God deigned to make him one of the angels, everything else is idle talk."

Galenus.

In another passage of the same book he says: "God spoke to Lycurgus, 'I am in doubt concerning you, whether to call you a man or an angel, but I incline to the latter.'"

Difference of denominating God in Arabic, Hebrew, and Syriac.

There are, however, certain expressions which are offensive according to the notions of one religion, whilst they are admissible according to those of another, which may pass in one language, whilst they are rejected by another. To this class belongs the word *apotheosis*, which has a bad sound in the ears of Muslims. If we consider the use of the word *god* in the Arabic language, we find that all the names by which the *pure truth*, *i.e.* Allâh, has been named, may somehow or other be applied to other beings besides him, except the word *Allâh*, which only applies to *God*, and which has been called his *greatest name*.

Page 18.

If we consider the use of the word in Hebrew and

Syriac, in which two languages the sacred books before the Koran were revealed, we find that in the Thora and the following books of prophets which are reckoned with the Thora as one whole, that word *Rabb* corresponds to the word *Allâh* in Arabic, in so far as it cannot in a genitive construction be applied to anybody besides God, and you cannot say the *rabb* of the house, the *rabb* of the property (which in Arabic is allowed). And, secondly, we find that the word *'Eloah* in Hebrew corresponds in its usage there to the word *Rabb* in Arabic (*i.e.* that in Hebrew the word אֱלֹהַּ may apply to other beings but *God*, like the word رَبّ in Arabic). The following passages occur in those books :—

"The sons of *Elohim* came in unto the daughters of men" (Gen. vi. 4), before the deluge, and cohabited with them.

"Satan entered together with the sons of *Elohim* into their meeting" (Job i. 6).

In the Thora of Moses God speaks to him : "I have made thee a *god* to Pharaoh" (Exod. vii. 1).

In the 82d Psalm of the Psalter of David the following occurs : "God standeth in the congregation of the *gods*" (Ps. lxxxii. 1), *i.e.* of the angels.

In the Thora the idols are called *foreign gods*. If the Thora had not forbidden to worship any other being but God, if it had not forbidden people to prostrate themselves before the idols, nay, even to mention them and to think of them, one might infer from this expression (*foreign gods*) that the order of the Bible refers only to the abolition of *foreign gods*, which would mean *gods that are not Hebrew ones* (as if the Hebrews had adored *national gods*, in opposition to the *gods* of their neighbours). The nations round Palestine were idol worshippers like the heathen Greeks, and the Israelites always rebelled against God by worshipping the idol of Baal (lit. *Ba'lâ*) and the idol of Ashtârôth, *i.e.* Venus.

From all this it is evident that the Hebrews used to

apply the term *being god*, grammatically a term like *being king*, to the angels, to the souls invested with divine power (v. p. 34); by way of comparison, also, to the images which were made to represent the bodies of those beings; lastly, metaphorically, to kings and to other great men.

Passing from the word *God* to those of *father* and *son*, we must state that Islam is not liberal in the use of them; for in Arabic the word *son* means nearly always as much as a *child* in the natural order of things, and from the ideas involved in parentage and birth can never be derived any expression meaning the Eternal Lord of creation. Other languages, however, take much more liberty in this respect; so that if people address a man by *father*, it is nearly the same as if they addressed him by *sir*. As is well known, phrases of this kind have become so prevalent among the Christians, that anybody who does not always use the words *father* and *son* in addressing people would scarcely be considered as one of them. By *the son* they understand most especially Jesus, but apply it also to others besides him. It is Jesus who orders his disciples to say in prayer, "O our *father* which art in heaven" (St. Matt. vi. 9); and informing them of his approaching death, he says that he is going to his *father* and to their *father* (St. John xx. 17). In most of his speeches he explains the word *the son* as meaning himself, that he is *the son of man*.

Besides the Christians, the Jews too use similar ex-
Page 19. pressions; for the 2d Book of Kings relates that God consoled David for the loss of his son, who had been borne to him by the wife of Uriah, and promised him another son from her, whom he would *adopt as his own son* (1 Chron. xxii. 9, 10). If the use of the Hebrew language admits that Salomo is by adoption a *son* of God, it is admissible that he who adopted was a *father*, viz. God.

The Manichæans stand in a near relationship to the Christians. Mânî expresses himself in a similar way in the book called *Kanz-al'iḥyâ* (*Thesaurus Vivificationis*): "The resplendent hosts will be called young women and virgins, fathers and mothers, sons, brothers, and sisters, because such is the custom in the books of the prophets. In the country of joy there is neither male nor female, nor are there organs of generation. All are invested with living bodies. Since they have divine bodies, they do not differ from each other in weakness and force, in length and shortness, in figure and looks; they are like similar lamps, which are lighted by the same lamp, and which are nourished by the same material. The cause of this kind of name-giving arises, in the last instance, from the rivalry of the two realms in mixing up with each other. When the low dark realm rose from the abyss of chaos, and was seen by the high resplendent realm as consisting of pairs of male and female beings, the latter gave similar outward forms to its own children, who started to fight that other world, so that it placed in the fight one kind of beings opposite the same kind of the other world."

Note on the Manichæans.

The educated among the Hindus abhor anthropomorphisms of this kind, but the crowd and the members of the single sects use them most extensively. They go even beyond all we have hitherto mentioned, so as to speak of wife, son, daughter, of the rendering pregnant and other physical processes, all in connection with God. They are even so little pious, that, when speaking of these things, they do not even abstain from silly and unbecoming language. However, nobody minds these classes and their theories, though they be numerous. The main and most essential point of the Hindu world of thought is that which the Brahmans think and believe, for they are specially trained for preserving and maintaining their religion. And this it is which we shall explain, viz. the belief of the Brahmans.

Notions of the educated Hindus. All created beings are a unity.

Regarding the whole creation (τὸ ὄν), they think that it is a unity, as has already been declared, because Vâsudeva speaks in the book called *Gîtâ:* "To speak accurately, we must say that all things are divine; for Vishṇu made himself the earth that the living beings should rest thereupon; he made himself water to nourish them thereby; he made himself fire and wind in order to make them grow; and he made himself the heart of every single being. He presented them with recollection and knowledge and the two opposite qualities, as is mentioned in the Veda."

How much does this resemble the expression of the author of the book of Apollonius, *De Causis Rerum*, as if the one had been taken from the other! He says: "There is in all men a divine power, by which all things, both material and immaterial, are apprehended." Thus in Persian the immaterial Lord is called *Khudhâ*, and in a derivative sense the word is also used to mean a man., *i.e.* a human lord.

Purusha. I. Those Hindus who prefer clear and accurate definitions to vague allusions call the soul *purusha*, which means *man*, because it is the living element in the existing world. Life is the only attribute which they give to it. They describe it as alternately knowing and not knowing, as not knowing *ἐν πράξει* (actually), and as knowing *ἐν δυνάμει* (potentially), gaining knowledge by acquisition. The not-knowing of *purusha* is
Page 20. the cause why action comes into existence, and its knowing is the cause why action ceases.

Avyakta. II. Next follows the general matter, *i.e.* the abstract *ὕλη*, which they call *avyakta*, *i.e.* a shapeless thing. It is dead, but has three powers potentially, not actually, which are called *sattva*, *rajas*, and *tamas*. I have heard that Buddhodana (*sic*), in speaking to his adherents the Shamanians, calls them *buddha*, *dharma*, *saṅgha*, as it were *intelligence*, *religion*, and *ignorance* (*sic*). The first power is rest and goodness, and hence come existing and growing. The second is exertion and fatigue, and hence come firmness and duration. The third is languor and irresolution, and hence come ruin and perishing. Therefore the first power is attributed to the angels, the second to men, the third to the animals. The ideas *before*, *afterwards*, and *thereupon* may be predicated of all these things only in the sense of a certain sequence and on account of the inadequacy of language, but not so as to indicate any ordinary notions of time.

Vyakta and prakṛiti.

III. Matter proceeding from δύναμις into πρᾶξις under the various shapes and with the *three primary forces* is called *vyakta*, i.e. *having shape*, whilst the union of the *abstract* ὕλη and of the *shaped matter* is called *prakṛiti*. This term, however, is of no use to us; we do not want to speak of an *abstract* matter, the term *matter* alone being sufficient for us, since the one does not exist without the other.

Ahaṅkâra.

IV. Next comes *nature*, which they call *ahaṅkâra*. The word is derived from the ideas of *overpowering*, *developing*, and *self-assertion*, because matter when assuming shape causes things to develop into new forms, and this growing consists in the changing of a foreign element and assimilating it to the growing one. Hence it is as if *Nature* were trying to overpower those *other* or foreign elements in this process of changing them, and were subduing that which is changed.

Mahâbhûta.

V.–IX. As a matter of course, each compound presupposes simple elements from which it is compounded and into which it is resolved again. The universal existences in the world are the five elements, *i.e.* according to the Hindus: heaven, wind, fire, water, and earth. They are called *mahâbhûta*, i.e. *having great natures*. They do not think, as other people do, that the fire is a hot dry body near the bottom of the ether. They understand by fire the common fire on earth which comes from an inflammation of smoke. The *Vâyu Purâṇa* says: "In the beginning were earth, water, wind,

Annotation from *Vâyu Purâṇa*.

and heaven, Brahman, on seeing sparks under the earth, brought them forward and divided them into three parts: the first, *pârthiva*, is the common fire, which requires wood and is extinguished by water; the second is *divya*, *i.e.* the sun; the third, *vidyut*, *i.e.* the lightning. The sun attracts the water; the lightning shines through the water. In the animals, also, there is fire in the midst of moist substances, which serve to nourish the fire and do not extinguish it."

Pañca mâtáras. Page 21.

X.–XIV. As these elements are compound, they presuppose simple ones which are called *pañca mâtáras*, *i.e.* five mothers. They describe them as the functions of the senses. The simple element of heaven is *śabda*, *i.e.* that which is heard; that of the wind is *sparśa*, *i.e.* that which is touched; that of the fire is *rûpa*, *i.e.* that which is seen; that of the water is *rasa*, *i.e.* that which is tasted; and that of the earth is *gandha*, *i.e.* that which is smelled. With each of these *mahâbhûta* elements (earth, water, &c.) they connect, firstly, *one* of the *pañca-mâtáras* elements, as we have here shown; and, secondly, all those which have been attributed to the *mahâbhûta* elements previously mentioned. So the earth has all five qualities; the water has them *minus* the smelling (= four qualities); the fire has them *minus* the smelling and tasting (*i.e.* three qualities); the wind has them *minus* smelling, tasting, and seeing (*i.e.* two qualities); heaven has them *minus* smelling, tasting, seeing, and touching (*i.e.* one quality).

I do not know what the Hindus mean by bringing *sound* into relation with heaven. Perhaps they mean something similar to what Homer, the poet of the ancient Greeks, said, "*Those invested with the seven melodies speak and give answer to each other in a pleasant tone.*" Thereby he meant the seven planets; as another poet says, "*The spheres endowed with different melodies are seven, moving eternally, praising the Creator, for it is he who holds them and embraces them unto the farthest end of the starless sphere.*"

Porphyry says in his book on the opinions of the most prominent philosophers about the nature of the sphere: "The heavenly bodies moving about in forms and shapes and with wonderful melodies, which are fixed for ever, as Pythagoras and Diogenes have explained, point to their Creator, who is without equal and without shape. People say that Diogenes had such subtle senses that he, and *he* alone, could hear the sound of the motion of the sphere."

All these expressions are rather hints than clear speech, but admitting of a correct interpretation on a scientific basis. Some successor of those philosophers, one of those who did not grasp the full truth, says: "Sight is watery, hearing airy, smelling fiery, tasting earthy, and touching is what the soul bestows upon everybody by uniting itself with it." I suppose this philosopher connects the sight with the water because he had heard of the moist substances of the eye and of their different classes (*lacuna*); he refers the smelling to the fire on account of frankincense and smoke; the tasting to the earth because of his nourishment which the earth yields him. As, then, the four elements are finished, he is compelled for the fifth sense, the touching, to have recourse to the soul.

The result of all these elements which we have enumerated, *i.e.* a compound of all of them, is the animal. The Hindus consider the plants as a species of animal as Plato also thinks that the plants have a sense, because they have the faculty of distinguishing between that which suits them and that which is detrimental to them. The animal is an animal as distinguished from a stone by virtue of its possession of the senses.

XV.–XIX. The senses are five, called *indriyâṇi*, the hearing by the ear, the seeing by the eye, the smelling by the nose, the tasting by the tongue, and the touching by the skin. Indriyâṇi.

XX. Next follows the will, which directs the senses Manas.

in the exercise of their various functions, and which dwells in the heart. Therefore they call it *manas*.

Karmendriyâṇi.

XXI.–XXV. The animal nature is rendered perfect by five *necessary functions*, which they call *karmendriyâṇi*, *i.e.* the senses of action. The former senses bring about learning and knowledge, the latter action and work. We shall call them the *necessaria*. They are: 1. To produce a sound for any of the different wants and wishes a man may have; 2. To throw the hands with force, in order to draw towards or to put away; 3. To walk with the feet, in order to seek something or to fly from it; 4, 5. The ejection of the superfluous elements of nourishment by means of the two openings created for the purpose.

Page 22.

Recapitulation of the twenty-five elements.

The whole of these elements are twenty-five, viz.:—

1. The general soul.
2. The abstract ὕλη.
3. The shaped matter.
4. The overpowering nature.

5–9. The simple mothers.

10–14. The primary elements.

15–19. The senses of apperception.

20. The directing will.

21–25. The instrumental *necessaria*.

The totality of these elements is called *tattva*, and all knowledge is restricted to them. Therefore Vyâsa the son of Parâśara speaks: "Learn twenty-five by distinctions, definitions, and divisions, as you learn a logical syllogism, and something which is a certainty, not merely studying with the tongue. Afterwards adhere to whatever religion you like; your end will be salvation."

(Chapter IV, pages 45–49, is a discussion of the relation between the soul and the body.)

CHAPTER V.

ON THE STATE OF THE SOULS, AND THEIR MIGRATIONS THROUGH THE WORLD IN THE METEMPSYCHOSIS.

As *the word of confession*, "There is no god but God, Muḥammad is his prophet," is the shibboleth of Islam, the Trinity that of Christianity, and the institute of the Sabbath that of Judaism, so metempsychosis is the shibboleth of the Hindu religion. Therefore he who does not believe in it does not belong to them, and is not reckoned as one of them. For they hold the following belief:—

Beginning, development, and ultimate result of metempsychosis.

Page 25.

The soul, as long as it has not risen to the highest absolute intelligence, does not comprehend the totality of objects at once, or, as it were, in no time. Therefore it must explore all particular beings and examine all the possibilities of existence; and as their number is, though not unlimited, still an enormous one, the soul wants an enormous space of time in order to finish the contemplation of such a multiplicity of objects. The soul acquires knowledge only by the contemplation of the individuals and the species, and of their peculiar actions and conditions. It gains experience from each object, and gathers thereby new knowledge.

However, these actions differ in the same measure as the three primary forces differ. Besides, the world is not left without some direction, being led, as it were, by a bridle and directed towards a definite scope. Therefore the imperishable souls wander about in perishable bodies conformably to the difference of their actions, as they prove to be good or bad. The object of the migration through the world of *reward* (*i.e.* heaven) is to direct the attention of the soul to the good, that it should become desirous of acquiring as much of it as possible. The object of its migration through the world of *punishment* (*i.e.* hell) is to direct its attention to the bad and abominable, that it should strive to keep as far as possible aloof from it.

The migration begins from low stages, and rises to higher and better ones, not the contrary, as we state on purpose, since the one is *a priori* as possible as the other. The difference of these lower and higher stages depends upon the difference of the actions, and this again results from the quantitative and qualitative diversity of the temperaments and the various degrees of combinations in which they appear.

This migration lasts until the object aimed at has been completely attained both for the soul and matter; the *lower* aim being the disappearance of the shape of matter, except any such new formation as may appear desirable; the *higher* aim being the ceasing of the desire of the soul to learn what it did not know before, the insight of the soul into the nobility of its own being and its independent existence, its knowing that it can dispense with matter after it has become acquainted with the mean nature of matter and the instability of its shapes, with all that which matter offers to the senses, and with the truth of the tales about its delights. Then the soul turns away from matter; the connecting links are broken, the union is dissolved. Separation and dissolution take place, and the soul returns to its home, carrying with itself as much of the bliss of knowledge as sesame develops grains and blossoms, afterwards never separating from its oil. The intelligent being, intelligence and its object, are united and become one.

It is now our duty to produce from their literature

Quotations from the book *Gîtâ*.

some clear testimonies as to this subject and cognate theories of other nations.

Vâsudeva speaks to Arjuna instigating him to the battle, whilst they stand between the two lines: "If you believe in predestination, you must know that neither they nor we are mortal, and do not go away without a return, for the souls are immortal and unchangeable. They migrate through the bodies, while man changes from childhood into youth, into manhood and infirm age, the end of which is the death of the body. Thereafter the soul proceeds on its return."

Further he says: "How can a man think of death and being killed who knows that the soul is eternal, not having been born and not perishing; that the soul is something stable and constant; that no sword can cut it, no fire burn it, no water extinguish it, and no wind wither it? The soul migrates from its body, after it has become old, into another, a different one, as the body, when its dress has become old, is clad in another. What then is your sorrow about a soul which does not perish? If it were perishable, it would be more becoming that you should not sorrow about a thing which may be dispensed with, which does not exist, and does not return into existence. But if you look more to your body than to your soul, and are in anxiety about its perishing, you must know that all that which is born dies, and that all that which dies returns into another existence. However, both life and death are not your concern. They are in the hands of God, from whom all things come and to whom they return."

Page 26.

In the further course of conversation Arjuna speaks to Vâsudeva: "How did you dare thus to fight Brahman, Brahman who was before the world was and before man was, whilst you are living among us as a being, whose birth and age are known?"

Thereupon Vâsudeva answered: "Eternity (pre-existence) is common to both of us and to him. How often have we lived together, when I knew the times of our life and death, whilst they were concealed from you! When I desire to appear in order to do some good, I array myself in a body, since one cannot be with man except in a human shape."

People tell a tale of a king, whose name I have forgotten, who ordered his people after his death to bury his body on a spot where never before had a dead person been buried. Now they sought for such a spot, but could not find it; finally, on finding a rock projecting out of the ocean, they thought they had found what they wanted. But then Vâsudeva spoke unto them, "This king has been burned on this identical rock already many times. But now do as you like; for the king only wanted to give you a lesson, and this aim of his has now been attained."

Vâsudeva says: "He who hopes for salvation and strives to free himself from the world, but whose heart is not obedient to his wish, will be rewarded for his action in the worlds of those who receive a good reward; but he does not attain his last object on account of his deficiency, therefore he will return to this world, and will be found worthy of entering a new shape of a kind of beings whose special occupation is devotion. Divine inspiration helps him to raise himself in this new shape by degrees to that which he already wished for in the first shape. His heart begins to comply with his wish; he is more and more purified in the different shapes, until he at last obtains salvation in an uninterrupted series of new births."

Further, Vâsudeva says: "If the soul is free from matter, it is knowing; but as long as it is clad in matter, the soul is not-knowing, on account of the turbid nature of matter. It thinks that it is an agent, and that the actions of the world are prepared for its sake. Therefore it clings to them, and it is stamped with the impressions of the senses. When, then, the soul leaves the body, the traces of the impressions of the senses remain in it, and are not completely eradicated, as it longs for the world of sense and returns towards it. And since it in these stages undergoes changes entirely opposed to each other, it is thereby subject to the influences of the *three primary forces*. What, therefore, can the soul do, its wing being cut, if it is not sufficiently trained and prepared?"

Page 27. Vâsudeva says: "The best of men is the perfectly wise one, for he loves God and God loves him. How many times has he died and been born again! During his whole life he perseveringly seeks for perfection till he obtains it."

Vishṇu-Dharma. In the *Vishṇu-Dharma*, Mârkaṇḍeya, speaking of the spiritual beings, says: "Brahman, Kârttikeya, son of Mahâdeva, Lakshmî, who produced the Amṛita, Daksha, who was beaten by Mahâdeva, Umâdevî, the wife of Mahâdeva, each of them has been in the middle of this *kalpa*, and they have been the same already many times."

Varâhamihira speaks of the influences of the comets, and of the calamities which befall men when they appear. These calamities compel them to emigrate from their homes, lean from exhaustion, moaning over their mishap, leading their children by the hand along the road, and speaking to each other in low tones, "We are punished for the sins of our kings;" whereupon others answer, "Not so. This is the retribution for what we have done in the former life, before we entered these bodies."

Mânî. When Mânî was banished from Êrânshahr, he went to India, learned metempsychosis from the Hindus, and transferred it into his own system. He says in the *Book of Mysteries*: "Since the Apostles knew that the souls are immortal, and that in their migrations they array themselves in every form, that they are shaped in every animal, and are cast in the mould of every figure, they asked Messiah what would be the end of those souls which did not receive the truth nor learn the origin of their existence. Whereupon he said, 'Any weak soul which has not received all that belongs to her of truth perishes without any rest or bliss.'" By *perishing* Mânî means her being punished, not her total disappearance. For in another place he says: "The partisans of Bardesanes think that the living soul rises and is purified in the carcase, not knowing that the latter is the enemy of the soul, that the carcase prevents the soul from rising, that it is a prison, and a painful punishment to the soul. If this human figure were a real existence, its creator would not let it wear out and suffer injury, and would not have compelled it to reproduce itself by the sperma in the uterus."

The following passage is taken from the book of Patañjali:—"The soul, being on all sides tied to ignorance, which is the cause of its being fettered, is like rice in its cover. As long as it is there, it is capable of growing and ripening in the transition stages between being born and giving birth itself. But if the cover is taken off the rice, it ceases to develop in this way, and becomes stationary. The retribution of the soul depends on the various kinds of creatures through which it wanders, upon the extent of life, whether it be long or short, and upon the particular kind of its happiness, be it scanty or ample." Patañjali.

The pupil asks: "What is the condition of the spirit when it has a claim to a recompense or has committed a crime, and is then entangled in a kind of new birth either in order to receive bliss or to be punished?"

The master says: "It migrates according to what it has previously done, fluctuating between happiness and misfortune, and alternately experiencing pain or pleasure." Page 28.

The pupil asks: "If a man commits something which

necessitates a retribution for him in a different shape from that in which he has committed the thing, and if between both stages there is a great interval of time and the matter is forgotten, what then?"

The master answers: "It is the nature of action to adhere to the spirit, for action is its product, whilst the body is only an instrument for it. Forgetting does not apply to spiritual matters, for they lie outside of time, with the nature of which the notions of long and short duration are necessarily connected. Action, by adhering to the spirit, frames its nature and character into a condition similar to that one into which the soul will enter on its next migration. The soul in its purity knows this, thinks of it, and does not forget it; but the light of the soul is covered by the turbid nature of the body as long as it is connected with the body. Then the soul is like a man who remembers a thing which he once knew, but then forgot in consequence of insanity or an illness or some intoxication which overpowered his mind. Do you not observe that little children are in high spirits when people wish them a long life, and are sorry when people imprecate upon them a speedy death? And what would the one thing or the other signify to them, if they had not tasted the sweetness of life and experienced the bitterness of death in former generations through which they had been migrating to undergo the due course of retribution?"

Quotations from Plato and Proclus.

The ancient Greeks agreed with the Hindus in this belief. Socrates says in the book *Phaedo:* "We are reminded in the tales of the ancients that the souls go from here to Hades, and then come from Hades to here; that the living originates from the dead, and that altogether things originate from their contraries. Therefore those who have died are among the living. Our souls lead an existence of their own in Hades. The soul of each man is glad or sorry at something, and contemplates this thing. This impressionable nature ties the soul to the body, nails it down in the body, and gives it, as it were, a bodily figure. The soul which is not pure cannot go to Hades. It quits the body still filled with its nature, and then migrates hastily into another body, in which it is, as it were, deposited and made fast. Therefore, it has no share in the living of the company of the unique, pure, divine essence."

Further he says: "If the soul is an independent being, our learning is nothing but remembering that which we had learned previously, because our souls were in some place before they appeared in this human figure. When people see a thing to the use of which they were accustomed in childhood, they are under the influence of this impressionability, and a cymbal, for instance, reminds them of the boy who used to beat it, whom they, however, had forgotten. Forgetting is the vanishing of knowledge, and knowing is the soul's remembrance of that which it had learned before it entered the body."

Proclus says: "Remembering and forgetting are peculiar to the soul endowed with reason. It is evident that the soul has always existed. Hence it follows that it has always been both knowing and for- Page 29.
getting, knowing when it is separated from the body, forgetting when it is in connection with the body. For, being separated from the body, it belongs to the realm of the spirit, and therefore it is knowing; but being connected with the body, it descends from the realm of the spirit, and is exposed to forgetting because of some forcible influence prevailing over it."

Ṣûfî doctrine.

The same doctrine is professed by those Ṣûfî who teach that this world is a sleeping soul and yonder world a soul awake, and who at the same time admit that God is immanent in certain places—*e.g.* in heaven —in the *seat* and the *throne* of God (mentioned in the Koran). But then there are others who admit that

God is immanent in the whole world, in animals, trees, and the inanimate world, which they call his *universal appearance.* To those who hold this view, the entering of the souls into various beings in the course of metempsychosis is of no consequence.

CHAPTER VI.

ON THE DIFFERENT WORLDS, AND ON THE PLACES OF RETRIBUTION IN PARADISE AND HELL.

The three *lokas.*

THE Hindus call the world *loka.* Its primary division consists of the upper, the low, and the middle. The upper one is called *svarloka, i.e.* paradise; the low, *nâgaloka, i.e.* the world of the serpents, which is hell; besides they call it *naraloka*, and sometimes also *pâtâla, i.e.* the lowest world. The middle world, that one in which we live, is called *madhyaloka* and *manushyaloka, i.e.* the world of men. In the latter, man has to earn, in the upper to receive his reward; in the low, to receive punishment. A man who deserves to come to *svarloka* or *nâgaloka* receives there the full recompense of his deeds during a certain length of time corresponding to the duration of his deeds, but in either of them there is only the soul, the soul free from the body.

For those who do not deserve to rise to heaven and to sink as low as hell there is another world called *tiryag-loka,* the irrational world of plants and animals, through the individuals of which the soul has to wander in the metempsychosis until it reaches the human being, rising by degrees from the lowest kinds of the vegetable world to the highest classes of the sensitive world. The stay of the soul in this world has one of the following causes: either the award which is due to the soul is not sufficient to raise it into heaven or to sink it into hell, or the soul is in its wanderings on the way back from hell; for they believe that a soul returning to the human world from heaven at once adopts a human body, whilst that one which returns there from hell has first to wander about in plants and animals before it reaches the degree of living in a human body.

Quotation from the *Vishṇu-Purâṇa.*

The Hindus speak in their traditions of a large number of hells, of their qualities and their names, and for each kind of sin they have a special hell. The number of hells is 88,000 according to the *Vishṇu-Purâṇa.* We shall quote what this book says on the subject:—

"The man who makes a false claim and who bears false witness, he who helps these two and he who ridicules people, come into the *Raurava* hell.

"He who sheds innocent blood, who robs others of their rights and plunders them, and who kills cows, comes into *Rodha.* Those also who strangle people come here.

"Whoso kills a Brahman, and he who steals gold, and their companions, the princes who do not look after their subjects, he who commits adultery with the family of his teacher, or who lies down with his mother-in-law, come into *Taptakumbha.*

Page 30.

"Whoso connives at the shame of his wife for greediness, commits adultery with his sister or the wife of has son, sells his child, is stingy towards himself with his property in order to save it, comes into *Mahâjwâla.*

"Whoso is disrespectful to his teacher and is not pleased with him, despises men, commits incest with animals, contemns the Veda and Purâṇas, or tries to make a gain by means of them in the markets, comes into *Śavala.*

"A man who steals and commits tricks, who opposes the straight line of conduct of men, who hates his father, who does not like God and men, who does not honour the gems which God has made glorious, and who considers them to be like other stones, comes into *Kṛimîśa.*

"Whoso does not honour the rights of parents and

grandparents, whoso does not do his duty towards the angels, the maker of arrows and spear-points, come to *Lâlâbhaksha*.

"The maker of swords and knives comes to *Viśasana*.

"He who conceals his property, being greedy for the presents of the rulers, and the Brahman who sells meat or oil or butter or sauce or wine, come to *Adhomukha*.

"He who rears cocks and cats, small cattle, pigs, and birds, comes to *Rudhirândha*.

"Public performers and singers in the markets, those who dig wells for drawing water, a man who cohabits with his wife on holy days, who throws fire into the houses of men, who betrays his companion and then receives him, being greedy for his property, come to *Rudhira*.

"He who takes the honey out of the beehive comes to *Vaitaraṇî*.

"Whoso takes away by force the property and women of others in the intoxication of youth comes to *Kṛishṇa*.

"Whoso cuts down the trees comes to *Asipatravana*.

"The hunter, and the maker of snares and traps, come to *Vahnijwâla*.

"He who neglects the customs and rules, and he who violates the laws—and he is the worst of all—come to *Sandaṁśaka*."

We have given this enumeration only in order to show what kinds of deeds the Hindus abhor as sins.

According to some Hindus, the migration through plants and animals takes the place of hell.

Some Hindus believe that the middle world, that one for earning, is the human world, and that a man wanders about in it, because he has received a reward which does not lead him into heaven, but at the same time saves him from hell. They consider heaven as a higher stage, where a man lives in a state of bliss which must be of a certain duration on account of the good deeds he has done. On the contrary, they consider the wandering about in plants and animals as a lower stage, where a man dwells for punishment for a certain length of time, which is thought to correspond to the wretched deeds he has done. People who hold this view do not know of another hell, but this kind of degradation below the degree of living as a human being.

Page 31.

Moral principles of metempsychosis.

All these degrees of retribution are necessary for this reason, that the seeking for salvation from the fetters of matter frequently does not proceed on the straight line which leads to absolute knowledge, but on lines chosen by guessing or chosen because others had chosen them. Not one action of man shall be lost, not even the last of all; it shall be brought to his account after his good and bad actions have been balanced against each other. The retribution, however, is not according to the deed, but according to the intention which a man had in doing it; and a man will receive his reward either in the form in which he lives on earth, or in that form into which his soul will migrate, or in a kind of intermediary state after he has left his shape and has not yet entered a new one.

Here now the Hindus quit the path of philosophical speculation and turn aside to traditional fables as regards the two places where reward or punishment is given, *e.g.* that man exists there as an incorporeal being, and that after having received the reward of his actions he again returns to a bodily appearance and human shape, in order to be prepared for his further destiny.

The *Sâṁkhya* criticises metempsychosis.

Therefore the author of the book *Sâṁkhya* does not consider the reward of paradise a special gain, because it has an end and is not eternal, and because this kind of life resembles the life of this our world; for it is not free from ambition and envy, having in itself various degrees and classes of existence, whilst cupidity and desire do not cease save where there is perfect equality.

Ṣûfî parallel.

The Ṣûfî, too, do not consider the stay in paradise a special gain for another reason, because there the soul delights in other things but the Truth, *i.e.* God, and its thoughts are diverted from the Absolute Good by things which are not the Absolute Good.

On the soul leaving the body, according to popular views.

We have already said that, according to the belief of the Hindus, the soul exists in these two places without a body. But this is only the view of the educated among them, who understand by the soul an independent being. However, the lower classes, and those who cannot imagine the existence of the soul without a body, hold about this subject very different views. One is this, that the cause of the agony of death is the soul's waiting for a shape which is to be prepared. It does not quit the body before there has originated a cognate being of similar functions, one of those which nature prepares either as an embryo in a mother's womb or as a seed in the bosom of the earth. Then the soul quits the body in which it has been staying.

Others hold the more traditional view that the soul does not wait for such a thing, that it quits its shape on account of its weakness whilst another body has been prepared for it out of the elements. This body is called *ativâhika*, i.e. *that which grows in haste*, because it does not come into existence by being born. The soul stays in this body a complete year in the greatest agony, no matter whether it has deserved to be rewarded or to be punished. This is like the Barzakh of the Persians, an intermediary stage between the periods of acting and earning and that of receiving award. For this reason the heir of the deceased must, according to Hindu use, fulfil the rites of the year for the deceased, duties which end with the end of the year, for then the soul goes to that place which is prepared for it.

Quotations from *Vishṇu Purâṇa* and the Sâṁkhya school.

We shall now give some extracts from their literature to illustrate these ideas. First from the *Vishṇu Purâṇa*.

"Maitreya asked Parâśara about the purpose of hell and the punishment in it, whereupon he answered: 'It is for distinguishing the good from the bad, knowledge

Page 32. from ignorance, and for the manifestation of justice. But not every sinner enters hell. Some of them escape hell by previously doing works of repentance and expiation. The greatest expiation is uninterruptedly thinking of Vishṇu in every action. Others wander about in plants, filthy insects and birds, and abominable dirty creeping things like lice and worms, for such a length of time as they desire it.' "

In the book *Sâṁkhya* we read: "He who deserves exaltation and reward will become like one of the angels, mixing with the hosts of spiritual beings, not being prevented from moving freely in the heavens and from living in the company of their inhabitants, or like one of the eight classes of spiritual beings. But he who deserves humiliation as recompense for sins and crimes will become an animal or a plant, and will wander about until he deserves a reward so as to be saved from punishment, or until he offers himself as expiation, flinging away the vehicle of the body, and thereby attaining salvation."

Muslim authors on metempsychosis.

A theosoph who inclines towards metempsychosis says: "The metempsychosis has four degrees:

"1. The *transferring*, *i.e.* the procreation as limited to the human species, because it *transfers* existence from one individual to another; the opposite of this is—

"2. The *transforming*, which concerns men in particular, since they are *transformed* into monkeys, pigs, and elephants.

"3. A stable condition of existence, like the condition of the plants. This is worse than *transferring*, because it is a stable condition of life, remains as it is through all time, and lasts as long as the mountains.

"4. The *dispersing*, the opposite of number 3, which applies to the plants that are plucked, and to animals immolated as sacrifice, because they vanish without leaving posterity."

Abû-Yaʿḳûb of Sijistân maintains in his book, called "*The disclosing of that which is veiled*," that the species are preserved; that metempsychosis always proceeds in one and the same species, never crossing its limits and passing into another species.

This was also the opinion of the ancient Greeks; for Johannes Grammaticus relates as the view of Plato that the rational souls will be clad in the bodies of animals, and that in this regard he followed the fables of Pythagoras. Quotations from Johannes Grammaticus and Plato.

Socrates says in the book *Phædo:* "The body is earthy, ponderous, heavy, and the soul, which loves it, wanders about and is attracted towards the place, to which it looks from fear of the shapeless and of Hades, the gathering-place of the souls. They are soiled, and circle round the graves and cemeteries, where souls have been seen appearing in shadowy forms. This phantasmagoria only occurs to such souls as have not been entirely separated, in which there is still a part of that towards which the look is directed."

Further he says: "It appears that these are not the souls of the good, but the souls of the wicked, which wander about in these things to make an expiation for the badness of their former kind of rearing. Thus they remain until they are again bound in a body on account of the desire for the bodily shape which has followed them. They will dwell in bodies the character of which is like the character which they had in the world. Whoso, *e.g.* only cares for eating and drinking will enter the various kinds of asses and wild animals; and he who preferred wrong and oppression will enter the various kinds of wolves, and falcons, and hawks."

Further he says about the gathering-places of the souls after death: "If I did not think that I am going first to gods who are wise, ruling, and good, Page 33. then afterwards to men, deceased ones, better than those here, I should be wrong not to be in sorrow about death."

Further, Plato says about the two places of reward and

of punishment: "When a man dies, a *daimon*, *i.e.* one of the guardians of hell, leads him to the tribunal of judgment, and a guide whose special office it is brings him, together with those assembled there, to Hades, and there he remains the necessary number of many and long cycles of time. Telephos says, 'The road of Hades is an even one.' I, however, say, 'If the road were even or only a single one, a guide could be dispensed with.' Now that soul which longs for the body, or whose deeds were evil and not just, which resembles souls that have committed murder, flies from there and encloses itself in every species of being until certain times pass by. Thereupon it is brought by necessity to that place which is suitable to it. But the pure soul finds companions and guides, gods, and dwells in the places which are suitable to it."

Further he says: "Those of the dead who led a middle sort of life travel on a vessel prepared for them over Acheron. After they have received punishment and have been purified from crime, they wash and receive honour for the good deeds which they did according to merit. Those, however, who had committed great sins, *e.g.* the stealing from the sacrifices of the gods, robberies on a great scale, unjust killing, repeatedly and consciously violating the laws, are thrown into Tartarus, whence they will never be able to escape."

Further: "Those who repented of their sins already during their lifetime, and whose crimes were of a somewhat lower degree, who, *e.g.* committed some act of violence against their parents, or committed a murder by mistake, are thrown into Tartarus, being punished there for a whole year; but then the wave throws them out to a place whence they cry to their antagonists, asking them to abstain from further retaliation, that they may be saved from the horrors of punishment. If those now agree, they *are* saved; if not, they are sent back into

Tartarus. And this, their punishment, goes on until their antagonists agree to their demands for being relieved. Those whose mode of life was virtuous are liberated from *these* places on *this* earth. They feel as though released from prison, and they will inhabit the pure earth."

Tartarus is a huge deep ravine or gap into which the rivers flow. All people understand by the punishment of hell the most dreadful things which are known to them, and the Western countries, like Greece, have sometimes to suffer deluges and floods. But the description of Plato indicates a place where there are glaring flames, and it seems that he means the sea or some part of the ocean, in which there is a whirlpool (*durdûr*, a pun upon *Tartarus*). No doubt these descriptions represent the belief of the men of those ages.

CHAPTER VII.

ON THE NATURE OF LIBERATION FROM THE WORLD, AND ON THE PATH LEADING THERETO.

First part: Moksha in general.

If the soul is bound up with the world, and its being bound up has a certain cause, it cannot be liberated from this bond save by the opposite of this identical cause. Now according to the Hindus, as we have already explained (p. 55), the reason of the bond is *ignorance*, and therefore it can only be liberated by *knowledge*, by comprehending all things in such a way as to define them both in general and in particular, rendering superfluous any kind of deduction and removing all doubts. For the soul distinguishing between things (τὰ ὄντα) by means of definitions, recognises its own self, and recognises at the same time that it is its noble lot to last for ever, and that it is the vulgar lot of matter to change and to perish in all kinds of shapes. Then it dispenses with matter, and perceives that that which it held to be good and delightful is in reality bad and painful. In this manner it attains real knowledge and turns away from being arrayed in matter. Thereby action ceases, and both matter and soul become free by separating from each other.

Page 34.

Moksha according to *Patañjali*.

The author of the book of *Patañjali* says: "The concentration of thought on the unity of God induces man to notice something besides that with which he is occupied. He who wants God, wants the good for the whole creation without a single exception for any reason whatever; but he who occupies himself exclusively with his own self, will for its benefit neither inhale, breathe, nor exhale it (*śvâsa* and *praśvâsa*). When a man attains to this degree, his spiritual power prevails over his bodily power, and then he is gifted with the faculty of doing eight different things by which detachment is realised; for a man can only dispense with that which he is able to do, not with that which is outside his grasp. These eight things are:—

"1. The faculty in man of making his body so thin that it becomes invisible to the eyes.

"2. The faculty of making the body so light that it is indifferent to him whether he treads on thorns or mud or sand.

"3. The faculty of making his body so big that it appears in a terrifying miraculous shape.

"4. The faculty of realising every wish.

"5. The faculty of knowing whatever he wishes.

"6. The faculty of becoming the ruler of whatever religious community he desires.

"7. That those over whom he rules are humble and obedient to him.

"8. That all distances between a man and any far-away place vanish."

Ṣûfî parallel.

The terms of the Ṣûfî as to the *knowing* being and his attaining the *stage of knowledge* come to the same effect, for they maintain that he has two souls—an eternal one, not exposed to change and alteration, by which he knows that which is hidden, the transcendental world, and performs wonders; and another, a human soul, which is liable to being changed and being born. From these and similar views the doctrines of the Christians do not much differ.

The different degrees of knowledge according to *Patañjali*.

The Hindus say: "If a man has the faculty to perform these things, he can dispense with them, and will reach the goal by degrees, passing through several stages:—

"1. The knowledge of things as to their names and

qualities and distinctions, which, however, does not yet afford the knowledge of definitions.

"2. Such a knowledge of things as proceeds as far as the definitions by which particulars are classed under the category of universals, but regarding which a man must still practise distinction.

"3. This distinction (*viveka*) disappears, and man comprehends things at once as a whole, but within *time*.

"4. This kind of knowledge is raised above *time*, and he who has it can dispense with names and epithets, which are only instruments of human imperfection. In this stage the *intellectus* and the *intelligens* unite with the *intellectum*, so as to be one and the same thing."

This is what *Patañjali* says about the knowledge which liberates the soul. In Sanskrit they call its liberation *Moksha*—i.e. *the end*. By the same term they call the last contact of the eclipsed and eclipsing bodies, or their separation in both lunar and solar eclipses, because it is *the end* of the eclipse, the moment when the two luminaries which were in contact with each other separate. Page 35.

According to the Hindus, the organs of the senses have been made for acquiring knowledge, and the pleasure which they afford has been created to stimulate people to research and investigation, as the pleasure which eating and drinking afford to the taste has been created to preserve the individual by means of nourishment. So the pleasure of *coitus* serves to preserve the species by giving birth to new individuals. If there were not special pleasure in these two functions, man and animals would not practise them for these purposes.

On knowledge according to the book *Gîtâ*.

In the book *Gîtâ* we read: "Man is created for the purpose of *knowing*; and because *knowing* is always the same, man has been gifted with the same organs.

If man were created for the purpose of *acting*, his organs would be *different*, as actions are *different* in consequence of the difference of the *three primary forces*. However, bodily nature is bent upon *acting* on account of its essential opposition to *knowing*. Besides, it wishes to invest action with *pleasures* which in reality are *pains*. But knowledge is such as to leave this nature behind itself prostrated on the earth like an opponent, and removes all darkness from the soul as an eclipse or clouds are removed from the sun."

Quotation from Plato's *Phædo*.

This resembles the opinion of Socrates, who thinks that the soul "being with the body, and wishing to inquire into something, then is deceived by the body. But by cogitations something of its desires becomes clear to it. Therefore, its cogitation takes place in that time when it is not disturbed by anything like hearing, seeing, or by any pain or pleasure, when it is quite by itself, and has as much as possible quitted the body and its companionship. In particular, the soul of the philosopher scorns the body, and wishes to be separate from it."

"If we in this our life did not make use of the body, nor had anything in common with it except in cases of necessity, if we were not inoculated with its nature, but were perfectly free from it, we should come near *knowledge* by getting rest from the ignorance of the body, and we should become pure by knowing ourselves as far as God would permit us. And it is only right to acknowledge that this is the truth."

The process of knowledge according to *Gîtâ* and another source.

Now we return and continue our quotation from the book *Gîtâ*.

"Likewise the other organs of the senses serve for acquiring knowledge. The *knowing person* rejoices in turning them to and fro on the field of knowledge, so that they are his spies. The apprehension of the senses is different according to time. The *senses* which serve the heart perceive only that which is present. The heart reflects over that which is present and remembers also the past. The *nature* takes hold of the present, claims it for itself in the past, and prepares to wrestle with it in future. The *reason* understands the nature of a thing, no regard being had of time or date, since past and future are the same for it. Its nearest helpers are *reflection* and *nature;* the most distant are the five senses. When the *senses* bring before reflection some particular object of knowledge, *reflection* cleans it from the errors of the functions of the senses, and hands it over to reason. Thereupon reason makes universal what was before particular, and communicates it to the *soul.* Thus the soul comes to know it."

Further, the Hindus think that a man becomes *knowing* in one of three ways :—

1. By being inspired, not in a certain course of time, but at once, at birth, and in the cradle, as, *e.g.* the sage Kapila, for he was born knowing and wise.

2. By being inspired after a certain time, like the children of Brahman, for they were inspired when they came of age.

3. By learning, and after a certain course of time, like all men who learn when their mind ripens.

Page 36.

Cupidity, wrath, and ignorance are the chief obstacles to Moksha.

Liberation through knowledge can only be obtained by abstaining from *evil.* The branches of evil are many, but we may classify them as *cupidity, wrath,* and *ignorance.* If the roots are cut the branches will wither. And here we have first to consider the rule of the two forces of *cupidity* and *wrath,* which are the greatest and most pernicious enemies of man, deluding him by the pleasure of eating and the delight of revenge, whilst in reality they are much more likely to lead him into pains and crimes. They make a man similar to the wild beasts and the cattle, nay, even to the demons and devils.

Next we have to consider that man must prefer the reasoning force of mind, by which he becomes similar to the highest angels, to the forces of cupidity and wrath; and, lastly, that he must turn away from the actions of the world. He cannot, however, *give up* these actions unless he does away with their causes, which are his lust and ambition. Thereby the second of the *three primary forces* is cut away. However, the abstaining *from action* takes place in two different ways:—

1. By laziness, procrastination, and ignorance according to the *third force*. This mode is not desirable, for it will lead to a blamable end.

2. By judicious selection and by preferring that which is better to that which is good, which way leads to a laudable end.

The abstaining from actions is rendered perfect in this way, that a man quits anything that might occupy him and shuts himself up against it. Thereby he will be enabled to restrain his senses from extraneous objects to such a degree that he does not any more know that there exists anything besides himself, and be enabled to stop all motions, and even the breathing. It is evident that a greedy man strains to effect his object, the man who strains becomes tired, and the tired man pants; so the panting is the result of greediness. If this greediness is removed, the breathing becomes like the breathing of a being living at the bottom of the sea, that does not want breath; and then the heart quietly rests on one thing, viz. the search for liberation and for arriving at the absolute unity.

Further quotations from *Gîtâ*.

In the book *Gîtâ* we read: "How is a man to obtain liberation who disperses his heart and does not concentrate it alone upon God, who does not exclusively direct his action towards him? But if a man turns away his cogitation from all other things and concentrates it upon the One, the light of his heart will be steady like the light of a lamp filled with clean oil, standing in a corner where no wind makes it flicker, and he will be occupied in such a degree as not to perceive anything that gives pain, like heat or cold, knowing that everything besides the One, *the Truth*, is a vain phantom."

In the same book we read: "Pain and pleasure have no effect on the real world, just as the continuous flow of the streams to the ocean does not affect its water. How could anybody ascend this mountain pass save him who has conquered *cupidity* and *wrath* and rendered them inert?"

On account of what we have explained it is necessary that cogitation should be continuous, not in any way to be defined by number; for a number always denotes *repeated times*, and repeated times presuppose a break in the cogitation occurring between two consecutive times. This would interrupt the continuity, and would prevent cogitation becoming united with the object of cogitation. And this is not the object kept in view, which is, on the contrary, *the continuity of cogitation.*

This goal is attained either in a *single shape, i.e.* a single stage of metempsychosis, or *in several shapes*, in this way, that a man perpetually practises virtuous behaviour and accustoms the soul thereto, so that this virtuous behaviour becomes to it a nature and an essential quality.

The nine commandments of the Hindu religion.

Virtuous behaviour is that which is prescribed by the religious law. Its principal laws, from which they derive many secondary ones, may be summed up in the following nine rules:—

1. A man shall not kill.
2. Nor lie.
3. Nor steal.
4. Nor whore.
5. Nor hoard up treasures. Page 37.
6. He is perpetually to practise holiness and purity.
7. He is to perform the prescribed fasting without an interruption and to dress poorly.

8. He is to hold fast to the adoration of God with praise and thanks.

9. He is always to have in mind the word *ôm*, the word of creation, without pronouncing it.

The injunction to abstain from killing as regards animals (No. 1) is only a special part of the general order to *abstain from doing anything hurtful.* Under this head falls also the robbing of another man's goods (No. 3), and the telling lies (No. 2), not to mention the foulness and baseness of so doing.

The abstaining from hoarding up (No. 5) means that a man is to give up toil and fatigue; that he who seeks the bounty of God feels sure that he is provided for; and that, starting from the base slavery of material life, we may, by the noble liberty of cogitation, attain eternal bliss.

Practising purity (No. 6) implies that a man knows the filth of the body, and that he feels called upon to hate it, and to love cleanness of soul. Tormenting oneself by poor dress (No. 7) means that a man should reduce the body, allay its feverish desires, and sharpen its senses. Pythagoras once said to a man who took great care to keep his body in a flourishing condition and to allow it everything it desired, "Thou art not lazy in building thy prison and making thy fetter as strong as possible."

The holding fast to meditation on God and the angels means a kind of familiar intercourse with them. The book *Sâṁkhya* says: "Man cannot go beyond anything in the wake of which he marches, it being a scope to him (*i.e.* thus engrossing his thoughts and detaining him from meditation on God)." The book *Gîtâ* says: "All that which is the object of a man's continuous meditating and bearing in mind is stamped upon him, so that he even unconsciously is guided by it. Since, now, the time of death is the time of remembering what we love, the soul on leaving the body is united with that object which we love, and is changed into it."

However, the reader must not believe that it is only the union of the soul with any forms of life that perish and return into existence that is perfect *liberation*, for the same book, *Gîtâ*, says: "He who knows when dying that God is everything, and that from him everything proceeds, *is liberated*, though his degree be lower than that of the saints."

Quotations from *Gîtâ*.

The same book says: "Seek deliverance from this world by abstaining from any connection with its follies, by having sincere intentions in all actions and when making offerings by fire to God, without any desire for reward and recompense; further, by keeping aloof from mankind." The real meaning of all this is that you should not prefer one because he is your friend to another because he is your enemy, and that you should beware of negligence in sleeping when others are awake, and in waking when others are asleep; for this, too, is a kind of being *absent* from them, though outwardly you are *present* with them. Further: Seek deliverance by guarding soul from soul, for the soul is an enemy if it be addicted to lusts; but what an excellent friend it is when it is *chaste!*"

Greek and Ṣûfî parallels.

Socrates, caring little for his impending death and being glad at the prospect of coming to his Lord, said: "My degree must not be considered by any one of you lower than that of the swan," of which people say that it is the bird of Apollo, the sun, and that it therefore knows what is hidden; that is, when feeling that it will soon die, sings more and more melodies from joy at the prospect of coming to its Lord. "At least my joy at my prospect of coming to the object of my adoration must not be less than the joy of this bird."

For similar reasons the Ṣûfî define *love* as being engrossed by the creature to the exclusion of God.

Second part: The *practical* path leading to Moksha

In the book of *Patañjali* we read: "We divide the path of liberation into three parts:—

"I. *The practical one* (*kriyâ-yoga*), a process of habituating the senses in a gentle way to detach themselves from the external world, and to concentrate themselves upon the internal one, so that they exclusively occupy themselves with God. This is in general the path of him who does not desire anything save what is sufficient to sustain life."

according to *Patañjali*, *Vishṇu-Dharma*, and *Gîtâ*.

Page 38.

In the book *Vishṇu-Dharma* we read: "The king Parîksha, of the family of Bhṛigu, asked Śatânîka, the head of an assembly of sages, who stayed with him, for the explanation of some notion regarding the deity, and by way of answer the sage communicated what *he* had heard from Śaunaka, Śaunaka from Uśanas, and Uśanas from Brahman, as follows: 'God is without first and without last; he has not been born from anything, and he has not borne anything save that of which it is impossible to say that it is *He*, and just as impossible to say that it is *Not-he*. How should I be able to ponder on the absolute good which is an outflow of his benevolence, and of the absolute bad which is a product of his wrath; and how could I know him so as to worship him as is his due, save by turning away from the world in general and by occupying myself exclusively with him, by perpetually cogitating on him?'

"It was objected to him: 'Man is weak and his life is a trifling matter. He can hardly bring himself to abstain from the necessities of life, and this prevents him from walking on the path of liberation. If we were living in the *first* age of mankind, when life extended to thousands of years, and when the world was good because of the non-existence of evil, we might hope that that which is necessary on this path should be done. But since we live in the *last* age, what, according to your opinion, is there in this revolving world that might protect him against the floods of the ocean and save him from drowning?'

"Thereupon Brahman spoke: 'Man wants nourishment, shelter, and clothing. Therefore in *them* there is no harm to him. But happiness is only to be found in abstaining from things besides them, from superfluous and fatiguing actions. Worship God, him alone, and venerate him; approach him in the place of worship with presents like perfumes and flowers; praise him and attach your heart to him so that it never leaves him. Give alms to the Brahmans and to others, and vow to God vows—special ones, like the abstaining from meat; general ones, like fasting. Vow to him animals which you must not hold to be something different from yourselves, so as to feel entitled to kill them. Know that he is everything. Therefore, whatever you do, let it be for his sake; and if you enjoy anything of the vanities of the world, do not forget him in your intentions. If you aim at the fear of God and the faculty of worshipping him, thereby you will obtain liberation, not by anything else.' "

The book *Gîtâ* says: "He who mortifies his lust does not go beyond the necessary wants; and he who is content with that which is sufficient for the sustaining of life will not be ashamed nor be despised."

The same book says: "If man is not without wants as regards the demands of human nature, if he wants nourishment to appease thereby the heat of hunger and exhaustion, sleep in order to meet the injurious influences of fatiguing motions and a couch to rest upon, let the latter be clean and smooth, everywhere equally high above the ground and sufficiently large that he may stretch out his body upon it. Let him have a place of temperate climate, not hurtful by cold nor by heat, and where he is safe against the approach of reptiles. All this helps him to sharpen the functions of his heart, that he may without any interruption concentrate his cogitation on the unity. For all things besides the necessities of life in the way of eating and clothing are pleasures of a kind which, in reality, are disguised pains. To acquiesce in them is impossible, and would end in the gravest inconvenience. There is pleasure only to him who kills the two intolerable enemies, *lust* and *wrath*, already during his life and not when he dies, who derives his rest and bliss from within, not from without; and who, in the final result, is able altogether to dispense with his senses." Page 39.

Vâsudeva spoke to Arjuna: "If you want the absolute good, take care of the nine doors of thy body, and know what is going in and out through them. Constrain thy heart from dispersing its thoughts, and quiet thy soul by thinking of the upper membrane of the child's brain, which is first soft, and then is closed and becomes strong, so that it would seem that there were no more need of it. Do not take perception of the senses for anything but the nature immanent in their organs, and therefore beware of following it."

The path of renunciation as the second part of the path of liberation according to *Gîtâ*.

II. The second part of the path of liberation is renunciation (the *via omissionis*), based on the knowledge of the evil which exists in the changing things of creation and their vanishing shapes. In consequence the heart shuns them, the longing for them ceases, and a man is raised above the *three primary forces* which are the cause of actions and of their diversity. For he who accurately understands the affairs of the world knows that the good ones among them are evil in reality, and that the bliss which they afford changes in the course of recompense into pains. Therefore he avoids everything which might aggravate his condition of being entangled in the world, and which might result in making him stay in the world for a still longer period.

The book *Gîtâ* says: "Men err in what is ordered and what is forbidden. They do not know how to distinguish between good and evil in actions. Therefore, giving up acting altogether and keeping aloof from it, this is *the* action."

The same book says: "The purity of knowledge is high above the purity of all other things, for by knowledge ignorance is rooted out and certainty is gained in exchange for doubt, which is a means of torture, for there is no rest for him who doubts."

It is evident from this that the first part of the path of liberation is instrumental to the second one.

Worship as the third part of the path of liberation according to *Gîtâ*.

III. The third part of the path of liberation which is to be considered as instrumental to the preceding two is *worship*, for this purpose, that God should help a man to obtain liberation, and deign to consider him worthy of such a shape of existence in the metempsychosis in which he may effect his progress towards beatitude.

The author of the book *Gîtâ* distributes the duties of worship among the *body*, the *voice*, and the *heart*.

What the *body* has to do is fasting, prayer, the fulfilment of the law, the service towards the angels and the sages among the Brahmans, keeping clean the body, keeping aloof from killing under all circumstances, and never looking at another man's wife and other property.

What the *voice* has to do is the reciting of the holy texts, praising God, always to speak the truth, to address people mildly, to guide them, and to order them to do good.

What the *heart* has to do is to have straight, honest intentions, to avoid haughtiness, always to be patient, to keep your senses under control, and to have a cheerful mind.

On Rasâyana as a path leading to Moksha.

The author (Patañjali) adds to the three parts of the path of liberation a fourth one of an illusory nature, called *Rasâyana*, consisting of alchemistic tricks with various drugs, intended to realise things which by nature are impossible. We shall speak of these things afterwards (*vide* chap. xvii.) They have no other relation to the theory of *Moksha* but this, that also in the tricks of Rasâyana everything depends upon the intention, the well-understood determination to carry them out, this determination resting on the firm belief in them, and resulting in the endeavour to realise them.

According to the Hindus, liberation is union with God; for they describe God as a being who can dispense with hoping for a recompense or with fearing opposition, unattainable to thought, because he is sublime beyond all unlikeness which is abhorrent and all likeness which is sympathetic, knowing himself not by a knowledge which comes to him like an accident, regarding something which had not in every phase before been known to him. And this same description the Hindus apply to *the liberated one*, for he is equal to God in all these things except in the matter of beginning, since he has not existed from all eternity, and except this, that before liberation he existed in *the world of entanglement*, knowing the objects of knowledge only by a phantasmagoric kind of knowing which he had acquired by absolute exertion, whilst the object of his knowing is still covered, as it were, by a veil. On the contrary, in the world of liberation all veils are lifted, all covers taken off, and obstacles removed. There the being is absolutely knowing, not desirous of learning anything unknown, separated from the soiled perceptions of the senses, united with the everlasting ideas. Therefore in the end of the book of *Patañjali*, after the pupil has asked about the nature of liberation, the master says: "If you wish, say, Liberation is the cessation of the functions of *the three forces*, and their returning to that home whence they had come. Or if you wish, say, It is the return of the soul as a *knowing* being into its own nature."

On the nature of Moksha itself.

Page 40.

Quotations from *Patañjali*.

The two men, pupil and master, disagree regarding him who has arrived at the stage of liberation. The anchorite asks in the book of Sâṁkhya, "Why does not *death* take place when *action* ceases?" The sage replies, "Because the cause of the separation is a certain condition of the soul whilst the spirit is still in the body. Soul and body are separated by a natural condition which severs their union. Frequently when

From *Sâṁkhya*.

the cause of an effect has already ceased or disappeared, the effect itself still goes on for a certain time, slackening, and by and by decreasing, till in the end it ceases totally; *e.g.* the silk-weaver drives round his wheel with his mallet until it whirls round rapidly, then he leaves it; however, it does not stand still, though the mallet that drove it round has been removed; the motion of the wheel decreases by little and little, and finally it ceases. It is the same case with the body. After the action of the body has ceased, its effect is still lasting until it arrives, through the various stages of motion and of rest, at the cessation of physical force and of the effect which had originated from preceding causes. Thus liberation is finished when the body has been completely prostrated."

From *Patañjali.*

In the book of Patañjali there is a passage which expresses similar ideas. Speaking of a man who restrains his senses and organs of perception, as the turtle draws in its limbs when it is afraid, he says that "he is not fettered, because the fetter has been loosened, and he is not liberated, because his body is still with him."

There is, however, another passage in the same book which does not agree with the theory of liberation as expounded above. He says: "The bodies are the snares of the souls for the purpose of acquiring recompense. He who arrives at the stage of liberation has acquired, in his actual form of existence, the recompense for all the doings of the past. Then he ceases to labour to acquire a title to a recompense in the future. He frees himself from the snare; he can dispense with the particular form of his existence, and moves in it quite freely without being ensnared by it. He has even the faculty of moving wherever he likes, and if he like, he might rise above the face of death. For the thick, cohesive bodies cannot oppose an obstacle to his *form* of existence (as, *e.g.* a mountain could not prevent him from passing through). How, then, could his body oppose an obstacle to his soul?"

Ṣûfî parallels.

Similar views are also met with among the Ṣûfî. Some Ṣûfî author relates the following story: "A company of Ṣûfî came down unto us, and sat down at some distance from us. Then one of them rose, prayed, and on having finished his prayer, turned towards me and spoke: 'O master, do you know here a place fit for us *to die* on?' Now I thought he meant *sleeping*, and so I pointed out to him a place. The man went there, threw himself on the back of his head, and remained motionless. Now I rose, went to him and shook him, but lo! he was already cold."

Page 41.

The Ṣûfî explain the Koranic verse, "We have made room for him on earth" (Sûra 18, 83), in this way: "If he wishes, the earth rolls itself up for him; if he wishes, he can walk on the water and in the air, which offer him sufficient resistance so as to enable him to walk, whilst the mountains do not offer him any resistance when he wants to pass through them."

On those who do not reach Moksha according to *Sâṁkhya*.

We next speak of those who, notwithstanding their greatest exertions, do not reach the stage of liberation. There are several classes of them. The book *Sâṁkhya* says: "He who enters upon the world with a virtuous character, who is liberal with what he possesses of the goods of the world, is recompensed in it in this way, that he obtains the fulfilment of his wishes and desires, that he moves about in the world in happiness, happy in body and soul and in all other conditions of life. For in reality good fortune is a recompense for former deeds, done either in the same shape or in some preceding shape. Whoso lives in this world piously but without knowledge will be raised and be rewarded, but not be liberated, because the means of attaining it are wanting in his case. Whoso is content and acquiesces in possessing the faculty of practising the above-mentioned eight commandments (*sic*, *vide* p. 74), whoso glories in them, is successful by means of them, and believes that *they* are liberation, will remain in the same stage."

A parable showing people in the various degrees of knowledge.

The following is a parable characterising those who vie with each other in the progress through the various stages of knowledge:—A man is travelling together with his pupils for some business or other towards the end of the night. Then there appears something standing erect before them on the road, the nature of which it is impossible to recognise on account of the darkness of night. The man turns towards his pupils, and asks them, one after the other, what it is? The first says: "I do not know what it is." The second says: "I do not know, and I have no means of learning what it is." The third says: "It is useless to examine what it is, for the rising of the day will reveal it. If it is something terrible, it will disappear at daybreak; if it is something else, the nature of the thing will anyhow be clear to us." Now, none of them had attained to knowledge, the first, because he was ignorant; the second, because he was incapable, and had no means of knowing; the third, because he was indolent and acquiesced in his ignorance.

The fourth pupil, however, did not give an answer. He stood still, and then he went on in the direction of the object. On coming near, he found that it was pumpkins on which there lay a tangled mass of something. Now he knew that a living man, endowed with free will, does not stand still in his place until such a tangled mass is formed on his head, and he recognised at once that it was a lifeless object standing erect. Further, he could not be sure if it was not a hidden place for some dunghill. So he went quite close to it, struck against it with his foot till it fell to the ground. Thus all doubt having been removed, he returned to his master and gave him the exact account. In such a way the master obtained the knowledge through the intermediation of his pupils.

With regard to similar views of the ancient Greeks we can quote Ammonius, who relates the following as a sentence of Pythagoras: "Let your desire and exertion in this world be directed towards the union with *the First Cause,* which is the cause of the cause of your existence, that you may endure for ever. You will be saved from destruction and from being wiped out; you will go to the world of the true sense, of the true joy, of the true glory, in everlasting joy and pleasures." Parallels from Greek authors, Ammonius, Plato, and Proclus.

Further, Pythagoras says: "How can you hope for the state of detachment as long as you are clad in bodies? And how will you obtain liberation as long as you are incarcerated in them?"

Ammonius relates: "Empedocles and his successors as far as Heracles (*sic*) think that the soiled souls always remain commingled with the world until they ask the universal soul for help. The universal soul intercedes for it with the *Intelligence,* the latter with the Creator. The Creator affords something of his light to Intelligence; Intelligence affords something of it to the universal soul, which is immanent in this world. Now the soul wishes to be enlightened by Intelligence, until at last the individual soul recognises the universal soul, unites with it, and is attached to its world. But this is a process over which many ages must pass. Then the soul comes to a region where there is neither place nor time, nor anything of that which is in the world, like transient fatigue or joy." Page 42.

Socrates says: "The soul on leaving space wanders to the holiness (τὸ καθαρόν) which lives for ever and exists eternally, being related to it. It becomes like holiness in duration, because it is by means of something like contact able to receive impressions from holiness. This, its susceptibility to impressions, is called *Intelligence.*"

Further, Socrates says: "The soul is very similar to the divine substance which does not die nor dissolve, and is the only *intelligibile* which lasts for ever; the body is the contrary of it. When soul and body unite, nature orders body to serve, the soul to rule; but when they separate, the soul goes to another place than that to which the body goes. There it is happy with things that are suitable to it; it reposes from being circumscribed in space, rests from folly, impatience, love, fear, and other human evils, on this condition, that it had always been pure and hated the body. If, however, it has sullied itself by connivance with the body, by serving and loving it so that the body was subservient to its lusts and desires, in this case it does not experience anything more real than the species of bodily things (τὸ σωματοειδές) and the contact with them."

Proclus says: "The body in which the rational soul dwells has received the figure of a globe, like the ether and its individual beings. The body in which both the rational and the irrational souls dwell has received an erect figure like man. The body in which only the irrational soul dwells has received a figure erect and curved at the same time, like that of the irrational animals. The body in which there is neither the one nor the other, in which there is nothing but the nourishing power, has received an erect figure, but it is at the same time curved and turned upside down, so that the head is planted in the earth, as is the case with the plants. The latter direction being the contrary to that of man, man is a heavenly tree, the root of which is directed towards its home, *i.e.* heaven, whilst the root of vegetables is directed towards *their* home, *i.e.* the earth."

Brahman compared to an Aśvattha tree according to *Patañjali.*

The Hindus hold similar views about nature. Arjuna asks, "What is Brahman like in the world?" Whereupon Vâsudeva answers, "Imagine him like an *Aśvattha* tree." This is a huge precious tree, well known among them, standing upside down, the roots being above, the branches below. If it has ample nourishment, it becomes quite enormous; the branches spread far, cling to the soil, and creep into it. Roots and branches above and below resemble each other to such a degree that it is difficult to say which is which.

"Brahman is the upper roots of this tree, its trunk is the Veda, its branches are the different doctrines and schools, its leaves are the different modes of interpretation; its nourishment comes from *the three forces;* the tree becomes strong and compact through the senses. The intelligent being has no other keen desire but that of felling this tree, *i.e.* abstaining from the world and its vanities. When he has succeeded in felling it, he wishes to settle in the place where it has grown, a place in which there is no returning in a further stage of metempsychosis. When he obtains this, he leaves behind himself all the pains of heat and cold, and coming from the light of sun and moon and common fires, he attains to the divine lights." Page 43.

Ṣûfî parallels.

The doctrine of *Patañjali* is akin to that of the Ṣûfî regarding being occupied in meditation on *the Truth* (*i.e.* God), for they say, "As long as you point to something, you are not a *monist;* but when *the Truth* seizes upon the object of your pointing and annihilates it, then there is no longer an indicating person nor an object indicated."

There are some passages in their system which show that they believe in the pantheistic union; *e.g.* one of them, being asked what is *the Truth* (God), gave the following answer: "How should I not know the being which is *I* in essence and *Not-I* in space? If I return once more into existence, thereby I am separated from him; and if I am neglected (*i.e.* not born anew and sent into the world), thereby I become light and become accustomed to the *union*" (*sic*).

Abû-Bekr Ash-shiblî says: "Cast off all, and you

will attain to us completely. Then you will exist; but you will not report about us to others as long as your doing is like ours."

Abû-Yazîd Albistâmî once being asked how he had attained *his* stage in Ṣufism, answered: "I cast off my own self as a serpent casts off its skin. Then I considered my own self, and found that *I* was *He*," *i.e.* God.

The Ṣûfî explain the Koranic passage (Sûra 2, 68), "*Then we spoke: Beat him with a part of her,*" in the following manner: "The order to kill that which is dead in order to give life to it indicates that the heart does not become alive by the lights of knowledge unless the body be killed by ascetic practice to such a degree that it does not any more exist as a reality, but only in a formal way, whilst your heart is a reality on which no object of the formal world has any influence."

Further they say: "Between man and God there are a thousand stages of light and darkness. Men exert themselves to pass through darkness to light, and when they have attained to the stations of light, there is no return for them."

(Chapter VIII, pages 89–98, gives a discussion of the various kinds of created beings according to Sankhya philosophy.)

CHAPTER IX.

ON THE CASTES, CALLED "COLOURS" (VARNA), AND ON THE CLASSES BELOW THEM.

Throne and altar.

IF a new order of things in political or social life is created by a man naturally ambitious of ruling, who by his character and capacity really deserves to be a ruler, a man of firm convictions and unshaken determination, who even in times of reverses is supported by good luck, in so far as people then side with him in recognition of former merits of his, such an order is likely to become consolidated among those for whom it was created, and to continue as firm as the deeply rooted mountains. It will remain among them as a generally recognised rule in all generations through the course of time and the flight of ages. If, then, this new form of state or society rests in some degree on religion, these twins, state and religion, are in perfect harmony, and their union represents the highest development of human society, all that men can possibly desire.

The kings of antiquity, who were industriously devoted to the duties of their office, spent most of their care on the division of their subjects into different classes and orders, which they tried to preserve from intermixture and disorder. Therefore they forbade people of different classes to have intercourse with each other, and laid upon each class a particular kind of work or art and handicraft. They did not allow anybody to transgress the limits of his class, and even punished those who would not be content with their class.

Castes of the ancient Persians.

All this is well illustrated by the history of the ancient Chosroes (Khusrau), for they had created great institutions of this kind, which could not be broken through by the special merits of any individual nor by bribery. When Ardashîr ben Bâbak restored the Persian empire, he also restored the classes or castes of the population in the following way:—

The first class were the knights and princes.

The second class the monks, the fire-priests, and the lawyers.

The third class the physicians, astronomers, and other men of science.

The fourth class the husbandmen and artisans.

And within these classes there were subdivisions, distinct from each other, like the species within a genus. All institutions of this kind are like a pedigree, as long as their origin is remembered; but when once their origin has been forgotten, they become, as it were, the stable property of the whole nation, nobody any more questioning its origin. And forgetting is the necessary result of any long period of time, of a long succession of centuries and generations.

Among the Hindus institutions of this kind abound. We Muslims, of course, stand entirely on the other side of the question, considering all men as equal, except in piety; and this is the greatest obstacle which prevents any approach or understanding between Hindus and Muslims.

The four castes.

The Hindus call their castes *varṇa*, i.e. *colours*, and from a genealogical point of view they call them *jâtaka*, i.e. *births*. These castes are from the very beginning only four.

Page 49.

I. The highest caste are the Brâhmaṇa, of whom the books of the Hindus tell that they were created from the head of Brahman. And as Brahman is only another name for the force called *nature*, and the head is the highest part of the animal body, the Brâhmaṇa are the choice part of the whole genus. Therefore the Hindus consider them as the very best of mankind.

II. The next caste are the Kshatriya, who were created, as they say, from the shoulders and hands of Brahman. Their degree is not much below that of the Brâhmaṇa.

III. After them follow the Vaiśya, who were created from the thigh of Brahman.

IV. The Śûdra, who were created from his feet.

Between the latter two classes there is no very great distance. Much, however, as these classes differ from each other, they live together in the same towns and villages, mixed together in the same houses and lodgings.

After the Śûdra follow the people called *Antyaja*, who render various kinds of services, who are not reckoned amongst any caste, but only as members of a certain craft or profession. There are eight classes of them, who freely intermarry with each other, except the fuller, shoemaker, and weaver, for no others would condescend to have anything to do with them. These eight guilds are the fuller, shoemaker, juggler, the basket and shield maker, the sailor, fisherman, the hunter of wild animals and of birds, and the weaver. The four castes do not live together with them in one and the same place. These guilds live near the villages and towns of the four castes, but outside them.

Low-caste people.

The people called Hâḍî, Ḍoma (Ḍomba), Caṇḍâla, and Badhatau (*sic*) are not reckoned amongst any caste or guild. They are occupied with dirty work, like the cleansing of the villages and other services. They are considered as one sole class, and distinguished only by their occupations. In fact, they are considered like illegitimate children; for according to general opinion they descend from a Śûdra father and a Brâhmaṇî mother as the children of fornication; therefore they are degraded outcasts.

Different occupations of the castes and guilds.

The Hindus give to every single man of the four castes characteristic names, according to their occupations and modes of life. *E.g.* the Brâhmaṇa is in general called by this name as long as he does his work staying at home. When he is busy with the service of one fire, he is called *ishṭin;* if he serves three fires, he is called *agnihôtrin;* if he besides offers an offering to the fire, he is called *dîkshita.* And as it is with the Brâhmaṇa, so is it also with the other castes. Of the classes *beneath* the castes, the Hâḍî are the best spoken of, because they keep themselves free from everything unclean. Next follow the Ḍôma, who play on the lute and sing. The still lower classes practise as a trade killing and the inflicting of judicial punishments. The worst of all are the Badhatau, who not only devour the flesh of dead animals, but even of dogs and other beasts.

Customs of the Brahmins.

Each of the four castes, when eating together, must form a group for themselves, one group not being allowed to comprise two men of different castes. If, further, in the group of the Brâhmaṇa there are two men who live at enmity with each other, and the seat of the one is by the side of the other, they make a barrier between the two seats by placing a board between them, or by spreading a piece of dress, or in some other way; and if there is only a line drawn between them, they are considered as separated. Since it is forbidden to eat the remains of a meal, every single man must have his own food for himself; for if any one of the party who are eating should take of the food from one and the same plate, that which remains in the plate becomes, after the first eater has taken part, to him who
Page 50.
wants to take as the second, *the remains of the meal,* and such is forbidden.

Such is the condition of the four castes. Arjuna

asked about the nature of the four castes and what must be their moral qualities, whereupon Vâsudeva answered:

"The Brâhmaṇa must have an ample intellect, a quiet heart, truthful speech, much patience; he must be master of his senses, a lover of justice, of evident purity, always directed upon worship, entirely bent upon religion.

"The Kshatriya must fill the hearts with terror, must be brave and high-minded, must have ready speech and a liberal hand, not minding dangers, only intent upon carrying the great tasks of his calling to a happy end.

"The Vaiśya is to occupy himself with agriculture, with the acquisition of cattle, and with trade.

"The Śûdra is to endeavour to render services and attention to each of the preceding classes, in order to make himself liked by them.

"If each member of these castes adheres to his customs and usages, he will obtain the happiness he wishes for, supposing that he is not negligent in the worship of God, not forgetting to remember him in his most important avocations. But if anybody wants to quit the works and duties of his caste and adopt those of another caste, even if it would bring a certain honour to the latter, it is a sin, because it is a transgression of the rule."

Further, Vâsudeva speaks, inspiring him with courage to fight the enemy: "Dost thou not know, O man with the long arm, that thou art a Kshatriya; that thy race has been created brave, to rush boldly to the charge, to care little for the vicissitudes of time, never to give way whenever their soul has a foreboding of coming misfortune? for only thereby is the reward to be obtained. If he conquers, he obtains power and good fortune. If he perishes, he obtains paradise and bliss. Besides, thou showest weakness in the presence of the enemy, and seemest melancholy at the prospect of killing this host; but it will be infinitely worse if thy name will spread as that of a timid, cowardly man, that thy reputation among the heroes and the experienced warriors will be gone, that thou wilt be out of their sight, and thy name no longer be remembered among them. I do not know a worse punishment than such a state. Death is better than to expose thyself to the consequences of ignominy. If, therefore, God has ordered thee to fight, if he has deigned to confer upon thy caste the task of fighting and has created thee for it, carry out his order and perform his will with a determination which is free from any desire, so that thy action be exclusively devoted to him."

Moksha and the various castes.

Hindus differ among themselves as to which of these castes is capable of attaining to liberation; for, according to some, only the Brâhmaṇa and Kshatriya are capable of it, since the others cannot learn the Veda, whilst according to the Hindu philosophers, liberation is common to all castes and to the whole human race, if their intention of obtaining it is perfect. This view is based on the saying of Vyâsa: "Learn to know the twenty-five things thoroughly. Then you may follow whatever religion you like; you will no doubt be liberated." This view is also based on the fact that Vâsudeva was a descendant of a Śûdra family, and also on the following saying of his, which he addressed to Arjuna: "God distributes recompense without injustice and without partiality. He reckons the good as bad if people in doing good forget him; he reckons the bad as good if people in doing bad remember him and do not forget him, whether those people be Vaiśya or Śûdra or women. How much more will this be the case when they are Brâhmaṇa or Kshatriya."

Page 51.

CHAPTER X.

ON THE SOURCE OF THEIR RELIGIOUS AND CIVIL LAW, ON PROPHETS, AND ON THE QUESTION WHETHER SINGLE LAWS CAN BE ABROGATED OR NOT.

Law and religion among the Greeks founded by their sages.

THE ancient Greeks received their religious and civil laws from sages among them who were called to the work, and of whom their countrymen believed that they received divine help, like Solon, Draco, Pythagoras, Minos, and others. Also their kings did the same; for Mianos (*sic*), when ruling over the islands of the sea and over the Cretans about two hundred years after Moses, gave them laws, pretending to have received them from Zeus. About the same time also Minos (*sic*) gave his laws.

At the time of Darius I., the successor of Cyrus, the Romans sent messengers to the Athenians, and received from them the laws in twelve books, under which they lived till the rule of Pompilius (Numa). This king gave them new laws; he assigned to the year twelve months, whilst up to that time it had only had ten months. It appears that he introduced his innovations against the will of the Romans, for he ordered them to use as instruments of barter in commerce pieces of pottery and hides instead of silver, which seems on his part to betray a certain anger against rebellious subjects.

Quotation from Plato's *Laws*.

In the first chapter of the *Book of Laws* of Plato, the Athenian stranger says: "Who do you think was the first who gave laws to you? Was he an angel or a man?" The man of Cnossus said: "He was an angel. In truth, with us it was Zeus, but with the Lacedæmonians, as they maintain, the legislator was Apollo."

Further, he says in the same chapter: "It is the duty of the legislator, if he comes from God, to make the acquisition of the greatest virtues and of the highest justice the object of his legislation."

He describes the laws of the Cretans as rendering perfect the happiness of those who make the proper use of them, because by them they acquire all the human good which is dependent upon the divine good.

The Athenian says in the second chapter of the same book: "The gods, pitying mankind as born for trouble, instituted for them feasts to the gods, the Muses, Apollo the ruler of the Muses, and to Dionysos, who gave men wine as a remedy against the bitterness of old age, that old men should again be young by forgetting sadness, and by bringing back the character of the soul from the state of affliction to the state of soundness."

Further he says: "They have given to men by inspiration the arrangements for dancing, and the equally weighed rhythm as a reward for fatigues, and that they may become accustomed to live together with them in feasts and joy. Therefore they call one kind of their music *praises*, with an implied allusion to the prayers to the gods."

The Ṛishis, the authors of Hindu law.

Page 52.

Such was the case with the Greeks, and it is precisely the same with the Hindus. For they believe that their religious law and its single precepts derive their origin from Ṛishis, their sages, the pillars of their religion, and not from the prophet, *i.e.* Nârâyaṇa, who, when coming into this world, appears in some human figure. But he only comes in order to cut away some evil matter which threatens the world, or to set the world right again when anything has gone wrong. Further, no law can be exchanged or replaced by another, for they use the laws simply as they find them. Therefore they can dispense with prophets, as far as law and worship are concerned, though in other affairs of the creation they sometimes want them.

Whether laws may be abrogated or not.

As for the question of the abrogation of laws, it seems that this is not impossible with the Hindus, for they say that many things which are now forbidden were allowed before the coming of Vâsudeva, *e.g.* the flesh of cows. Such changes are necessitated by the change of the nature of man, and by their being too feeble to bear the whole burden of their duties. To these changes also belong the changes of the *matrimonial system* and of *the theory of descent*. For in former times there were three modes of determining descent or relationship:

Different matrimonial systems.

1. The child born to a man by his legitimate wife is the child of the father, as is the custom with us and with the Hindus.

2. If a man marries a woman and has a child by her; if, further, the marriage-contract stipulates that the children of the woman will belong to *her* father, the child is considered as the child of its grandfather who made that stipulation, and not as the child of its father who engendered it.

3. If a stranger has a child by a married woman, the child belongs to her husband, since the wife being, as it were, the soil in which the child has grown, is the property of the husband, always presupposing that the sowing, *i.e.* the cohabitation, takes place with his consent.

The story of Pâṇḍu and Vyâsa.

According to this principle, Pâṇḍu was considered as the son of Śântanu; for this king had been cursed by an anchorite, and in consequence was unable to cohabit with his wives, which was the more provoking to him as he had not yet any children. Now he asked Vyâsa, the son of Parâśara, to procreate for him children from his wives in his place. Pâṇḍu sent him one, but she was afraid of him when he cohabitated with her, and trembled, in consequence of which she conceived a sickly child of yellow hue. Then the king sent him a second woman; she, too, felt much reverence for him, and wrapped herself up in her veil, and in consequence she gave birth to Dhṛitarâshṭra, who was blind and unhealthy. Lastly, he sent him a third woman, whom he enjoined to put aside all fear and reverence with regard to the saint. Laughing and in high spirits, she went in to him, and conceived from him a child of moon-like beauty, who excelled all men in boldness and cunning.

Birth of Vyâsa.

The four sons of Pâṇḍu had one wife in common, who stayed one month with each of them alternately. In the books of the Hindus it is told that Parâśara, the hermit, one day travelled in a boat in which there was also a daughter of the boatman. He fell in love with her, tried to seduce her, and finally she yielded; but there was nothing on the bank of the river to hide them from the looks of the people. However, instantaneously there grew a tamarisk-tree to facilitate their purpose. Now he cohabited with her behind the tamarisk, and made her conceive, whereupon she became pregnant with this his excellent son Vyâsa.

All these customs have now been abolished and abrogated, and therefore we may infer from their tradition that in principle *the abrogation of a law is allowable.*

Various kinds of marriage with Tibetans and Arabs.

As regards unnatural kinds of marriage, we must state that such exist still in our time, as they also existed in the times of Arab heathendom; for the people inhabiting the mountains stretching from the region of Panchîr into the neighbourhood of Kashmîr live under the rule that several brothers have one wife in common. Among the heathen Arabs, too, marriage was of different kinds:—

Page 53.

1. An Arab ordered his wife to be sent to a certain

man to demand sexual intercourse with him; then he abstained from her during the whole time of her pregnancy, since he wished to have from her a generous offspring. This is identical with the third kind of marriage among the Hindus.

2. A second kind was this, that the one Arab said to the other, "Cede me your wife, and I will cede you mine," and thus they exchanged their wives.

3. A third kind is this, that several men cohabited with one wife. When, then, she gave birth to a child, she declared who was the father; and if she did not know it, the fortune-tellers had to know it.

4. The *Nikâḥ-elmakt* (= *matrimonium exosum*), *i.e.* when a man married the widow of his father or of his son, the child of such a marriage was called *ḍaizan*. This is nearly the same as a certain Jewish marriage, for the Jews have the law that a man must marry the widow of his brother, if the latter has not left children, and create a line of descent for his deceased brother; and the offspring is considered as that of the deceased man, not as that of the real father. Thereby they want to prevent his memory dying out in the world. In Hebrew they call a man who is married in this way *Yâbhâm*.

Marriage among the ancient Iranians.

There was a similar institution among the Magians. In the book of Tausar, the great *herbadh*, addressed to Padashvâr-girshâh, as an answer to his attacks on Ardashîr the son of Bâbak, we find a description of the institution of a man's being married as the substitute for another man, which existed among the Persians. If a man dies without leaving male offspring, people are to examine the case. If he leaves a wife, they marry her to his nearest relative. If he does not leave a wife, they marry his daughter or the nearest related woman to the nearest related male of the family. If there is no woman of his family left, they woo by means of the money of the deceased a woman for his family, and marry her to some male relative. The child of such a marriage is considered as the offspring of the deceased.

Whoever neglects this duty and does not fulfil it, kills innumerable souls, since he cuts off the progeny and the name of the deceased to all eternity.

We have here given an account of these things in order that the reader may learn by the comparative treatment of the subject how much superior the institutions of Islam are, and how much more plainly this contrast brings out all customs and usages, differing from those of Islam, in their essential foulness.

CHAPTER XI.

ABOUT THE BEGINNING OF IDOL-WORSHIP, AND A DESCRIPTION OF THE INDIVIDUAL IDOLS.

Origin of idol-worship in the nature of man.

It is well known that the popular mind leans towards the sensible world, and has an aversion to the world of abstract thought which is only understood by highly educated people, of whom in every time and every place there are only few. And as common people will only acquiesce in pictorial representations, many of the leaders of religious communities have so far deviated from the right path as to give such imagery in their books and houses of worship, like the Jews and Christians, and, more than all, the Manichæans. These words of mine would at once receive a sufficient illustration if, for example, a picture of the Prophet were made, or of Mekka and the Ka'ba, and were shown to an uneducated man or woman. Their joy in looking at the thing would bring them to kiss the picture, to rub their cheeks against it, and to roll themselves in the dust before it, as if they were seeing not the picture, but the original, and were in this way, as if they were present in the holy places, performing the rites of pilgrimage, the great and the small ones.

This is the cause which leads to the manufacture of idols, monuments in honour of certain much venerated persons, prophets, sages, angels, destined to keep alive their memory when they are absent or dead, to create for them a lasting place of grateful veneration in the hearts of men when they die. But when much time passes by after the setting up of the monument, generations and centuries, its origin is forgotten, it becomes a matter of custom, and its veneration a rule for general practice. This being deeply rooted in the nature of man, the legislators of antiquity tried to influence them from this weak point of theirs. Therefore they made the veneration of pictures and similar monuments obligatory on them, as is recounted in historic records, both for the times before and after the Deluge. Some people even pretend to know that all mankind, before God sent them his prophets, were one large idolatrous body.

Page 54.

The followers of the Thora fix the beginning of idolatry in the days of Serûgh, the great-grandfather of Abraham. The Romans have, regarding this question, the following tradition:—Romulus and Romanus (!), the two brothers from the country of the Franks, on having ascended the throne, built the city of Rome. Then Romulus killed his brother, and the consequence was a long succession of intestine troubles and wars. Finally, Romulus humiliated himself, and then he dreamt that there would only be peace on condition that he placed his brother on the throne. Now he got a golden image made of him, placed it at his side, and henceforward he used to say, "*We* (not *I*) have ordered thus and thus," which since has become the general use of kings. Thereupon the troubles subsided. He founded a feast and a play to amuse and to gain over those who bore him ill-will on account of the murder of his brother. Besides, he erected a monument to the sun, consisting of four images on four horses, the green one for the earth, the blue for the water, the red for the fire, and the white for the air. This monument is still in Rome in our days.

Story of Romulus and Remus.

Since, however, here we have to explain the system and the theories of the Hindus on the subject, we shall now mention their ludicrous views; but we declare at once

Idol-worship as restricted to the low classes of people.

that they are held only by the common uneducated people. For those who march on the path to liberation, or those who study philosophy and theology, and who desire abstract truth which they call *sâra*, are entirely free from worshipping anything but God alone, and would never dream of worshipping an image manufactured to represent him. A tradition illustrative of this is that which Śaunaka told the king Parîksha in these words:—

There was once a king called Ambarîsha, who had obtained an empire as large as he had wished for. But afterwards he came to like it no longer; he retired from the world, and exclusively occupied himself with worshipping and praising God for a long time. Finally, God appeared to him in the shape of Indra, the prince of the angels, riding on an elephant. He spoke to the king: "Demand whatever you like, and I will give it you."

Story of King Ambarîsha and Indra.

The king answered: "I rejoice in seeing thee, and I am thankful for the good fortune and help thou hast given; but I do not demand anything from thee, but only from him who created thee."

Indra said: "The object of worship is to receive a noble reward. Realise, therefore, your object, and accept the reward from him from whom hitherto you have obtained your wishes, and do not pick and choose, saying, 'Not from thee, but from another.'"

The king answered: "The earth has fallen to my lot, but I do not care for all that is in it. The object of my worship is to see the Lord, and that thou canst not give me. Why, therefore, should I demand the fulfilment of my desire from thee?"

Indra said: "The whole world and whoever is upon it are obedient to me. Who are you that you dare to oppose me?"

The king answered: "I, too, hear and obey, but I worship *him* from whom thou hast received this power, who is the lord of the universe, who has protected thee against the attacks of the two kings, Bali and Hiraṇyâksha. Therefore let me do as *I* like, and turn away from me with my farewell greeting."

Indra said: "If you will absolutely oppose me, I will kill you and annihilate you."

The king answered: "People say that happiness is envied, but not so misfortune. He who retires from the world is envied by the angels, and therefore they will try to lead him astray. I am one of those who have retired from the world and entirely devoted themselves to worship, and I shall not give it up as long as
Page 55. I live. I do not know myself to be guilty of a crime for which I should deserve to be killed by thee. If thou killest me without any offence on my part, it is thy concern. What dost thou want from me? If my thoughts are entirely devoted to God, and nothing else is blended with them, thou art not able to do me any harm. Sufficient for me is the worship with which I am occupied, and now I return to it."

As the king now went on worshipping, the Lord appeared to him in the shape of a man of the grey lotus colour, riding on a bird called Garuḍa, holding in one of the four hands the *śaṅkha*, a sea-shell which people blow when riding on elephants; in the second hand the *cakra*, a round, cutting, orbicular weapon, which cuts everything it hits right through; in the third an amulet, and in the fourth *padma*, *i.e.* the red lotus. When the king saw him, he shuddered from reverence, prostrated himself and uttered many praises. The Lord quieted his terrified mind and promised him that he should obtain everything he wished for. The king spoke: "I had obtained an empire which nobody disputed with me; I was in conditions of life not troubled by sorrow or sickness. It was as if the whole world belonged to me. But then I turned away from it, after I had understood that the good of the world is really bad in the end. I do not wish for anything except what I now have. The only thing I now wish for is to be liberated from this fetter."

The Lord spoke: "That you will obtain by keeping aloof from the world, by being alone, by uninterrupted meditation, and by restraining your senses to yourself."

The king spoke: "Supposing that I am able to do so through that sanctity which the Lord has deigned to bestow upon me, how should any other man be able to do so? for man wants eating and clothing, which connects him with the world. How is he to think of anything else?"

The Lord spoke: "Occupy yourself with your empire in as straightforward and prudent a way as possible: turn your thoughts upon me when you are engaged in civilising the world and protecting its inhabitants, in giving alms, and in everything you do. And if you are overpowered by human forgetfulness, make to yourself an image like that in which you see me; offer to it perfumes and flowers, and make it a memorial of me, so that you may not forget me. If you are in sorrow, think of me; if you speak, speak in my name; if you act, act for me."

The king spoke: "Now I know what I have to do in general, but honour me further by instructing me in the details."

The Lord spoke: "That I have done already. I have inspired your judge Vasishṭha with all that is required. Therefore rely upon him in all questions."

Then the figure disappeared from his sight. The king returned into his residence and did as he had been ordered.

From that time, the Hindus say, people make idols, some with four hands like the appearance we have described, others with two hands, as the story and description require, and conformably to the being which is to be represented.

Nârada and the voice from the fire.

Another story of theirs is the following:—Brahman had a son called Nârada, who had no other desire but that of seeing the Lord. It was his custom, when he walked about, to hold a stick. If he threw it down, it became a serpent, and he was able to do miracles with it. He never went without it. One day being engrossed in meditation on the object of his hopes, he saw a fire from afar. He went towards it, and then a voice spoke to him out of the fire: "What you demand and wish is impossible. You cannot see me save thus." When he looked in that direction, he saw a fiery appearance in something like human shape. Henceforward it has been the custom to erect idols of certain shapes.

Page 56.

The idol of Multân called Âditya.

A famous idol of theirs was that of Multân, dedicated to the sun, and therefore called *Âditya*. It was of wood and covered with red Cordovan leather; in its two eyes were two red rubies. It is said to have been made in the last Kṛitayuga. Suppose that it was made in the very end of Kṛitayuga, the time which has since elapsed amounts to 216,432 years. When Muhammad Ibn Alḳâsim Ibn Almunabbih conquered Multân, he inquired how the town had become so very flourishing and so many treasures had there been accumulated, and then he found out that this idol was the cause, for there came pilgrims from all sides to visit it. Therefore he thought it best to have the idol where it was, but he hung a piece of cow's-flesh on its neck by way of mockery. On the same place a mosque was built. When then the Ḳarmatians occupied Multân, Jalam Ibn Shaibân, the usurper, broke the idol into pieces and killed its priests. He made his mansion, which was a castle built of brick on an elevated place, the mosque instead of the old mosque, which he ordered to be shut from hatred against anything that had been done under the dynasty of the Caliphs of the house of 'Umayya. When afterwards the blessed Prince Maḥmûd swept away their rule from those countries, he made again the old mosque the place of the Friday-worship, and the second one was left to decay. At present it is only a barn-floor, where bunches of Ḥinnâ (*Lawsonia inermis*) are bound together.

If we now subtract from the above-mentioned number of years the hundreds, tens, and units, *i.e.* the 432 years, as a kind of arbitrary equivalent for the sum of about 100 years, by which the rise of the Ḳarmatians preceded our time, we get as the remainder 216,000 years for the time of the end of the Ḳritayuga, and about the epoch of the era of the Hijra. How, then, could wood have lasted such a length of time, and particularly in a place where the air and the soil are rather wet? God knows best!

The idol of Tâneshar called Cakra-svâmin.

The city of Tâneshar is highly venerated by the Hindus. The idol of that place is called *Cakrasvâmin*, *i.e.* the owner of the *cakra*, a weapon which we have already described (page 114). It is of bronze, and is nearly the size of a man. It is now lying in the hippodrome in Ghazna, together with the *Lord of Somanâth*, which is a representation of the *penis* of Mahâdeva, called *Linga*. Of Somanâth we shall hereafter speak in the proper place. This Cakrasvâmin is said to have been made in the time of Bhârata as a memorial of wars connected with this name.

The idol Śârada in Kashmîr.

In Inner Kashmîr, about two or three days' journey from the capital in the direction towards the mountains of Bolor, there is a wooden idol called *Śârada*, which is much venerated and frequented by pilgrims.

Quotation from the Saṁhitâ of Varâhamihira.

We shall now communicate a whole chapter from the book *Saṁhitâ* relating to the construction of idols, which will help the student thoroughly to comprehend the present subject.

Varâhamihira says: "If the figure is made to represent Râma the son of Daśaratha, or Bali the son of Virocana, give it the height of 120 digits," *i.e.* of *idol digits*, which must be reduced by one-tenth to become *common digits*, in this case 108.

"To the idol of Vishṇu give eight hands, or four, or two, and on the left side under the breast give him the figure of the woman Śrî. If you give him eight hands, place in the right hands a sword, a club of gold or iron, an arrow, and make the fourth hand as if it were draw-
Page 57. ing water; in the left hands give him a shield, a bow, a *cakra*, and a conch.

"If you give him four hands, omit the bow and the arrow, the sword and shield.

"If you give him two hands, let the right hand be drawing water, the left holding a conch.

"If the figure is to represent Baladeva, the brother of Nârâyaṇa, put earrings into his ears, and give him eyes of a drunken man.

"If you make both figures, Nârâyaṇa and Baladeva, join with them their sister *Bhagavatî* (Durgâ=Ekânanśâ), her left hand resting on her hip a little away from the side, and her right hand holding a lotus.

"If you make her four-handed, place in the right hands a rosary and a hand drawing water; in the left hands, a book and a lotus.

"If you make her eight-handed, place in the left hands the *kamaṇḍalu*, *i.e.* a pot, a lotus, bow and book; in the right hands, a rosary, a mirror, an arrow, and a water-drawing hand.

"If the figure is to represent Sâmba, the son of Vishṇu, put only a club in his right hand. If it is to represent Pradyumna, the son of Vishṇu, place in his right hand an arrow, in his left hand a bow. And if you make their two wives, place in their right hand a sword, in the left a buckler.

"The idol of Brahman has four faces towards the four sides, and is seated on a lotus.

"The idol of Skanda, the son of Mahâdeva, is a boy riding on a peacock, his hand holding a *śakti*, a weapon like a double-edged sword, which has in the middle a pestle like that of a mortar.

"The idol Indra holds in its hand a weapon called *vajra* of diamond. It has a similar handle to the *śakti*, but on each side it has two swords which join at the handle. On his front place a third eye, and make him ride on a white elephant with four tusks.

"Likewise make on the front of the idol of Mahâdeva a third eye right above, on his head a crescent, in his hand a weapon called *śûla*, similar to the club but with three branches, and a sword; and let his left hand hold his wife Gaurî, the daughter of Himavant, whom he presses to his bosom from the side.

"To the idol Jina, *i.e.* Buddha, give a face and limbs as beautiful as possible, make the lines in the palms of his hands and feet like a lotus, and represent him seated on a lotus; give him grey hair, and represent him with a placid expression, as if he were the father of creation.

"If you make Arhant, the figure of another body of Buddha, represent him as a naked youth with a fine face, beautiful, whose hands reach down to the knees, with the figure of Śrî, his wife, under the left breast.

"The idol of Revanta, the son of the sun, rides on a horse like a huntsman.

"The idol of Yima, the angel of death, rides on a buffalo, and holds a club in his hand.

"The idol of Kubera, the treasurer, wears a crown, has a big stomach and wide hips, and is riding on a man.

"The idol of the sun has a red face like the pith of the red lotus, beams like a diamond, has protruding limbs, rings in the ears, the neck adorned with pearls which hang down over the breast, wears a crown of several compartments, holds in his hands two lotuses, and is clad in the dress of the Northerners which reaches down to the ankle.

"If you represent the Seven Mothers, represent several Page 58.
of them together in one figure, Brahmâṇî with four faces

towards the four directions, Kaumârî with six faces, Vaishṇavî with four hands, Vârâhî with a hog's head on a human body, Indrâṇî with many eyes and a club in her hand, Bhagavatî (Durgâ) sitting as people generally sit, Câmuṇḍâ ugly, with protruding teeth and a slim waist. Further join with them the sons of Mahâdeva, Kshetrapâla with bristling hair, a sour face, and an ugly figure, but Vinâyaka with an elephant's head on a human body, with four hands, as we have heretofore described."

The worshippers of these idols kill sheep and buffaloes with axes (*kuṭâra*), that they may nourish themselves with their blood. All idols are constructed according to certain measures determined by *idol-fingers* for every single limb, but sometimes they differ regarding the measure of a limb. If the artist keeps the right measure and does not make anything too large nor too small, he is free from sin, and is sure that the being which he represented will not visit him with any mishap. "If he makes the idol one cubit high and together with the throne two cubits, he will obtain health and wealth. If he makes it higher still, he will be praised.

"But he must know that making the idol too large, especially that of the Sun, will hurt the ruler, and making it too small will hurt the artist. If he gives it a thin belly, this helps and furthers the famine in the country; if he gives it a lean belly, this ruins property.

"If the hand of the artist slips so as to produce something like a wound, he will have a wound in his own body which will kill him.

"If it is not completely even on both sides, so that the one shoulder is higher than the other, his wife will perish.

"If he turns the eye upward, he will be blind for lifetime; if he turns it downward, he will have many troubles and sorrows."

If the statue is made of some precious stone, it is better than if it were made of wood, and wood is better than clay. "The benefits of a statue of precious stone will be common to all the men and women of the empire. A golden statue will bring power to him who erected it, a statue of silver will bring him renown, one of bronze will bring him an increase of his rule, one of stone the acquisition of landed property."

The Hindus honour their idols on account of those who erected them, not on account of the material of which they are made. We have already mentioned that the idol of Multân was of wood. *E.g.* the *linga* which Râma erected when he had finished the war with the demons was of sand, which he had heaped up with his own hand. But then it became petrified all at once, since the astrologically correct moment for the erecting of the monument fell before the moment when the workmen had finished the cutting of the stone monument which Râma originally had ordered. Regarding the building of the temple and its peristyle, the cutting of the trees of four different kinds, the astrological determination of the favourable moment for the erection, the celebration of the rites due on such an occasion, regarding all this Râma gave very long and tedious instructions. Further, he ordered that servants and priests to minister to the idols should be nominated from different classes of the people. "To the idol of Vishṇu are devoted the class called Bhâgavata; to the idol of the Sun, the Maga, *i.e.* the Magians; to the idol of Mahâdeva, a class of saints, anchorites with long hair, who cover their skin with ashes, hang on their persons the bones of dead people, and swim in the pools. The Brâhmaṇa are devoted to the Eight Page 59.
Mothers, the Shamanians to Buddha, to Arhant the class called *Nagna*. On the whole, to each idol certain people are devoted who constructed it, for those know best how to serve it."

Quotations from *Gîtâ* showing that God is not to be confounded with the idols.

Our object in mentioning all this mad raving was to teach the reader the accurate description of an idol, if he happens to see one, and to illustrate what we have said before, that such idols are erected only for uneducated low-class people of little understanding; that the Hindus never made an idol of any supernatural being, much less of God; and, lastly, to show how the crowd is kept in thraldom by all kinds of priestly tricks and deceits. Therefore the book *Gîtâ* says: "Many people try to approach me in their aspirations through something which is different from me; they try to insinuate themselves into my favour by giving alms, praise, and prayer to something besides me. I, however, confirm and help them in all these doings of theirs, and make them attain the object of their wishes, because I am able to dispense with them."

In the same book Vâsudeva speaks to Arjuna: "Do you not see that most of those who wish for something address themselves in offering and worshipping to the several classes of *spiritual beings*, and to the sun, moon, and other celestial bodies? If now God does not disappoint their hopes, though he in no way stands in need of their worship, if he even gives them more than they asked for, and if he gives them their wishes in such a way as though they were receiving them from that to which they had addressed their prayers—viz. the idol—they will proceed to worship those whom they address, because they have not learned to know him, whilst *he*, by admitting this kind of intermediation, carries their affairs to the desired end. But that which is obtained by desires and intermediation is not lasting, since it is only as much as is deserved for any particular merit. Only that is lasting which is obtained from God alone, when people are disgusted with old age, death, and birth (and desire to be delivered therefrom by *Mokska*)."

This is what Vâsudeva says. When the ignorant crowd

get a piece of good luck by accident or something at which they had aimed, and when with this some of the preconcerted tricks of the priests are brought into connection, the darkness in which they live increases vastly, not their intelligence. They will rush to those *figures* of idols, maltreating their own figures before them by shedding their own blood and mutilating their own bodies.

The ancient Greeks, also, considered the idols as mediators between themselves and the *First Cause*, and worshipped them under the names of the stars and the highest substances. For they described the First Cause, not with positive, but only with negative predicates, since they considered it too high to be described by human qualities, and since they wanted to describe it as free from any imperfection. Therefore they could not address it in worship.

When the heathen Arabs had imported into their country idols from Syria, they also worshipped them, hoping that they would intercede for them with God.

Plato says in the fourth chapter of the *Book of Laws*: "It is necessary to any one who gives perfect honours (to the gods) that he should take trouble with the *mystery* of the gods and Sakînât, and that he should not make special idols masters over the ancestral gods. Further, it is the greatest duty to give honours as much as possible to the parents while they live."

By *mystery* Plato means a special kind of *devotion*. The word is much used among the Ṣâbians of Ḥarrân, the dualistic Manichæans, and the theologians of the Hindus.

Galenus says in the book *De Indole Animæ*: "At the time of the Emperor Commodus, between 500–510 years after Alexander, two men went to an idol-mer- Page 60.
chant and bargained with him for an idol of Hermes. The one wanted to erect it in a temple as a memorial of Hermes, the other wanted to erect it on a tomb as a

memorial of the deceased. However, they could not settle the business with the merchant, and so they postponed it until the following day. The idol-merchant dreamt the following night that the idol addressed him and spoke to him: 'O excellent man! I am thy work. I have received through the work of thy hands a figure which is thought to be the figure of a star. Now I am no longer a stone, as people called me heretofore; I am now known as Mercury. At present it stands in thy hands to make me either a memorial of something imperishable or of something that has perished already.'"

There is a treatise of Aristotle in which he answers certain questions of the Brahmins which Alexander had sent him. There he says: "If you maintain that some Greeks have fabled that the idols speak, that the people offer to them and think them to be spiritual beings, of all this we have no knowledge, and we cannot give a sentence on a subject we do not know." In these words he rises high above the class of fools and uneducated people, and he indicates by them that he does not occupy himself with such things. It is evident that the first cause of idolatry was the desire of commemorating the dead and of consoling the living; but on this basis it has developed, and has finally become a foul and pernicious abuse.

The former view, that idols are only memorials, was also held by the Caliph Mu'âwiya regarding the idols of Sicily. When, in the summer of A.H. 53, Sicily was conquered, and the conquerors sent him golden idols adorned with crowns and diamonds which had been captured there, he ordered them to be sent to Sind, that they should be sold there to the princes of the country; for he thought it best to sell them as objects costing sums of so-and-so many denars, not having the slightest scruple on account of their being objects of abominable idolatry, but simply considering the matter from a political, not from a religious point of view.

CHAPTER XII.

ON THE VEDA, THE PURÂṆAS, AND OTHER KINDS OF THEIR NATIONAL LITERATURE.

VEDA means knowledge of that which was before unknown. It is a religious system which, according to the Hindus, comes from God, and was promulgated by the mouth of Brahman. The Brahmins recite the Veda without understanding its meaning, and in the same way they learn it by heart, the one receiving it from the other. Only few of them learn its explanation, and still less is the number of those who master the contents of the Veda and their interpretation to such a degree as to be able to hold a theological disputation. Sundry notes relating to the Veda.

The Brahmins teach the Veda to the Kshatriyas. The latter learn it, but are not allowed to teach it, not even to a Brahmin. The Vaiśya and Śûdra are not allowed to hear it, much less to pronounce and recite it. If such a thing can be proved against one of them, the Brahmins drag him before the magistrate, and he is punished by having his tongue cut off.

The Veda contains commandments and prohibitions, detailed statements about reward and punishment intended to encourage and to deter; but most of it contains hymns of praise, and treats of the various kinds of sacrifices to the fire, which are so numerous and difficult that you could hardly count them.

They do not allow the Veda to be committed to writing, because it is recited according to certain modu- The Veda transmitted by memory.

lations, and they therefore avoid the use of the pen, since it is liable to cause some error, and may occasion an addition or a defect in the written text. In consequence it has happened that they have several times Page 61. forgotten the Veda and lost it. For they maintain that the following passage occurs in the conversations between God and Brahman relating to the beginning of all things, according to the report of Śaunaka who had received it from the planet Venus: "You will forget the Veda at the time when the earth will be submerged; it will then go down to the depths of the earth, and none but the fish will be able to bring it out again. Therefore I shall send the fish, and it will deliver the Veda into your hands. And I shall send the boar to raise the earth with its tusks and to bring it out of the water."

Further, the Hindus maintain that the Veda, together with all the rites of their religion and country, had been obliterated in the last Dvâpara-yuga, a period of time of which we shall speak in the proper place, until it was renewed by Vyâsa, the son of Parâśara.

The *Vishṇu Purâṇa* says: "At the beginning of each Manvantara period there will be created anew a lord of a period whose children will rule over the whole earth, and a prince who will be the head of the world, and angels to whom men will bring fire-offerings, and the *Great Bear*, who will renew the Veda which is lost at the end of each period."

Vasukra commits the Veda to writing.

This is the reason why, not long before our time, Vasukra, a native of Kashmîr, a famous Brahmin, has of his own account undertaken the task of explaining the Veda and committing it to writing. He has taken on himself a task from which everybody else would have recoiled, but he carried it out because he was afraid that the Veda might be forgotten and entirely vanish out of the memories of men, since he observed that the characters of men grew worse and worse, and that they did not care much for virtue, nor even for duty.

There are certain passages in the Veda which, as they maintain, must not be recited within dwellings, since they fear that they would cause an abortion both to women and the cattle. Therefore they step out into the open field to recite them there. There is hardly a single verse free from such and similar minatory injunctions.

As we have already mentioned, the books of the Hindus are metrical compositions like the Rajaz poems of the Arabs. Most of them are composed in a metre called *śloka*. The reason of this has already been explained. Galenus also prefers metrical composition, and says in his book ***Κατὰ γένη***: "The single signs which denote the weights of medicines become corrupt by being copied; they are also corrupted by the wanton mischief of some envious person. Therefore it is quite right that the books of Damocrates on medicines should be preferred to others, and that they should gain fame and praise, since they are written in a Greek metre. If all books were written in this way it would be the best;" the fact being that a prose text is much more exposed to corruption than a metrical one.

The Veda, however, is not composed in this common metre, śloka, but in another. Some Hindus say that no one could compose anything in the same metre. However, their scholars maintain that this is possible indeed, but that they refrain from trying it merely from veneration for the Veda.

The four pupils of Vyâsa and the four Vedas.

According to their tradition, Vyâsa divided it into four parts: *Ṛigveda*, *Yajurveda*, *Sâmaveda*, and *Atharvaṇaveda*.

Vyâsa had four *śishya*, *i.e.* pupils. He taught a separate Veda to each of them, and made him carry it in his memory. They are enumerated in the same order as the four parts of the Veda: *Paila*, *Vaiśaṁpâyana*, *Jaimini*, *Sumantu*.

On the Rigveda.

Each of the four parts has a peculiar kind of recitation. The first is Ṛigveda, consisting of metrical compositions called *ṛic*, which are of different lengths. It is called Ṛigveda as being the totality of the *ṛic*. It treats of the sacrifices to the fire, and is recited in three different ways. First, in a uniform manner of reading, just as every other book is read. Secondly, in such a way that a pause is made after every single word. Thirdly, in a method which is the most meritorious, and for which plenty of reward in heaven is promised. First you read a short passage, each word of which is distinctly pronounced; then you repeat it together with a part of that which has not yet been recited. Next you recite the added portion alone, and then you repeat it together with the next part of that which has not yet been recited, &c., &c. Continuing to do so till the end, you will have read the whole text twice.

Page 62.

On the Yajurveda.

The Yajurveda is composed of *kâṇḍin*. The word is a derivative noun, and means *the totality of the kâṇḍin*. The difference between this and the Ṛigveda is that it may be read as a text connected by the rules of Saṁdhi, which is not allowed in the case of Ṛigveda. The one as well as the other treats of works connected with the fire and the sacrifices.

I have heard the following story about the reason why the Ṛigveda cannot be recited as a text connected by the rules of Saṁdhi:—

The story of Yâjnavalkya.

Yâjnavalkya stayed with his master, and his master had a Brahmin friend who wanted to make a journey. Therefore he asked the master to send somebody to his house to perform there during his absence the rites to *Homa*, *i.e.* to his fire, and to prevent it from being extinguished. Now the master sent his pupils to the house of his friend one after the other. So it came to be the turn of Yâjnavalkya, who was beautiful to look at and handsomely dressed. When he began the work which he was sent for, in a place where the wife of the absent man was present, she conceived an aversion to his fine attire, and Yâjnavalkya became aware of it, though she concealed it. On having finished, he took the water to sprinkle it over the head of the woman, for this holds with them the place of the blowing after an incantation, since blowing is disliked by them and considered as something impure. Then the woman said, "Sprinkle it over this column." So he did, and at once the column became green. Now the woman repented having missed the blessing of his pious action; therefore on the following day she went to the master, asking him to send her the same pupil whom he had sent the day before. Yâjnavalkya, however, declined to go except in his turn. No urging had any effect upon him; he did not mind the wrath of his master, but simply said, "Take away from me all that you have taught me." And scarcely had he spoken the word, when on a sudden he had forgotten all he knew before. Now he turned to the Sun and asked him to teach him the Veda. The Sun said, "How is that possible, as I must perpetually wander, and you are incapable of doing the same?" But then Yâjnavalkya clung to the chariot of the Sun and began to learn the Veda from him; but he was compelled to interrupt the recitation here and there on account of the irregularity of the motion of the chariot.

The Sâmaveda treats of the sacrifices, commandments, and prohibitions. It is recited in a tone like a chant, and hence its name is derived, because *sâman* means *the sweetness of recitation*. The cause of this kind of recital is, that Nârâyaṇa, when he appeared on earth in the shape of Vâmana, and came to the king Bali, changed himself into a Brahman and began to recite the Sâmaveda with a touching melody, by which he exhilarated the king, in consequence of which there happened to him the well-known story. (Sâmaveda and Âtharvaṇaveda.)

The Âtharvaṇaveda is as a text connected by the

rules of Saṁdhi. It does not consist of the same compositions as the Ṛig and Yajur Vedas, but of a third kind called *bhara*. It is recited according to a melody with a nasal tone. This Veda is less in favour with the Hindus than the others. It likewise treats of the sacrifices to the fire, and contains injunctions regarding the dead and what is to be done with them.

List of the Purâṇas.

As to the Purâṇas, we first mention that the word means *first, eternal.* There are eighteen Purâṇas, most of them called by the names of animals, human or angelic beings, because they contain stories about them, or because the contents of the book refer in some way to them, or because the book consists of answers which the creature whose name forms the title of the book has given to certain questions.

Page 63.

The Purâṇas are of human origin, composed by the so-called Ṛishis. In the following I give a list of their names, as I have heard them, and committed them to writing from dictation:—

1. *Âdi-purâṇa, i.e.* the first.
2. *Matsya-purâṇa, i.e.* the fish.
3. *Kûrma-purâṇa, i.e.* the tortoise.
4. *Varâha-purâṇa, i.e.* the boar.
5. *Narasiṁha-purâṇa, i.e.* a human being with a lion's head.
6. *Vâmana-purâṇa, i.e.* the dwarf.
7. *Vâyu-purâṇa, i.e.* the wind.
8. *Nanda-purâṇa, i.e.* a servant of Mahâdeva.
9. *Skanda-purâṇa, i.e.* a son of Mahâdeva.
10. *Âditya-purâṇa, i.e.* the sun.
11. *Soma-purâṇa, i.e.* the moon.
12. *Sâmba-purâṇa, i.e.* the son of Vishṇu.
13. *Brahmâṇḍa-purâṇa, i.e.* heaven.
14. *Mârkaṇḍeya-purâṇa, i.e.* a great Ṛishi.
15. *Târkshya-purâṇa, i.e.* the bird Garuḍa.
16. *Vishṇu-purâṇa, i.e.* Nârâyaṇa.
17. *Brahma-purâṇa, i.e.* the nature charged with the preservation of the world.
18. *Bhavishya-purâṇa, i.e.* future things.

Of all this literature I have only seen portions of the Matsya, Âditya, and Vâyu Purâṇas.

Another somewhat different list of the Purâṇas has been read to me from the *Vishṇu-Purâṇa*. I give it here *in extenso*, as in all questions resting on tradition it is the duty of an author to give those traditions as completely as possible:—

1. *Brahma.*
2. *Padma, i.e.* the red lotus.
3. *Vishṇu.*
4. *Śiva, i.e.* Mahâdeva.
5. *Bhâgavata, i.e.* Vâsudeva.
6. *Nârada, i.e.* the son of Brahma.
7. *Mârkaṇḍeya.*
8. *Agni, i.e.* the fire.
9. *Bhavishya, i.e.* the future.
10. *Brahmavaivarta, i.e.* the wind.
11. *Liṅga, i.e.* an image of the αἰδοῖα of Mahâdeva.
12. *Varâha.*
13. *Skanda.*
14. *Vâmana.*
15. *Kûrma.*
16. *Matsya, i.e.* the fish.
17. *Garuḍa, i.e.* the bird on which Vishṇu rides.
18. *Brahmâṇḍa.*

These are the names of the Purâṇas according to the *Vishṇu-Purâṇa*.

The book *Smṛiti* is derived from the Veda. It contains commandments and prohibitions, and is composed by the following twenty sons of Brahman:— A list of *Smṛiti* books.

1. Âpastamba.	11. Yâjnavalkya.
2. Parâśara.	12. Atri.
3. Śâtâtapa.	13. Hârîta.
4. Saṁvarta.	14. Likhita.
5. Daksha.	15. Śaṅkha.
6. Vasishṭha.	16. Gautama.
7. Aṅgiras.	17. Vṛihaspati.
8. Yama.	18. Kâtyâyana.
9. Vishṇu.	19. Vyâsa.
10. Manu.	20. Uśanas.

Besides, the Hindus have books about the jurisprudence of their religion, on theosophy, on ascetics, on the process of becoming god and seeking liberation from the world, as, *e.g.* the book composed by Gauḍa the anchorite, which goes by his name; the book *Sâṁkhya*, composed by Kapila, on divine subjects; the book of *Patañjali*, on the search for liberation and for the union of the soul with the object of its meditation; the book *Nyâyabhâshâ*, composed by Kapila, on the Veda and its interpretation, also showing that it has been created, and distinguishing within the Veda between such injunctions as are obligatory only in certain cases, and those which are obligatory in general; further, the book *Mîmâṁsâ*, composed by Jaimini, on the same subject; the book *Laukâyata*, composed by Bṛihaspati, treating of the subject that in all investigations we must exclusively rely upon the apperception of

Page 64. the senses; the book *Agastyamata*, composed by Agastya, treating of the subject that in all investigations we must use the apperception of the senses as well as tradition; and the book *Vishṇu-dharma*. The word *dharma* means *reward*, but in general it is used for *religion*; so that this title means *The religion of God*, who in this case is understood to be Nârâyaṇa. Further, there are the books of the six pupils of Vyâsa, viz. *Devala*, *Śukra*, *Bhârgava*, *Vṛihaspati*, *Yâjnavalkya*, and *Manu*. The Hindus have numerous books about all the branches of science. How could anybody know the titles of all of them, more especially if he is not a Hindu, but a foreigner?

Mahâbhârata.

Besides, they have a book which they hold in such veneration that they firmly assert that everything which occurs in other books is found also in this book, but not all which occurs in this book is found in other books. It is called *Bhârata*, and composed by Vyâsa the son of Parâśara at the time of the great war between the children of Pâṇḍu and those of Kuru. The title itself gives an indication of those times. The book has 100,000 Ślokas in eighteen parts, each of which is called *Parvan*. Here we give the list of them:—

1. *Sabhâ-parva, i.e.* the king's dwelling.
2. *Araṇya, i.e.* going out into the open field, meaning the exodus of the children of Pâṇḍu.
3. *Virâṭa, i.e.* the name of a king in whose realm they dwelt during the time of their concealment.
4. *Udyoga, i.e.* the preparing for battle.
5. *Bhîshma.*
6. *Droṇa* the Brahmin.
7. *Karṇa* the son of the Sun.
8. *S'alya* the brother of *Duryodhana*, some of the greatest heroes who did the fighting, one *always* coming forward after his predecessor had been killed.
9. *Gadâ, i.e.* the club.
10. *Sauptika, i.e.* the killing of the sleepers, when Aśvatthâman the son of Droṇa attacked the city of Pâñcâla during the night and killed the inhabitants.
11. *Jalapradânika, i.e.* the successive drawing of water for the dead, after people have washed off the impurity caused by the touching of the dead.
12. *Strî, i.e.* the lamentations of the women.
13. *S'ânti*, containing 24,000 Ślokas on eradicating hatred from the heart, in four parts:
    (1.) *Râjadharma*, on the reward of the kings.
    (2.) *Dânadharma*, on the reward for almsgiving.
    (3.) *Âpaddharma*, on the reward of those who are in need and trouble.
    (4). *Mokshadharma*, on the reward of him who is liberated from the world.
14. *Aśvamedha, i.e.* the sacrifice of the horse which is sent out together with an army to wander through the world. Then they proclaim in public that it belongs to the king of the world, and that he who does not agree thereto is to come forward to fight. The Brahmans follow the horse, and celebrate sacrifices to the fire in those places where the horse drops its dung.
15. *Mausala, i.e.* the fighting of the Yâdavas, the tribe of Vâsudeva, among themselves.
16. *Âśramavâsa, i.e.* leaving one's own country.
17. *Prasthâna, i.e.* quitting the realm to seek liberation.
18. *Svargârohaṇa, i.e.* journeying towards Paradise.

These eighteen parts are followed by another one which is called *Harivaṁśa-Parvan,* which contains the traditions relating to Vâsudeva.

In this book there occur passages which, like riddles, admit of manifold interpretations. As to the reason of Page 65, this the Hindus relate the following story:—Vyâsa asked Brahman to procure him somebody who might write for him the *Bhârata* from his dictation. Now he intrusted with this task his son Vinâyaka, who is represented as an idol with an elephant's head, and made it obligatory on him never to cease from writing. At the same time Vyâsa made it obligatory on him to write only that which he understood. Therefore Vyâsa, in the course of his dictation, dictated such sentences as compelled the writer to ponder over them, and thereby Vyâsa gained time for resting awhile.

(Chapter XIII, pages 135–151, contains a technical comparison of Sanskrit and Arabic meters.)

CHAPTER XIV.

HINDU LITERATURE IN THE OTHER SCIENCES, ASTRONOMY, ASTROLOGY, ETC.

Times unfavourable to the progress of science.

THE number of sciences is great, and it may be still greater if the public mind is directed towards them at such times as they are in the ascendancy and in general favour with all, when people not only honour science itself, but also its representatives. To do this is, in the first instance, the duty of those who rule over them, of kings and princes. For they alone could free the minds of scholars from the daily anxieties for the necessities of life, and stimulate their energies to earn more fame and favour, the yearning for which is the pith and marrow of human nature.

The present times, however, are not of this kind. They are the very opposite, and therefore it is quite impossible that a new science or any new kind of research should arise in our days. What we have of sciences is nothing but the scanty remains of bygone better times.

If a science or an idea has once conquered the whole earth, every nation appropriates part of it. So do also the Hindus. Their belief about the cyclical revolutions of times is nothing very special, but is simply in accordance with the results of scientific observation.

On the Siddhântas.

The science of astronomy is the most famous among them, since the affairs of their religion are in various ways connected with it. If a man wants to gain the title of an astronomer, he must not only know scientific or mathematical astronomy, but also astrolcgy. The book known among Muslims as *Sindhind* is called by them *Siddhânta*, i.e. *straight*, not crooked nor changing. By this name they call every standard book on astronomy, even such books as, according to our opinion, do not come up to the mark of our so-called *Zîj*, *i.e.* handbooks of mathematical astronomy. They have five Siddhântas:—

I. *Sûrya-siddhânta*, *i.e.* the Siddhânta of the sun, composed by Lâṭa.

II. *Vasishṭha-siddhânta*, so called from one of the stars of the Great Bear, composed by Vishṇucandra.

III. *Pulisa-siddhânta*, so called from Paulisa, the Greek, from the city of Saintra, which I suppose to be Alexandria, composed by Pulisa.

IV. *Romaka-siddhânta*, so called from the Rûm, *i.e.* the subjects of the Roman Empire, composed by Śrîsheṇa.

V. *Brahma-siddhânta*, so called from Brahman, composed by Brahmagupta, the son of Jishṇu, from the town of Bhillamâla between Multân and Anhilwâra, 16 *yojana* from the latter place (?).

The authors of these books draw from one and the same source, the book *Paitâmaha*, so called from *the first father*, *i.e.* Brahman.

Varâhamihira has composed an astronomical handbook of small compass called *Pañca-siddhântikâ*, which name ought to mean that it contains the pith and marrow of the preceding five Siddhântas. But this is not the case, nor is it so much better than they as to be called the most correct one of the five. So the name does not indicate anything but the fact that the number of Siddhântas is five.

Brahmagupta says: "Many of the Siddhântas are Sûrya, others Indu, Pulisa, Romaka, Vasishṭha, and Yavana, *i.e.* the Greeks; and though the Siddhântas are many, they differ only in words, not in the subject-matter. He who studies them properly will find that they agree with each other."

Up to the present time I have not been able to procure any of these books save those of Pulisa and of Brahmagupta. I have commenced translating them, but have not yet finished my work. Meanwhile I shall give here a table of contents of the *Brahma-siddhânta*, which in any case will be useful and instructive.

Page 74.

Contents of the *Brahma-siddhânta*.

Contents of the twenty-four chapters of the *Brahma-siddhânta* —

1. On the nature of the globe and the figure of heaven and earth.

2. On the revolutions of the planets; on the calculation of time, *i.e.* how to find the time for different longitudes and latitudes; how to find the mean places of the planets; how to find the sine of an arc.

3. On the correction of the places of the planets.

4. On three problems: how to find the shadow, the bygone portion of the day and the *ascendens*, and how to derive one from the other.

5. On the planets becoming visible when they leave the rays of the sun, and their becoming invisible when entering them.

6. On the first appearance of the moon, and about her two cusps.

7. On the lunar eclipse.

8. On the solar eclipse.

9. On the shadow of the moon.

10. On the meeting and conjunction of the planets.

11. On the latitudes of the planets.

12. A critical investigation for the purpose of distinguishing between correct and corrupt passages in the texts of astronomical treatises and handbooks.

13. On arithmetic; on plane measure and cognate subjects.

14. Scientific calculation of the mean places of the planets.

15. Scientific calculation of the correction of the places of the planets.

16. Scientific calculation of the three problems (v. chap. 4).

17. On the deflection of eclipses.

18. Scientific calculation of the appearance of the new moon and her two cusps.

19. On *Kuṭṭaka, i.e.* the pounding of a thing. The pounding of oil-producing substances is here compared with *the most minute and detailed research.* This chapter treats of algebra and related subjects, and besides it contains other valuable remarks of a more or less arithmetical nature.

20. On the shadow.

21. On the calculation of the measures of poetry and on metrics.

22. On cycles and instruments of observation.

23. On time and the four measures of time, the *solar*, the *civil*, the *lunar*, and the *sidereal.*

24. About numeral notation in the metrical books of this kind.

These, now, are twenty-four chapters, according to his own statement, but there is a twenty-fifth one, called *Dhyâna-graha-adhyâya,* in which he tries to solve the problems by speculation, not by mathematical calculation. I have not enumerated it in this list, because the pretensions which he brings forward in this chapter are repudiated by mathematics. I am rather inclined to think that that which he produces is meant to be the *ratio metaphysica* of all astronomical methods, otherwise how could any problem of this science be solved by anything save by mathematics?

On the literature of Tantras and Karaṇas.

Such books as do not reach the standard of a Siddhânta are mostly called *Tantra* or *Karaṇa.* The former means *ruling under a governor*, the latter means *following, i.e.* following behind the Siddhânta. Under *governors* they understand the *Âcâryas, i.e.* the sages, anchorites, the followers of Brahman.

There are two famous *Tantras* by *Âryabhaṭa* and *Balabhadra*, besides the *Rasâyana-tantra* by *Bhânuyaśas* (?). About what Rasâyana means we shall give a separate chapter (chap. xvii.)

As for *Karaṇas*, there is one (*lacuna*) called by his name, besides the *Karaṇa-khaṇḍa-khâdyaka* by Brahmagupta. The last word, *khaṇḍa*, means a kind of their sweetmeats. With regard to the reason why he gave his book this title, I have been told the following:—

Sugrîva, the Buddhist, had composed an astronomical handbook which he called *Dadhi-sâgara, i.e.* the sea of sour-milk; and a pupil of his composed a book of the same kind which he called *Kûra-babayâ* (?), *i.e.* a mountain of rice. Afterwards he composed another book which he called *Lavaṇa-mushṭi, i.e.* a handful of salt. Therefore Brahmagupta called his book the *Sweetmeat—khâdyaka*—in order that all kinds of victuals (sour-milk, rice, salt, &c.) should occur in the titles of the books on this science.

The contents of the book *Karaṇa-khaṇḍa-khâdyaka*
Page 75. represent the doctrine of Âryabhaṭa. Therefore Brahmagupta afterwards composed a second book, which he called *Uttara-khaṇḍa-khâdyaka, i.e.* the explanation of the *Khaṇḍa-khâdyaka*. And this book is again followed by another one called *Khaṇḍa-khâdyaka-tippâ* (*sic*), of which I do not know whether it is composed by Brahmagupta or somebody else. It explains the reasons and the nature of the calculations employed in the *Khaṇḍa-khâdyaka*. I suppose it is a work of Balabhadra's.

Further, there is an astronomical handbook composed by Vijayanandin, the commentator, in the city of Benares, entitled *Karaṇa-tilaka, i.e.* the blaze on the front of the Karaṇas; another one by Vitteśvara the son of Bhadatta (? Mihdatta), of the city of Nâgarapura, called *Karaṇa-sâra, i.e.* that which has been derived from the Karaṇa; another one, by Bhânuyaśas (?), is called *Karaṇa-para-tilaka*, which shows, as I am told, how the corrected places of the stars are derived from one another.

There is a book by Utpala the Kashmirian called *Râhunrâkaraṇa* (?), *i.e.* breaking the Karaṇas; and another called *Karaṇa-pâta*, *i.e.* killing the Karaṇas. Besides there is a book called *Karaṇa-cûḍâmaṇi* of which I do not know the author.

There are more books of the same kind with other titles, *e.g.* the great *Mânasa*, composed by Manu, and the commentary by Utpala; the small *Mânasa*, an epitome of the former by Puñcala (?), from the southern country; *Daśagîtikâ*, by Âryabhaṭa; *Âryâshṭaśata*, by the same; *Lokânanda*, so called from the name of the author; *Bhaṭṭila* (?), so called from its author, the Brahman Bhaṭṭila. The books of this kind are nearly innumerable.

On astrological literature, the so-called Saṁhitâs.

As for astrological literature, each one of the following authors has composed a so-called *Saṁhitâ*, viz.:—

Mâṇḍavya.	Balabhadra.
Parâśara.	Divyatattva.
Garga.	Varâhamihira.
Brahman.	

Saṁhitâ means *that which is collected*, books containing something of everything, *e.g.* forewarnings relating to a journey derived from meteorological occurrences; prophecies regarding the fate of dynasties; the knowledge of lucky and unlucky things; prophesying from the lines of the hand; interpretation of dreams, and taking auguries from the flight or cries of birds. For Hindu scholars believe in such things. It is the custom of their astronomers to propound in their Saṁhitâs also the whole science of meteorology and cosmology.

The Jâtakas, *i.e.* books on nativities.

Each one of the following authors has composed a book, *Jâtaka*, *i.e.* book of nativities, viz.:—

Parâśara.	Jîvaśarman.
Satya.	Mau, the Greek.
Maṇittha.	

Varâhamihira has composed two Jâtakas, a small and a large one. The latter of these has been explained by Balabhadra, and the former I have translated into Arabic. Further, the Hindus have a large book on the science of the astrology of nativities called *Sârâvalî*, *i.e.* the chosen one, similar to the *Vazîdaj* (= Persian *guzîda* ?), composed by Kalyâṇa-Varman, who gained high credit for his scientific works. But there is another book still larger than this, which comprehends the whole of astrological sciences, called *Yavana*, *i.e.* belonging to the Greeks.

Of Varâhamihira there are several small books, *e.g.* *Shaṭ-pañcâśikâ*, fifty-six chapters on astrology; *Horâ-pañca-hotṛiya* (?), on the same subject.

Travelling is treated of in the book *Yogayâtrâ* and the book *Tikanî*(?)-*yâtrâ*, marriage and marrying in the book *Vivâha-paṭala*, architecture in the book (*lacuna*).

The art of taking auguries from the flight or cries of birds, and of the foretelling by means of piercing a needle into a book, is propounded in the work called *Srudhava* (? śrotavya), which exists in three different copies. Mahâdeva is said to be the author of the first, Vimalabuddhi the author of the second, and Baṅgâla the author of the third. Similar subjects are treated in the book *Gûḍhâmana* (?), *i.e.* the knowledge of the unknown, composed by Buddha, the originator of the sect of the red robe-wearers, the Shamanians; and in the book *Praśna Gûḍhâmana* (?), *i.e.* questions of the science of the unknown, composed by Utpala.

Besides, there are Hindu scholars of whom we know
Page 76. the names, but not the title of any book of theirs, viz.:—

Pradyumna.	Sârasvata.
Saṅgahila (Śṛiṅkhala ?).	Pîruvâna (?).
Divâkara.	Devakîrtti.
Parêśvara.	Prithûdaka-svâmin.

Medical literature.

Medicine belongs to the same class of sciences as astronomy, but there is this difference, that the latter stands in close relation to the religion of the Hindus. They have a book called by the name of its author, *i.e.* *Caraka*, which they consider as the best of their whole literature on medicine. According to their belief, Caraka was a Ṛishi in the last Dvâpara-yuga, when his name was *Agniveśa*, but afterwards he was called *Caraka*, *i.e.* the intelligent one, after the first elements of medicine had been laid down by certain Ṛishis, the children of *Sûtra*. These latter had received them from Indra, Indra from Aśvin, one of the two physicians of the Devas, and Aśvin had received them from Prajâpati, *i.e.* Brahman, *the first father*. This book has been translated into Arabic for the princes of the house of the Barmecides.

The Hindus cultivate numerous other branches of science and literature, and have a nearly boundless literature. I, however, could not comprehend it with my knowledge. I wish I could translate the book *Pañcatantra*, known among us as the book of Kalîla and Dimna. It is far spread in various languages, in Persian, Hindî, and Arabic—in translations of people who are not free from the suspicion of having altered the text. For instance, ʿAbdallâh Ibn Almuḳaffaʿ has added in his Arabic version the chapter about Barzôya, with the intention of raising doubts in the minds of people of feeble religious belief, and to gain and prepare them for the propagation of the doctrines of the Manichæans. And if he is open to suspicion in so far as he has added something to the text which he had simply to translate, he is hardly free from suspicion in his capacity as translator. On Pañcatantra.

(Chapter XV, pages 160–169. Lists of Indian weights and measures with Arabic equivalents. Among those frequently used, a *farsakh* equals four miles, and a *yojana* is eight miles.)

CHAPTER XVI.

NOTES ON THE WRITING OF THE HINDUS, ON THEIR ARITHMETIC AND RELATED SUBJECTS, AND ON CERTAIN STRANGE MANNERS AND CUSTOMS OF THEIRS.

Page 81.

On various kinds of writing material.

THE tongue communicates the thought of the speaker to the hearer. Its action has therefore, as it were, a momentary life only, and it would have been impossible to deliver by oral tradition the accounts of the events of the past to later generations, more particularly if they are separated from them by long periods of time. This has become possible only by a new discovery of the human mind, by the art of writing, which spreads news over space as the winds spread, and over time as the spirits of the deceased spread. Praise therefore be unto Him who has arranged creation and created everything for the best!

The Hindus are not in the habit of writing on hides, like the Greeks in ancient times. Socrates, on being asked why he did not compose books, gave this reply: "I do not transfer knowledge from the living hearts of men to the *dead* hides of sheep." Muslims, too, used in the early times of Islam to write on hides, *e.g.* the treaty between the Prophet and the Jews of Khaibar and his letter to Kisrâ. The copies of the Koran were written on the hides of gazelles, as are still nowadays the copies of the Thora. There occurs this passage in the Koran (Sûra vi. 91): "They make it *karâṭîs*," *i.e.* *τομάρια*. The *kirṭâs* (or *charta*) is made in Egypt, being cut out of the papyrus stalk. Written on this material, the orders of the Khalifs went out into all the world until shortly before our time. Papyrus has this advantage over vellum, that you can neither rub out nor change anything on it, because thereby it would be destroyed. It was in China that paper was first manufactured. Chinese prisoners introduced the fabrication of paper into Samarḳand, and thereupon it was made in various places, so as to meet the existing want.

The Hindus have in the south of their country a slender tree like the date and cocoa-nut palms, bearing edible fruits and leaves of the length of one yard, and as broad as three fingers one put beside the other. They call these leaves *târî* (*tâla* or *târ*=*Borassus flabelliformis*), and write on them. They bind a book of these leaves together by a cord on which they are arranged, the cord going through all the leaves by a hole in the middle of each.

In Central and Northern India people use the bark of the *tûz* tree, one kind of which is used as a cover for bows. It is called *bhûrja*. They take a piece one yard long and as broad as the outstretched fingers of the hand, or somewhat less, and prepare it in various ways. They oil and polish it so as to make it hard and smooth, and then they write on it. The proper order of the single leaves is marked by numbers. The whole book is wrapped up in a piece of cloth and fastened between two tablets of the same size. Such a book is called *pûthî* (cf. *pusta, pustaka*). Their letters, and whatever else they have to write, they write on the bark of the *tûz* tree.

On the Hindu alphabet.

As to the writing or alphabet of the Hindus, we have already mentioned that it once had been lost and forgotten; that nobody cared for it, and that in consequence people became illiterate, sunken into gross ignorance, and entirely estranged from science. But then Vyâsa, the son of Parâśara, rediscovered their alphabet of fifty letters by an inspiration of God. A letter is called *akshara*.

Some people say that originally the number of their letters was less, and that it increased only by degrees. This is possible, or I should even say necessary. As for the Greek alphabet, a certain *Asîdhas* (*sic*) had formed sixteen characters to perpetuate science about the time when the Israelites ruled over Egypt. Thereupon *Kîmush* (*sic*) and *Agenon* (*sic*) brought them to the Greeks. By adding four new signs they obtained an alphabet of twenty letters. Later on, about the time when Socrates was poisoned, Simonides added four
Page 82. other signs, and so the Athenians at last had a complete alphabet of twenty-four letters, which happened during the reign of Artaxerxes, the son of Darius, the son of Artaxerxes, the son of Cyrus, according to the chronographers of the West.

The great number of the letters of the Hindu alphabet is explained, firstly, by the fact that they express every letter by a separate sign if it is followed by a vowel or a diphthong or a *hamza* (*visarga*), or a small extension of the sound beyond the measure of the vowel; and, secondly, by the fact that they have consonants which are not found together in any other language, though they may be found scattered through different languages—sounds of such a nature that *our* tongues, not being familiar with them, can scarcely pronounce them, and that *our* ears are frequently not able to distinguish between many a cognate pair of them.

The Hindus write from the left to the right like the Greeks. They do not write on the basis of a line, above which the heads of the letters rise whilst their tails go down below, as in Arabic writing. On the contrary, their ground-line is above, a straight line above every single character, and from this line the letter hangs down and is written under it. Any sign *above* the line is nothing but a grammatical mark to denote the pronunciation of the character above which it stands.

On the local alphabets of the Hindus.

The most generally known alphabet is called *Siddha-mâtṛikâ*, which is by some considered as originating from Kashmîr, for the people of Kashmîr use it. But it is also used in Varânaṣî. This town and Kashmîr are the high schools of Hindu sciences. The same writing is used in Madhyadeśa, *i.e.* the middle country, the country all around Kanauj, which is also called Âryâvarta.

In Mâlava there is another alphabet called *Nâgara*, which differs from the former only in the shape of the characters.

Next comes an alphabet called *Ardhanâgarî*, *i.e. half-nâgara*, so called because it is compounded of the former two. It is used in Bhâtiya and some parts of Sindh.

Other alphabets are the *Malwârî*, used in Malwashau, in Southern Sind, towards the sea-coast; the *Saindhava*, used in Bahmanwâ or Almanṣûra; the *Karnâṭa*, used in Karnâṭadeśa, whence those troops come which in the armies are known as *Kannara;* the *Andhrî*, used in Andhradeśa; the *Dirwarî* (*Drâviḍî*), used in Dirwaradeśa (Draviḍadeśa); the *Lârî*, used in Lâradeśa (Lâṭadeśa); the *Gaurî* (*Gauḍî*), used in Pûrvadeśa, *i.e.* the Eastern country; the *Bhaikshukî*, used in Udunpûr in Pûrvadeśa. This last is the writing of Buddha.

On the word Om.

The Hindus begin their books with *Om*, the word of creation, as we begin them with "In the name of God." The figure of the word *om* is . This figure does not consist of letters; it is simply an image invented to represent this word, which people use, believing that it will bring them a blessing, and meaning thereby a confession of the unity of God. Similar to this is the manner in which the Jews write the name of God, viz. by three Hebrew *yods*. In the Thora the word is written *YHVH* and pronounced

Adonai; sometimes they also say *Yah.* The word *Adonai,* which they pronounce, is not expressed in writing.

On their numeral signs.

The Hindus do not use the letters of their alphabet for numerical notation, as we use the Arabic letters in the order of the Hebrew alphabet. As in different parts of India the letters have different shapes, the numeral signs, too, which are called *aṅka,* differ. The numeral

Page 83.

signs which *we* use are derived from the finest forms of the Hindu signs. Signs and figures are of no use if people do not know what they mean, but the people of Kashmîr mark the single leaves of their books with figures which look like drawings or like the Chinese characters, the meaning of which can only be learned by a very long practice. However, they do not use them when reckoning in the sand.

In arithmetic all nations agree that all the *orders* of numbers (*e.g.* one, ten, hundred, thousand) stand in a certain relation to the ten; that each order is the tenth part of the following and the tenfold of the preceding. I have studied the names of the *orders* of the numbers in various languages with all kinds of people with whom I have been in contact, and have found that no nation goes beyond the thousand. The Arabs, too, stop with the thousand, which is certainly the most correct and the most natural thing to do. I have written a separate treatise on this subject.

Those, however, who go beyond the thousand in their numeral system are the Hindus, at least in their arithmetical technical terms, which have been either freely invented or derived according to certain etymologies, whilst in others both methods are blended together. They extend the names of the *orders* of numbers until the 18th *order* for religious reasons, the mathematicians being assisted by the grammarians with all kinds of etymologies.

The 18th *order* is called *Parârdha, i.e.* the half of

heaven, or, more acurately, *the half of that which is above.* For if the Hindus construct periods of time out of Kalpas, the unit of this *order* is *a day of God* (*i.e.* a half *nychthemeron*). And as we do not know any body larger than heaven, half of it (*parârdha*), as *a half of the greatest body,* has been compared with *a half of the greatest day.* By doubling it, by uniting night to day, we get the *whole* of the greatest day. There can be no doubt that the name *Parârdha* is accounted for in this way, and that *parâr* means *the whole of heaven.*

The following are the names of the eighteen *orders* of numbers:— The eighteen orders of numeration.

1. *Ekaṁ.*	10. *Padma.*
2. *Daśaṁ.*	11. *Kharva.*
3. *S'ataṁ.*	12. *Nikharva.*
4. *Sahasraṁ.*	13. *Mahâpadma.*
5. *Ayuta.*	14. *S'aṅku.*
6. *Laksha.*	15. *Samudra.*
7. *Prayuta.*	16. *Madhya.*
8. *Koṭi.*	17. *Antya.*
9. *Nyarbuda.*	18. *Parârdha.*

I shall now mention some of their differences of opinion relating to this system.

Some Hindus maintain *that there is a 19th order beyond the Parârdha, called Bhûri, and that this is the limit of reckoning.* But in reality *reckoning* is unlimited; it has only a technical limit, which is conventionally adopted as the last of the *orders* of numbers. By the word *reckoning* in the sentence above they seem to mean *nomenclature,* as if they meant to say that the language has no *name* for any reckoning beyond the 19th *order.* It is known that the unit of this *order, i.e.* one *bhûri,* is equal to one-fifth of the *greatest day,* but on this subject they have no tradition. In their tradition there are only traces of combinations of the *greatest day,* as we shall hereafter explain. Therefore this 19th order is an addition of an artificial and hyper-accurate nature. Variations occurring in the eighteen orders.

Page 84. According to others, the limit of reckoning is *koṭi;* and starting from *koṭi* the succession of the *orders* of numbers would be *koṭi,* thousands, hundreds, tenths; for the number of Devas is expressed in *kôṭis.* According to their belief there are thirty-three *koṭis* of Devas, eleven of which belong to each of the three beings, Brahman, Narâyaṇa, and Mahâdeva.

The names of the *orders* beyond that of the 18th have been invented by the grammarians, as we have said already (p. 174).

Further, we observe that the popular name of the 5th *order* is *Daśa sahasra,* that of the 7th *order, Daśa laksha;* for the two names which we have mentioned in the list above (*Ayuta* and *Prayuta*) are rarely used.

The book of Âryabhaṭa of Kusumapura gives the following names of the *orders* from the ten till 10 *koṭi*:—

Ayutaṁ.	*Koṭi padma.*
Niyutaṁ.	*Parapadma.*
Prayutaṁ.	

Further, it is noteworthy that some people establish a kind of etymological relationship between the different names; so they call the 6th *order Niyuta,* according to the analogy of the 5th, which is called *Ayuta.* Further, they call the 8th *order Arbuda,* according to the analogy of the 9th, which is called *Nyarbuda.*

There is a similar relation between *Nikharva* and *Kharva,* the names of the 12th and 11th *orders,* and between *Śaṅku* and *Mahâśaṅku,* the names of the 13th and 14th *orders.* According to this analogy *Mahâpadma* ought to follow immediately after *Padma,* but this latter is the name of the 10th, the former the name of the 13th *order.*

These are differences of theirs which can be traced back to certain reasons; but besides, there are many differences without any reason, which simply arise from people dictating these names without observing any fixed order, or from the fact that they hate to avow their ignorance by a frank *I do not know*,—a word which is difficult to them in any connection whatsoever.

The *Pulisa-siddhânta* gives the following list of the *orders* of the numbers :—

4. *Sahasraṁ.*	8. *Koṭi.*
5. *Ayutaṁ.*	9. *Arbudaṁ.*
6. *Niyutaṁ.*	10. *Kharva.*
7. *Prayutaṁ.*	

The following *orders*, from the 11th till the 18th, are the same as those of the above-mentioned list.

The Hindus use the numeral signs in arithmetic in the same way as we do. I have composed a treatise showing how far, possibly, the Hindus are ahead of us in this subject. We have already explained that the Hindus compose their books in Ślokas. If, now, they wish, in their astronomical handbooks, to express some numbers of the various *orders*, they express them by words used to denote certain numbers either in one *order* alone or at the same time in two *orders* (*e.g.* a word meaning either 20 or both 20 and 200). For each number they have appropriated quite a great quantity of words. Hence, if one word does not suit the metre, you may easily exchange it for a synonym which suits. Brahmagupta says: "If you want to write *one*, express it by everything which is unique, as *the earth, the moon*; *two* by everything which is double, as, *e.g. black* and *white*; *three* by everything which is threefold; the *nought* by *heaven*, the *twelve* by the names of the sun."

Numeral notation.

I have united in the following table all the expressions for the numbers which I used to hear from them; for the knowledge of these things is most essential for deciphering their astronomical handbooks

Whenever I shall come to know all the meanings of these words, I will add them, if God permits!

0 = *śûnya* and *kha*, both meaning *point*.
gagana, *i.e.* heaven.
viyat, *i.e.* heaven.
âkâśa, *i.e.* heaven.
ambara, *i.e.* heaven.
abhra, *i.e.* heaven.

1 = *âdi*, *i.e.* the beginning.
śaśin.
indu.
śîtâ.
urvarâ, *dharaṇî*.
pitâmaha, *i.e.* the first father.
candra, *i.e.* the moon.
śîtâṁśu, *i.e.* the moon.
rûpa.
raśmi.

2 = *yama*.
aśvin.
ravicandra.
locana, *i.e.* the two eyes.
akshi.
dasra.
yamala.
paksha, *i.e.* the two halves of a month.
netra, *i.e.* the two eyes.

3 = *trikâla*, *i.e.* the three parts of time.
trijagat.
trayaṁ.
pâvaka, *vaiśvânara*, *dahana*, *tapana*, *hutâśana*, *jvalana*, *agni*, *i.e.* fire.
[*triguṇa*,] *i.e.* the three first forces.
loka, *i.e.* the worlds, earth, heaven, and hell.
trikaṭu.

4 = *veda*, *i.e.* their sacred code, because it has four parts.
samudra, *sâgara*, *i.e.* the sea.
abdhi.
dadhi.
diś, *i.e.* the four cardinal points.
jalâśaya.
kṛita.

5 = *śara*.
artha.
indriya, *i.e.* the five senses.
sâyaka.
اخون
vâṇa.
bhûta.
ishu.
Pâṇḍava, *i.e.* the five royal brothers.
pattrin, *mârgaṇa*.

6 = *rasa*.
aṅga.
shaṭ.
الدرم (?) *i.e.* the year.
ṛitu (?).
mâsârdhaṁ.

7 = *aga*.
mahîdhara.
parvata, *i.e.* the mountains.
saptan.
naga, *i.e.* the mountains.
adri.
muni.

8 = *vasu*, *ashṭa*.
dhî, *maṅgala*.
gaja, *nâga*.
dantin.

9 = *go*, *chidra*.
nanda, *pavana*.
randhra, *antara*.
navan = 9.

10 = *diś, khendu.*
âśâ, Râvaṇa-śiras.

11 = *Rudra,* the destroyer of the world.
Mahâdeva, i.e. the prince of the angels.
îśvara.
akshauhiṇî, i.e. the army Kuru had.

12 = *sûrya,* because there are twelve suns.
âditya.
arka, i.e. the sun.
mâsa, bhânu.
sahaśrâṁśu.

13 = *viśva.*

14 = *manu,* the lords of the fourteen *manvantaras.*

15 = *tithi, i.e.* the lunar days in each half month.

16 = *ashṭi, nṛipa, bhûpa.*

17 = *atyashṭi.*

18 = *dhṛiti.* Page 88.

19 = *atidhṛiti.*

20 = *nakha, kṛiti.*

21 = *utkṛiti.*

22 =

23 =

24 =

25 = *tattva, i.e.* the twenty-five things, through the knowledge of which liberation is obtained.

As far as I have seen and heard of the Hindus, they do not usually go beyond twenty-five with this kind of numerical notation.

Strange manners and customs of the Hindus. Page 89.

We shall now speak of certain strange manners and customs of the Hindus. The strangeness of a thing evidently rests on the fact that it occurs but rarely, and that we seldom have the opportunity of witnessing it. If such strangeness reaches a high degree, the thing becomes a curiosity, or even something like a miracle, which is no longer in accordance with the ordinary laws of nature, and which seems chimerical as long as it has not been witnessed. Many Hindu customs differ from those of our country and of our time to such a degree as to appear to us simply monstrous. One might almost think that they had intentionally changed them into the opposite, for *our* customs do not resemble theirs, but are the very reverse; and if ever a custom of *theirs* resembles one of *ours,* it has certainly just the opposite meaning.

They do not cut any of the hair of the body. Originally they went naked in consequence of the heat, and by not cutting the hair of the head they intended to prevent sunstroke.

They divide the moustache into single plaits in order to preserve it. As regards their not cutting the hair of the genitals, they try to make people believe that the cutting of it incites to lust and increases carnal desire. Therefore such of them as feel a strong desire for cohabitation never cut the hair of the genitals.

They let the nails grow long, glorying in their idleness, since they do not use them for any business or work, but only, while living a *dolce far niente* life, they scratch their heads with them and examine the hair for lice.

The Hindus eat singly, one by one, on a tablecloth of dung. They do not make use of the remainder of a meal, and the plates from which they have eaten are thrown away if they are earthen.

They have red teeth in consequence of chewing areca-nuts with betel-leaves and chalk.

They drink wine before having eaten anything, then they take their meal. They sip the stall of cows, but they do not eat their meat.

They beat the cymbals with a stick.

They use turbans for trousers. Those who want little dress are content to dress in a rag of two fingers' breadth, which they bind over their loins with two cords; but those who like much dress, wear trousers lined with so much cotton as would suffice to make a number of counterpanes and saddle-rugs. These trousers have no (visible) openings, and they are so huge that the feet are not visible. The string by which the trousers are fastened is at the back.

Their *ṣidâr* (a piece of dress covering the head and the upper part of breast and neck) is similar to the trousers, being also fastened at the back by buttons.

The lappets of the *kurṭakas* (short shirts from the shoulders to the middle of the body with sleeves, a female dress) have slashes both on the right and left sides.

They keep the shoes tight till they begin to put them on. They are turned down from the calf before walking (?).

In washing they begin with the feet, and then wash the face. They wash themselves before cohabiting with their wives.

*Cœunt stantes velut palus vitis, dum mulieres ab imo sursum moventur velut occupatæ in arando, maritus vero plane otiosus manet.**

On festive days they besmear their bodies with dung instead of perfumes.

The men wear articles of female dress; they use cosmetics, wear earrings, arm-rings, golden seal-rings on the ring-finger as well as on the toes of the feet.

Miseret eos catamiti et viri qui rebus venereis frui non potest pushaṇḍila *dicti, qui penem bucca devorans semen elicit sorbendum.*

In cacando faciem vertunt versus murum retegentes pudenda ut videantur a prætereuntibus.

Sacra faciunt virilibus liṅga *dictis, quæ est imago veretri Mahadevæ.**

They ride without a saddle, but if they put on a saddle, they mount the horse from its right side. In travelling they like to have somebody riding behind them.

They fasten the *kuṭhâra*, *i.e.* the dagger, at the waist on the right side.

They wear a girdle called *yajnopavîta*, passing from the left shoulder to the right side of the waist.

In all consultations and emergencies they take the Page 90.
advice of the women.

When a child is born people show particular attention to the man, not to the woman.

Of two children they give the preference to the younger, particularly in the eastern parts of the country; for they

* See page 186 for translation.

maintain that the elder owes his birth to predominant lust, whilst the younger owes his origin to mature reflection and a calm proceeding.

In shaking hands they grasp the hand of a man from the convex side.

They do not ask permission to enter a house, but when they leave it they ask permission to do so.

In their meetings they sit cross-legged.

They spit out and blow their noses without any respect for the elder ones present, and they crack their lice before them. They consider the *crepitus ventris* as a good omen, sneezing as a bad omen.

They consider as unclean the weaver, but as clean the cupper and the flayer, who kills dying animals for money either by drowning or by burning.

They use black tablets for the children in the schools, and write upon them along the long side, not the broad side, writing with a white material from the left to the right. One would think that the author of the following verses had meant the Hindus:—

> "How many a writer uses paper as black as charcoal,
> Whilst his pen writes on it with white colour.
> By writing he places a bright day in a dark night,
> Weaving like a weaver, but without adding a woof."

They write the title of a book at the end of it, not at the beginning.

They magnify the nouns of their language by giving them the feminine gender, as the Arabs magnify them by the diminutive form.

If one of them hands over a thing to another, he expects that it should be thrown to him as we throw a thing to the dogs.

If two men play at *Nard* (backgammon), a third one throws the dice between them.

They like the juice which flows over the cheeks of

the rutting elephant, which in reality has the most horrid smell.

In playing chess they move the elephant straight on, not to the other sides, one square at a time, like the pawn, and to the four corners also one square at a time, like the queen (*firzân*). They say that these five squares (*i.e.* the one straight forward and the others at the corners) are the places occupied by the trunk and the four feet of the elephant. On the Indian chess.

They play chess—four persons at a time—with a pair of dice. Their arrangement of the figures on the chess-board is the following:—

Tower (*rukh*).	Horse.	Elephant	King.			Pawn.	Tower.
Pawn.	Pawn.	Pawn.	Pawn.			Pawn.	Horse.
						Pawn.	Elephant.
						Pawn.	King.
King.	Pawn.						
Elephant.	Pawn.						
Horse.	Pawn.			Pawn.	Pawn.	Pawn.	Pawn.
Tower.	Pawn.			King.	Elephant.	Horse.	Tower.

As this kind of chess is not known among us, I shall here explain what I know of it.

The four persons playing together sit so as to form a square round a chess-board, and throw the two dice alternately. Of the numbers of the dice the five and
Page 91. six are blank (*i.e.* do not count as such). In that case, if the dice show five or six, the player takes one instead of the five, and four instead of the six, because the figures of these two numerals are drawn in the following manner:—

6			5
4	3	2	1

so as to exhibit a certain likeness of form to 4 and 1, viz. in the Indian signs.

The name *Shâh* or *king* applies here to the *queen* (*firzân*).

Each number of the dice causes a move of one of the figures.

The 1 moves either the pawn or the king. Their moves are the same as in the common chess. The king may be taken, but is not required to leave his place.

The 2 moves the tower (*rukh*). It moves to the third square in the direction of the diagonal, as the elephant moves in *our* chess.

The 3 moves the horse. Its move is the generally known one to the third square in oblique direction.

The 4 moves the elephant. It moves in a straight line, as the tower does in our chess, unless it be prevented from moving on. If this is the case, as sometimes happens, one of the dice removes the obstacle, and enables it to move on. Its smallest move is one square, the greatest fifteen squares, because the dice sometimes show two 4, or two 6, or a 4 and a 6. In consequence of one of these numbers, the elephant moves along the whole side on the margin of the chess-board; in consequence of the other number, it moves along the other side on the other margin of the board, in case there is no impediment in its way. In consequence of these two numbers, the elephant, in the course of his moves, occupies the two ends of the diagonal.

The pieces have certain values, according to which the player gets his share of the stake, for the pieces are taken and pass into the hands of the player. The value of the king is 5, that of the elephant 4, of the horse 3, of the tower 2, and of the pawn 1. He who takes a king gets 5. For two kings he gets 10, for three kings 15, if the winner is no longer in possession of his own king. But if he has still his own king, and takes all three kings, he gets 54, a number which represents a progression based on general consent, not on an algebraic principle.

The innate perversity of the Hindu character.

If the Hindus claim to differ from us, and to be something better than we, as we on our side, of course, do *vice versâ*, we might settle the question by an experiment to be made with their boys. I never knew a Hindu boy who had only recently come into Muhammadan territory who was not thoroughly versed in the manners and customs of the people, but at the same time he would place the shoes before his master in a wrong order, the right one to the left foot, and *vice versâ*; he would, in folding, turn his master's garments inside out, and spread the carpets so that the under part is uppermost, and more of the kind. All of which is a consequence of the innate perversity of the Hindu nature.

Customs of the heathen Arabs.

However, I must not reproach the Hindus only with their heathen practices, for the heathen Arabs too committed crimes and obscenities. They cohabited with menstruating and pregnant women; several men agreed to cohabit with the same woman in the same period of menstruation; they adopted the children of others, of their guests, of the lover of their daughter, not to mention that in some kinds of their worship they whistled on their fingers and clapped with their hands, and that they ate unclean and dead animals. Islam has abolished all those things among the Arabs, as it has also abolished them in those parts of India the people of which have become Muḥammadans. Thanks be unto God!

Translation of Latin passages page 181:

In washing they begin with the feet, and then wash the face. They wash themselves before cohabiting with their wives.

They cohabit like a stake entwined by a vine, or rather, while their wives move back and forth as if they were plowing, the husband remains completely motionless.

Pity those boys like Ganymede, and men who cannot enjoy sexual relations, called *pushandila,* who entice men, sucking their penises, and drinking their semen. While defecating, they turn their faces toward a wall, bearing their private parts so they can be seen by the passerby.

They make objects consecrated to the male organ called a *lingam,* which is the image of the god Mahadeva.

CHAPTER XVII.

ON HINDU SCIENCES WHICH PREY ON THE IGNORANCE OF PEOPLE.

On alchemy among the Hindus in general.

Page 92.

WE understand by witchcraft, making by some kind of delusion a thing appear to the senses as something different from what it is in reality. Taken in this sense, it is far spread among people. Understood, however, as common people understand it, as the producing of something which is impossible, it is a thing which does not lie within the limits of reality. For as that which is impossible cannot be produced, the whole affair is nothing but a gross deception. Therefore witchcraft in this sense has nothing whatever to do with science.

One of the species of witchcraft is alchemy, though it is generally not called by this name. But if a man takes a bit of cotton and makes it appear as a bit of gold, what would you call this but a piece of witchcraft? It is quite the same as if he were to take a bit of silver and make it appear as gold, only with this difference, that the latter is a generally-known process, *i.e.* the gilding of silver, the former is not.

The Hindus do not pay particular attention to alchemy, but no nation is entirely free from it, and one nation has more bias for it than another, which must not be construed as proving intelligence or ignorance; for we find that many intelligent people are entirely given to alchemy, whilst ignorant people ridicule the art and its adepts. Those intelligent people, though boisterously exulting over their make-believe science, are not to be blamed for occupying themselves with alchemy, for their motive is simply excessive eagerness for acquiring fortune and for avoiding misfortune. Once a sage was asked why scholars always flock to the doors of the rich, whilst the rich are not inclined to call at the doors of scholars. "The scholars," he answered, "are well aware of the use of money, but the rich are ignorant of the nobility of science." On the other hand, ignorant people are not to be praised, although they behave quite quietly, simply because they abstain from alchemy, for their motives are objectionable ones, rather practical results of innate ignorance and stupidity than anything else.

The adepts in this art try to keep it concealed, and shrink back from intercourse with those who do not belong to them. Therefore I have not been able to learn from the Hindus which methods they follow in this science, and what element they principally use, whether a mineral or an animal or a vegetable one. I only heard them speaking of the process of *sublimation*, of *calcination*, of *analysis*, and of the *waxing of talc*, which they call in their language *tâlaka*, and so I guess that they incline towards the mineralogical method of alchemy.

The science of Rasâyana.

They have a science similar to alchemy which is quite peculiar to them. They call it *Rasâyana*, a word composed with *rasa*, *i.e.* gold. It means an art which is restricted to certain operations, drugs, and compound medicines, most of which are taken from plants. Its principles restore the health of those who were ill beyond hope, and give back youth to fading old age, so that people become again what they were in the age near puberty; white hair becomes black again, the keenness of the senses is restored as well as the capacity for juvenile agility, and even for cohabitation, and the life of people in this world is even extended to a long period. And why not? Have we not already mentioned on the authority of Patañjali (v. p. 88) that one of the methods leading to liberation is *Rasâyana?* What man would hear this, being inclined to take it for truth, and not dart off into foolish joy and not honour the master of such a wonderful art by popping the choicest bit of his meal into his mouth?

Nâgârjuna, the author of a book on Rasâyana.

A famous representative of this art was Nâgârjuna, a native of the fort Daihak, near Somanâth. He excelled in it, and composed a book which contains the substance of the whole literature on this subject, and is very rare. He lived nearly a hundred years before our time.

Page 93.

The alchemist Vyâḍi in the time of King Vikramditya.

In the time of the King Vikramâditya, of whose era we shall speak hereafter, there lived in the city of Ûjain a man of the name of Vyâḍi, who had turned his whole attention to this science, and had ruined on account of it both his life and property, but all his zeal did not even avail him so much as to help him to things which, under ordinary circumstances, are easily obtained. Becoming restricted in his means, he conceived a disgust to that which had been the object of all his exertions, and sat down on the bank of a river sighing, sorrowful, and despairing. He held in his hand his *pharmacopœia*, from which he used to take the prescriptions for his medicines, but now he began to throw one leaf of it after the other into the water. A harlot happened to sit on the bank of the same river farther down, who, on seeing the leaves pass by, gathered them, and fished up some relating to *Rasâyana.* Vyâḍi did not notice her till all the leaves of his book had gone. Then the woman came to him, asking why he had done so with his book, whereupon he answered, "Because I have derived no advantage from it. I have not obtained what I ought to have obtained; for *its* sake I have become bankrupt after having had great treasures, and now I am miserable after having so long been in the hope of obtaining happiness." The harlot spoke: "Do not give up a pursuit in which you have spent your life; do not despair of the possibility of a thing which all sages before you have shown to be true. Perhaps the obstacle which prevents you from realising your plans is only of an accidental nature, which may perhaps be removed by an accident. I have much solid cash. It is all yours that you may spend it on the realisation of your plans." Thereupon Vyâḍi resumed his work.

However, books of this kind are written in an enigmatic style. So he happened to misunderstand a word in the prescription of a medicine, which meant *oil* and *human blood*, both being required for it. It was written *raktâmala*, and he thought it meant *red myrobalanon*. When he used the medicine it had no effect whatsoever. Now he began to concoct the various drugs, but the flame touched his head and dried up his brain. Therefore he oiled himself with oil, pouring it in great quantity over his skull. One day he rose to step away from the fireplace for some business or other, but as there happened to be a peg projecting from the roof right above his head, he knocked his head against it, and the blood began to flow. On account of the pain which he felt, he looked downward, and in consequence some drops of blood mixed with oil dropped from the upper part of his skull into the caldron without his noticing it. When, then, the concocting process was finished and he and his wife besmeared themselves with the concoction in order to try it, they both flew up into the air. Vikramâditya on hearing of this affair left his castle, and proceeded to the market-place in order to see them with his own eyes. Then the man shouted to him, "Open thy mouth for my saliva." The king, however, being disgusted, did not do it, and so the saliva fell down near the door, and immediately the threshold was filled with gold.

Vyâḍi and the woman flew to any place they liked. He has composed famous books on this science. People say that both man and wife are still alive.

Story about the piece of silver in the door of the Government-house in Dhâra.

A similar tale is the following:—In the city of Dhâra, the capital of Mâlava, which is in our days ruled by Bhojadeva, there lies in the door of the Government-house an oblong piece of pure silver, in which the outlines of the limbs of a man are visible. Its origin is accounted for by the following story:—Once in olden times a man went to a king of theirs, bringing him a *Rasâyana*, the use of which would make him immortal, victorious, invincible, and capable of doing everything he desired. He asked the king to come alone to the place of their meeting, and the king gave orders to keep in readiness all the man required.

Page 94.

The man began to boil the oil for several days, until at last it acquired consistency. Then he spoke to the king: "Spring into it and I shall finish the process." But the king, terrified at what he saw, had not the courage to dive into it. The man, on perceiving his cowardice, spoke to him: "If you have not sufficient courage, and will not do it for yourself, will you allow me myself to do it?" Whereupon the king answered, "Do as you like." Now he produced several packets of drugs, and instructed him that when such and such symptoms should appear, he should throw upon him this or that packet. Then the man stepped forward to the caldron and threw himself into it, and at once he was dissolved and reduced into pulp. Now the king proceeded according to his instruction, but when he had nearly finished the process, and there remained only one packet that was not yet thrown into the mass, he began to be anxious, and to think what might happen to his realm, in case the man should return to life as an *immortal, victorious, invincible* person, as has above been mentioned. And so he thought it preferable not to throw the last packet into the mass. The consequence was that the caldron became cold, and the dissolved man became consolidated in the shape of the said piece of silver.

The Hindus tell a tale about Vallabha, the king of the city of Vallabhî, whose era we have mentioned in the proper chapter.

Story of the fruit-seller Raṅka and the king Vallabha.

A man of the rank of a *Siddha* asked a herdsman with reference to a plant called *Thohar*, of the species of the *Lactaria*, from which milk flows when they are torn off, whether he had ever seen *Lactaria* from which blood flows instead of milk. When the herdsman declared he had, he gave him some drink-money that he should show it to him, which he did. When the man now saw the plant, he set fire to it, and threw the dog of the herdsman into the flame. Enraged thereby, the herdsman caught the man, and did with him the same as he had done to his dog. Then he waited till the fire was extinguished, and found both the man and the dog, but turned into gold. He took the dog with him, but left the man on the spot.

Now some peasant happened to find it. He cut off a finger, and went to a fruit-seller who was called *Raṅka*, i.e. *the poor*, because he was an utter pauper, and evidently near bankruptcy. After the peasant had bought from him what he wanted, he returned to the golden man, and then he found that in the place where the cut off finger had been, a new finger had grown. He cut it off a second time, and bought again from the same fruit-seller all that he wanted. But when the fruit-seller asked him whence he had the finger, he was stupid enough to tell him. So Raṅka went out to the body of the Siddha, and brought it on a carriage to his house. He stayed in his old abode, but managed by degrees to buy the whole town. The king Vallabha desired to own the same town, and asked him to cede it to him for money, but Raṅka declined. Being however afraid of the king's resentment, he fled to the lord of Almanṣûra, made him presents of money, and asked him to help him by a naval force. The lord of Almanṣûra complied with his desire, and assisted him. So he made a night-attack upon the king Vallabha, and killed him and his people, and destroyed his town. People say that still in our time there are such traces left in that country as are found in places which were destroyed by an unexpected night-attack.

The greediness of the ignorant Hindu princes for gold-making does not know any limit. If any one of them wanted to carry out a scheme of gold-making, and people advised him to kill a number of fine little children, the monster would not refrain from such a crime; he would throw them into the fire. If this precious science of Rasâyana were banished to the utmost limits of the world, where it is unattainable to anybody, it would be the best.

According to the Eranian tradition, Isfandiyâd is said to have spoken when dying: "Kâûs had been given the power and the miraculous things mentioned in the Book of the Law. Finally he went to the mountain Ḳâf as a decrepit man, bent down by old age, but he returned thence as a lively youth of well-proportioned figure and full of force, having made the clouds his carriage, as God allowed him." An Eranian tradition. Page 95.

As regards charms and incantations, the Hindus have a firm belief in them, and they, as a rule, are much inclined towards them. The book which treats of those things is considered as a work of Garuḍa, a bird on which Nârâyaṇa rode. Some people describe this bird in such a way as to indicate a Ṣifrid-bird and its doings. It is an enemy of fish, catching them. As a rule, animals have by nature an aversion to their opponents, and try to beware of them; here, however, there is an exception to this rule. For when this bird flutters above the water and swims on it, the fish rise from the On the bird Garuḍa.

deep to the surface, and make it easy to him to catch them, as if he had bound them by his spell. Others describe it with such characteristics as might indicate a stork. The *Vâyu Purâṇa* attributes to it a pale colour. On the whole, Garuḍa comes nearer to a stork than to a Ṣifrid, as the stork is by nature, like Garuḍa, a destroyer of snakes.

The effect of charms on the bite of serpents.

Most of their charms are intended for those who have been bitten by serpents. Their excessive confidence in them is shown by this, which I heard a man say, that he had seen a dead man who had died from the bite of a serpent, but after the charm had been applied he had been restored to life, and remained alive, moving about like all others.

Another man I heard as he told the following story: "He had seen a man who had died from the bite of a serpent. A charm was applied, and in consequence he rose, spoke, made his will, showed where he had deposited his treasures, and gave all necessary information about them. But when he inhaled the smell of a dish, he fell down dead, life being completely extinct."

It is a Hindu custom that when a man has been bitten by a venomous serpent, and they have no charmer at hand, they bind the bitten man on a bundle of reeds, and place on him a leaf on which is written a blessing for that person who will accidentally light upon him, and save him by a charm from destruction.

I, for my part, do not know what I am to say about these things, since I do not believe in them. Once a man who had very little belief in reality, and much less in the tricks of jugglers, told me that he had been poisoned, and that people had sent him some Hindus possessing the knowledge of charms. They sang their charms before him, and this had a quieting effect upon him, and soon he felt that he became better and better, whilst they were drawing lines in the air with their hands and with twigs.

I myself have witnessed that in hunting gazelles they caught them with the hand. One Hindu even went so far as to assert that he, without catching the gazelle, would drive it before him and lead it straight into the kitchen. This, however, rests, as I believe I have found out, simply on the device of slowly and constantly accustoming the animals to one and the same melody. Our people, too, practise the same when hunting the ibex, which is more wild even than the gazelle. When they see the animals resting, they begin to walk round them in a circle, singing one and the same melody so long until the animals are accustomed to it. Then they make the circle more and more narrow, till at last they come near enough to shoot at the animals which lie there in perfect rest. Hunting practices.

The shooters of Ḳaṭâ-birds have a custom of beating copper-vessels during the night with one and the same kind of beat, and they manage to catch them with the hand. If, however, the beat is changed, the birds fly off in all directions.

All these things are peculiar customs which have nothing whatsoever to do with charms. Sometimes the Hindus are considered as sorcerers because of their playing with balls on raised beams or on tight ropes, but tricks of this kind are common to all nations. Page 96.

CHAPTER XVIII.

VARIOUS NOTES ON THEIR COUNTRY, THEIR RIVERS, AND THEIR OCEAN. ITINERARIES OF THE DISTANCES BETWEEN THEIR SEVERAL KINGDOMS, AND BETWEEN THE BOUNDARIES OF THEIR COUNTRY.

The inhabitable world and the ocean.

THE reader is to imagine the inhabitable world, ἡ οἰκουμένη, as lying in the northern half of the earth, and more accurately in one-half of this half—*i.e.* in one of the quarters of the earth. It is surrounded by a sea, which both in west and east is called *the comprehending one;* the Greeks call its western part near their country ὠκεανός. This sea separates the inhabitable world from whatever continents or inhabitable islands there may be beyond it, both towards west and east; for it is not navigable on account of the darkness of the air and the thickness of the water, because there is no more any road to be traced, and because the risk is enormous, whilst the profit is nothing. Therefore people of olden times have fixed marks both on the sea and its shores which are intended to deter from entering it.

The inhabitable world does not reach the north on account of the cold, except in certain places where it penetrates into the north in the shape, as it were, of tongues and bays. In the south it reaches as far as the coast of the ocean, which in west and east is connected with the *comprehending ocean.* This southern ocean is navigable. It does not form the utmost southern limit of the inhabitable world. On the contrary, the latter stretches still more southward in the shape of large and small islands which fill the ocean. In this southern region land and water dispute with each other their position, so that in one place the continent protrudes into the sea, whilst in another the sea penetrates deeply into the continent.

The continent protrudes far into the sea in the western half of the earth, and extends its shores far into the south. On the plains of this continent live the western negroes, whence the slaves are brought; and there are the Mountains of the Moon, and on them are the sources of the Nile. On its coast, and the islands before the coast, live the various tribes of the Zanj. There are several bays or gulfs which penetrate into the continent on this western half of the earth—the bay of Berberâ, that of Klysma (the Red Sea), and that of Persia (the Persian Gulf); and between these gulfs the western continent protrudes more or less into the ocean.

In the eastern half of the earth the sea penetrates as deeply into the northern continent as the continent in the western half protrudes into the southern sea, and in many places it has formed bays and estuaries which run far into the continent—bays being parts of the sea, estuaries being the outlets of rivers towards the sea. This sea is mostly called from some island in it or from the coast which borders it. Here, however, we are concerned only with that part of the sea which is bordered by the continent of India, and therefore is called the *Indian Ocean*.

The orographic system of Asia and Europe.

As to the orographic configuration of the inhabitable world, imagine a range of towering mountains like the vertebræ of a pine stretching through the middle latitude of the earth, and in longitude from east to west, passing through China, Tibet, the country of the Turks, Kâbul, Badhakhshân, Ṭokhâristân, Bâmiyân, Elghôr, Khurâsân, Media, Âdharbaijân, Armenia, the Roman

Empire, the country of the Franks, and of the Jalâliḳa (Gallicians). Long as this range is, it has also a considerable breadth, and, besides, many windings which enclose inhabited plains watered by streams which descend from the mountains both towards north and south. One of these plains is India, limited in the south by the above-mentioned Indian Ocean, and on

Page 97.

all three other sides by the lofty mountains, the waters of which flow down to it. But if you have seen the

India, a recent alluvial formation.

soil of India with your own eyes and meditate on its nature—if you consider the rounded stones found in the earth however deeply you dig, stones that are huge near the mountains and where the rivers have a violent current; stones that are of smaller size at greater distance from the mountains, and where the streams flow more slowly; stones that appear pulverised in the shape of sand where the streams begin to stagnate near their mouths and near the sea—if you consider all this, you could scarcely help thinking that India has once been a sea which by degrees has been filled up by the alluvium of the streams.

First orientation regarding Madhyadeśa, Kanoj, Mâhûra, and Tânêshar.

The middle of India is the country round Kanoj (Kanauj), which they call *Madhyadeśa*, *i.e.* the middle of the realms. It is the middle or centre from a geographical point of view, in so far as it lies half way between the sea and the mountains, in the midst between the hot and the cold provinces, and also between the eastern and western frontiers of India. But it is a political centre too, because in former times it was the residence of their most famous heroes and kings.

The country of Sindh lies to the west of Kanoj. In marching from our country to Sindh we start from the country of Nîmrôz, *i.e.* the country of Sijistân, whilst marching to *Hind* or India proper we start from the side of Kâbul. This, however, is not the only possible road. You may march into India from all sides, supposing that you can remove the obstacles in the way.

In the mountains which form the frontier of India towards the west there are tribes of the Hindus, or of people near akin to them—rebellious savage races—which extend as far as the farthermost frontiers of the Hindu race.

Kanoj lies to the west of the Ganges, a very large town, but most of it is now in ruins and desolate since the capital has been transferred thence to the city of Bârî, east of the Ganges. Between the two towns there is a distance of three to four days' marches.

As Kanoj (*Kanyâkubja*) has become famous by the children of Pâṇḍu, the city of Mâhûra (*Mathurâ*) has become famous by Vâsudeva. It lies east of the river Jaun (*Yamunâ*). The distance between Mâhûra and Kanoj is 28 *farsakh*.

Tânêshar (*Sthânêśvara*) lies between the two rivers to the north both of Kanoj and Mâhûra, at a distance of nearly 80 *farsakh* from Kanoj, and nearly 50 *farsakh* from Mâhûra.

The river Ganges rises in the mountains which have already been mentioned. Its source is called *Gangâ-dvâra.* Most of the other rivers of the country also rise in the same mountains, as we have already mentioned in the proper place.

(Chapter XVIII, page 199 line 13 from bottom to page 212, lists more distances between Indian cities. There is also a brief description of the coasts. Chapter XIX, pages 213–220, is concerned with the planets and the signs of the Zodiac. Chapter XX, pages 221–227, is a discussion of the Hindu and Greek idea of the world as a primordial egg.)

CHAPTER XXI.

DESCRIPTION OF EARTH AND HEAVEN ACCORDING TO THE RELIGIOUS VIEWS OF THE HINDUS, BASED UPON THEIR TRADITIONAL LITERATURE.

On the seven earths. Page 112.

THE people of whom we have spoken in the preceding chapter think that the earths are seven like seven covers one above the other, and the upper one they divide into seven parts, differing from our astronomers, who divide it into κλίματα, and from the Persians, who divide it into *Kishvar*. We shall afterwards give a clear explanation of their theories derived from the first authorities of their religious law, to expose the matter to fair criticism. If something in it appears strange to us, so as to require a commentary, or if we perceive some coincidence with others, even if both parties missed the mark, we shall simply put the case before the reader, not with the intention of attacking or reviling the Hindus, but solely in order to sharpen the minds of those who study these theories.

Differences in the sequence of the earths explained as resulting from the copiousness of the language.

They do not differ among themselves as to the number of earths nor as to the number of the parts of the upper earth, but they differ regarding their names and the order of these names. I am inclined to derive this difference from the great verbosity of their language, for they call one and the same thing by a multitude of names. For instance, they call the sun by a thousand different names according to their own statement, just as the Arabs call the lion by nearly as many. Some of these names are original, while others are derived from the changing conditions of his life or his actions and faculties. The Hindus and their like boast of this copiousness, whilst in reality it is one of the greatest faults of the language. For it is the task of language to give a name to everything in creation and to its effects, a name based on general consent, so that everybody, when hearing this name pronounced by another man, understands what he means. If therefore one and the same name or word means a variety of things, it betrays a defect of the language and compels the hearer to ask the speaker what he means by the word. And thus the word in question must be dropped in order to be replaced either by a similar one of a sufficiently clear meaning, or by an epithet describing what is really meant. If one and the same thing is called by many names, and this is not occasioned by the fact that every tribe or class of people uses a separate one of them, and if, in fact, one single name would be sufficient, all the other names save this one are to be classified as mere nonsense, as a means of keeping people in the dark, and throwing an air of mystery about the subject. And in any case this copiousness offers painful difficulties to those who want to learn the whole of the language, for it is entirely useless, and only results in a sheer waste of time.

Frequently it has crossed my mind that the authors of books and the transmitters of tradition have an aversion to mentioning the earths in a definite arrangement, and limit themselves to mentioning their names, or that the copyists of the books have arbitrarily altered the text. For those men who explained and translated the text to me were well versed in the language, and were not known as persons who would commit a wanton fraud.

The earths according to the *Âditya-Purâṇa.*

The following table exhibits the names of the earths, as far as I know them. We rely chiefly on that list, which has been taken from the *Âditya-purâṇa,* because it follows a certain rule, combining every single earth and heaven with a single member of the members of the sun. The heavens are combined with the members from the skull to the womb, the earths with the members from the navel to the foot. This mode of comparison illustrates their sequence and preserves it from confusion:—

Page 113.

The Number of the Earths.	*Âditya-Purâṇa.*		*Vishṇu-Purâṇa.*	*Vâyu-Purâṇa.*		Vernacular Names.
	What Members of the Sun they Represent.	Their Names.		Their Names.	Their Epithets.	
I.	The navel.	Tâla.	Atala.	Âbhâstala.	Kṛishṇa-bhûmi, the dark earth.	Amśu (?)
II.	The thighs.	Sutâla.	Vitala.	Ilâ (?)	S'ukla-bhûmi, the bright earth.	Ambaratâla.
III.	The knees.	Pâtâla.	Nitala.	Nitala.	Rakta-bhûmi, the red earth.	S'arkara (?) (Sakkaru).
IV.	Under the knees.	Âśâla (?)	Gabhastimat.	Gabhastala.	Pîta-bhûmi, the yellow earth.	Gabhastimat.
V.	The calves.	Viśâla (?)	Mahâkhya (?)	Mahâtala.	Pâshâṇa-bhûmi, the earth of marble.	Mahâtala.
VI.	The ankles.	Mṛittâla.	Sutala.	Sutala.	S'ilâtala, the earth of brick.	Sutâla.
VII.	The feet.	Rasâtala.	Jâgara (?)	Pâtâla.	Suvarṇa-varṇa, the gold-coloured earth.	Rasâtala.

THE SPIRITUAL BEINGS LIVING ON THE SEVEN EARTHS ACCORDING TO THE VÂYU-PURÂṆA.

Page 114.

Of the Dânavas—Namuci, Śaṅkukarṇa, Kabandha (?), Nishkubâda (?), Śûladanta, Lohita, Kaliṅga, Śvâpada; and the master of the serpents—Dhanañjaya, Kâliya.

Of the Daityas—Surakshas, Mahâjambha, Hayagrîva, Kṛishṇa, Janarta (?), Śaṅkhâkhsha, Gomukha; and of the Râkshasa—Nîla, Megha, Krathanaka, Mahoshṇîsha, Kambala, Aśvatara, Takshaka.

Of the Dânavas—Rada (?), Anuhlâda, Agnimukha, Târakâksha, Triśira, Śiśumâra; and of the Râkshasa—Cyavana, Nanda, Viśâla. And there are many cities in this world.

Of the Daityas—Kâlanemi, Gajakarṇa, Uñjara (?); and of the Râkshasa—Sumâli, Muñja, Vṛikavaktra, and the large birds called Garuḍa.

Of the Daityas—Virocana, Jayanta (?), Agnijihva, Hiraṇyâksha; and of the Râkshasa—Vidyujjihva, Mahâmegha; the serpent Karmâra, Svastikajaya.

Of the Daityas—Kesari; and of the Râkshasa—Ûrdhvakuja (?), Śataśîrsha, *i.e.* having a hundred heads, a friend of Indra; Vâsuki, a serpent.

The king Bali; and of the Daitya Mucukunda. In this world there are many houses for the Râkshasa, and Vishṇu resides there, and Śesha, the master of the serpents.

On the seven heavens. Quotations from Johannes Grammaticus, Plato, and Aristotle.

After the earths follow the heavens, consisting of seven stories, one above the other. They are called *loka*, which means "*gathering-place.*" In a similar manner also the Greeks considered the heavens as gathering-places. So Johannes Grammaticus says in his refutation of Proclus: "Some philosophers thought that the sphere called γαλαξίας, i.e. *milk*, by which they mean the milky way, is a dwelling-place for rational souls." The poet Homer says: "Thou hast made the pure heaven an eternal dwelling-place for the gods. The winds do not shake it, the rains do not wet it, and the snow does not destroy it. For in it there is resplendent clearness without any covering cloud."

Plato says: "God spoke to the seven planets: You are the gods of the gods, and I am the father of the actions; I am he who made you so that no dissolution

Page 115. is possible; for anything bound, though capable of being loosened, is not exposed to destruction, as long as its order is good."

Aristotle says in his letter to Alexander: "The world is the order of the whole creation. That which is above the world, and surrounds it on the sides, is the dwelling-place of the gods. Heaven is full of the gods to which we give the name of stars." In another place of the same book he says, "The earth is bounded by the water, the water by the air, the air by the fire, the fire by the *αἰθήρ*. Therefore the highest place is the dwelling-place of the gods, and the lowest, the home of the aquatic animals."

There is a similar passage in the *Vâyu-Purâṇa* to this effect, that the earth is held in its grasp by the water, the water by the pure fire, the fire by the wind, the wind by heaven, and heaven by its lord.

The names of the *lokas* do not differ like those of the earths. There is a difference of opinion only regarding their order. We exhibit the names of the *lokas* in a table similar to the former (p. 230).

The Number of the Heavens.	What members of the Sun they represent according to the *Âditya-Purâṇa*.	Their Names according to the *Âditya*, *Vâyu* and *Vishṇu Purâṇas*.
I.	The stomach.	Bhûrloka.
II.	The breast.	Bhuvarloka.
III.	The mouth.	Svarloka.
IV.	The eyebrow.	Maharloka.
V.	The forehead.	Janaloka.
VI.	Above the forehead.	Tapoloka.
VII.	The skull.	Satyaloka.

Criticisms on the commentator of Patañjali. Page 116.

This theory of the earths is the same with all Hindus, except alone the commentator of the book of Patañjali. He had heard that the *Pitaras*, or *fathers*, had their gathering-place in the sphere of the moon, a tradition built on the theories of the astronomers. In consequence he made the lunar sphere the first heaven, whilst he ought to have identified it with *Bhûrloka.* And because by this method he had one heaven too many, he dropped the *Svarloka*, the place of reward.

The same author differs besides in another point. As the seventh heaven, Satyaloka, is in the Purâṇas also called *Brahmaloka,* he placed the Brahmaloka above the Satyaloka, whilst it would have been much more reasonable to think that in this case one and the same thing is called by two different names. He ought to have omitted the Brahmaloka, to have identified Pitṛiloka with Bhûrloka, and not to have left out the Svarloka.

So much about the seven earths and the seven heavens. We shall now speak of the division of the surface of the uppermost earth and of related subjects.

The system of Dvîpas and *seas.*

Dîp (*dvîpa*) is the Indian word for *island.* Hence the words *Sangaladîp* (Siṃhaladvîpa), which we call Serendîb, and the *Dîbajât* (Maledives, Laccadives). The latter are numerous islands, which become, so to speak, decrepit, are dissolved and flattened, and finally disappear below the water, whilst at the same time other formations of the same kind begin to appear above the water like a streak of sand which continually grows and rises and extends. The inhabitants of the former island leave their homes, settle on the new one and colonise it.

According to the religious traditions of the Hindus, the earth on which we live is round and surrounded by a sea. On the sea lies an earth like a collar, and on this earth lies again a round sea like a collar. The number of dry collars, called *islands,* is seven, and likewise that of the seas. The size of both *dvîpas* and seas rises in such a progression that each *dvîpa* is the double of the preceding *dvîpa,* each sea the double of the preceding sea, *i.e.* in the progression of the powers of two. If the middle earth is reckoned as one, the size of all seven earths represented as collars is 127. If the sea surrounding the middle earth is counted as one, the size of all seven seas represented as collars is 127. The total size of both earths and seas is 254.

The size of the Dvîpas and seas, according to the commentator of Patañjali and the *Vâyu-Purâṇa*.

The commentator of the book of Patañjali has adopted as the size of the middle earth 100,000 *yojana*. Accordingly, the size of all the earths would be 12,700,000 *yojana*. Further he adopts as the size of the sea which surrounds the middle earth 200,000 *yojana*. Accordingly, the size of all the seas would be 25,400,000 *yojana*, and the total size of all the earths and seas 38,100,000 *yojana*. However, the author himself has not made these additions. Therefore we cannot compare his numbers with ours. But the *Vâyu-Purâṇa* says that the diameter of the totality of earths and seas is 37,900,000 *yojana*, a number which does not agree with the above-mentioned sum of 38,100,000 *yojana*. It cannot be accounted for, unless we suppose that the number of earths is only six, and that the progression begins with the number 4 instead of 2. Such a number of seas (*i.e.* 6) may possibly be explained in this way, that the seventh one has been dropped, because the author only wanted to find the size of the continents, which induced him to leave the last surrounding sea out of the calculation. But if he once mentions the continents he must also mention all the seas which surround them. Why he has commenced the progression with 4 instead of 2, I cannot account for by any of the principles of the calculation as they have been laid down.

Each *dvîpa* and sea has a separate name. As far as we know them, we place them before the reader in the following table, and hope that the reader will excuse us for so doing.

(Chapter XXI, pages 235–238, has more material on geography from the *Puranas*. Chapter XXII, pages 239–242, deals with the Hindu ideas of the earth's poles.)

CHAPTER XXIII.

ON MOUNT MERU ACCORDING TO THE BELIEF OF THE AUTHORS OF THE PURÂṆAS AND OF OTHERS.

Brahmagupta on the earth and Mount Meru.

We begin with the description of this mountain, since it is the centre of the Dvîpas and seas, and, at the same time, the centre of Jambûdvîpa. Brahmagupta says: "Manifold are the opinions of people relating to the description of the earth and to Mount Meru, particularly among those who study the Purâṇas and the religious literature. Some describe this mountain as rising above the surface of the earth to an excessive height. It is situated under the pole, and the stars revolve round its foot, so that rising and setting depends upon Meru. It is called Meru because of its having the faculty of doing this, and because it depends alone upon the influence of its head that sun and moon become visible. The day of the angels who inhabit Meru lasts six months, and their night also six months."

Brahmagupta quotes the following passage from the book of *Jina, i.e.* Buddha: "Mount Meru is quadrangular, not round."

Balabhadra on the same subject.

The commentator Balabhadra says: "Some people say that the earth is flat, and that Mount Meru is an illuminating, light-giving body. However, if such were the case, the planets would not revolve round the horizon of the inhabitants of Meru; and if it were shining it would be visible because of its height, as the pole above it is visible. According to some, Meru consists of gold; according to others it consists of jewels. Âryabhaṭa thinks that it has not absolute height, but only the height of *one yojana*, and that it is round, not quadrangular, the realm of the angels; that it is invisible, although shining, because it is very distant from

Page 122.

the inhabited earth, being situated entirely in the high north, in the cold zone, in the centre of a desert called *Nandana-vana*. However, if it were of a great height, it would not be possible on the 66th degree of latitude for the whole Tropic of Cancer to be visible, and for the sun to revolve on it, being always visible without ever disappearing."

The author criticises Balabhadra.

All that Balabhadra produces is foolish both in words and matter, and I cannot find why he felt himself called upon to write a commentary if he had nothing better to say.

If he tries to refute the theory of the flatness of the earth by the planets revolving round the horizon of Meru, this argument would go nearer proving the theory than refuting it. For if the earth were a flat expanse, and everything high on earth were parallel to the perpendicular height of Meru, there would be no change of horizon, and the same horizon would be the equinox for all places on earth.

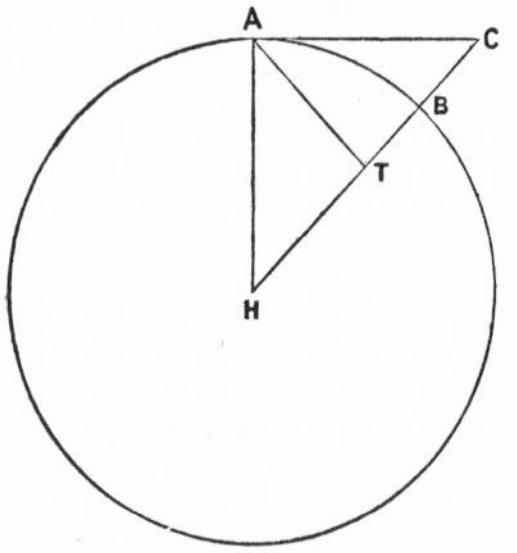

The statements of Âryabhaṭa examined by the author.

On the words of Âryabhaṭa as quoted by Balabhadra we make the following remarks.

Let A B be the globe of the earth round the centre H. Further, A is a place on the earth in the 66th degree of latitude. We cut off from the circle the arc A B, equal to the greatest declination. Then B is the place in the zenith of which the pole stands.

Further, we draw the line A C touching the globe in

the point A. This line lies in the plane of the horizon as far as the human eye reaches round the earth.

We join the points A and H with each other, and draw the line H B C, so that it is met in C by the line A C. Further, we let fall the perpendicular A T on H C. Now, it is evident that—

A T is the sine of the greatest declination ;
T B the versed sine of the greatest declination ;
T H the sine of the complement of the greatest declination.

And as we here occupy ourselves with Âryabhaṭa, we shall, according to his system, change the sines in *kardajât*. Accordingly—

A T = 1397.
T H = 3140.
B T = 298.

Because the angle H A C is a right angle, we have the equation—

H T : T A = T A : T C.

And the square of A T is 1,951,609. If we divide it by T H, we get as quotient 622.

The difference between this number and T B is 324, which is B C. And the relation of B C to B H, the latter being *sinus totus* = 3438, is the same as the relation of the number of *yojanas* of B C to the *yojanas* of B H. The latter number is, according to Âryabhaṭa, 800. If it is multiplied by the just-mentioned difference of 324 we get the sum of 259,200. And if we divide this number by the *sinus totus* we get 75 as quotient, which is the number of *yojanas* of B C, equal to 600 *miles* or 200 *farsakh*.

If the perpendicular of a mountain is 200 *farsakh*, the ascent will be nearly the double. Whether Mount Meru has such a height or not, nothing of it can be visible in the 66th degree of latitude, and it would not cover anything of the Tropic of Cancer at all (so as to intercept from it the light of the sun). And if for those

latitudes (66° and 23°) Meru is under the horizon, it is also under the horizon for all places of less latitude. If you compare Meru with a luminous body like the sun, you know that the sun sets and disappears under the earth. Indeed Meru may be compared with the earth.
Page 123. It is not invisible to us because of its being far away in the cold zone, but because it lies below the horizon, because the earth is a globe, and everything heavy is attracted towards its centre.

Âryabhaṭa further tries to prove that Mount Meru has only a moderate height by the fact that the Tropic of Cancer is visible in places the latitude of which is equal to the complement of the greatest declination. We must remark that this argument is not valid, for we know the conditions of the lines of latitude and other lines in those countries only through ratiocination, not from eyesight nor from tradition, because they are uninhabited and their roads are impassable.

If a man has come from those parts to Âryabhaṭa and told him that the Tropic of Cancer is visible in that latitude, we may meet this by stating that a man has also come to *us* from the same region telling us that one part of it is there invisible. The only thing which covers the Tropic of Cancer is this mountain Meru. If Meru did not exist, the whole tropic would be visible. Who, now, has been able to make out which of the two reports deserves most credit?

In the book of Âryabhaṭa of Kusumapura we read that the mountain Meru is in Himavant, the cold zone, not higher than a *yojana*. In the translation, however, it has been rendered so as to express that it is not higher than Himavant by more than a *yojana*.

This author is not identical with the elder Âryabhaṭa, but he belongs to his followers, for he quotes him and follows his example. I do not know which of these two namesakes is meant by Balabhadra.

In general, what we know of the conditions of the

place of this mountain we know only by ratiocination. About the mountain itself they have many traditions. Some give it the height of one *yojana*, others more; some consider it as quadrangular, others as an octagon. We shall now lay before the reader what the Ṛishis teach regarding this mountain.

Matsya-Purâṇa on Mount Meru and the mountains of the earth.

The *Matsya-Purâṇa* says: "It is golden and shining like fire which is not dulled by smoke. It has four different colours on its four sides. The colour of the eastern side is white like the colour of the Brahmins, that of the northern is red like that of the Kshatriya, that of the southern is yellow like the colour of the Vaiśya, and that of the western is black like the colour of the Śûdra. It is 86,000 *yojana* high, and 16,000 of these *yojana* lie within the earth. Each of its four sides has 34,000 *yojana*. There are rivers of sweet water running in it, and beautiful golden houses inhabited by the spiritual beings, the Deva, by their singers the Gandharva, and their harlots the Apsaras. Also Asuras, Daityas, and Râkshasas are living in it. Round the mountain lies the pond Mânasa, and around it to all four sides are the *Lokapâla*, *i.e.* the guardians of the world and its inhabitants. Mount Meru has seven *knots*, *i.e.* great mountains, the names of which are Mahendra, Malaya, Sahya, Śuktibâm (?), Ṛikshabâm (?), Vindhya, Pâriyâtra. The small mountains are nearly innumerable; they are those which are inhabited by mankind.

"The great mountains round Meru are the following: *Himavant*, always covered with snow, inhabited by the Râkshasa, Piśâca, and Yaksha. *Hemakûṭa*, the golden, inhabited by the Gandharva and Apsaras. *Nishadha*, inhabited by the Nâga or snakes, which have the following seven princes: Ananta, Vâsuki, Takshaka, Karkoṭaka, Mahâpadma, Kambala, Aśvatara. *Nîla*, peacock-like, of many colours, inhabited by the Siddha and Brahmarshi, the anchorites. The mountain Page 124.

Śveta, inhabited by the Daitya and Dânava. The mountain *Śṛiṅgavant*, inhabited by the Pitaras, the fathers and grandfathers of the Deva. Not far to the north of this mountain there are mountain-passes full of jewels and of trees which remain during a whole kalpa. And in the centre of these mountains is Ilâvṛita, the highest of all. The whole is called *Purushaparvata*. The region between the Himavant and the Śṛiṅgavant is called Kailâsa, the play-ground of the Râkshasa and Apsaras."

Quotations from the *Vishṇu*, *Vâyu*, and *Âditya Purâṇas*.

The *Vishṇu-Purâṇa* says: "The great mountains of the middle earth are Śrî-parvata, Malaya-parvata, Mâlyavant, Vindhya, Trikûṭa, Tripurântika, and Kailâsa. Their inhabitants drink the water of the rivers, and live in eternal bliss."

The *Vâyu-Purâṇa* contains similar statements about the four sides and the height of Meru as the hitherto quoted Purâṇas. Besides, it says that on each side of it there is a quadrangular mountain, in the east the Mâlyavant, in the north Ânîla, in the west the Gandhamâdana, and in the south the Nishadha.

The *Âditya-Purâṇa* gives the same statement about the size of each of its four sides which we have quoted from the *Matsya-Purâṇa*, but I have not found in it a statement about the height of Meru. According to this Purâṇa, its east side is of gold, the west of silver, the south of rubies, the north of different jewels.

The commentator of Patañjali on the same subject.

The extravagant notions of the dimensions of Meru would be impossible if they had not the same extravagant notions regarding the earth, and if there is no limit fixed to guesswork, guesswork may without any hindrance develop into lying. For instance, the commentator of the book of Patañjali not only makes Meru quadrangular, but even oblong. The length of one side he fixes at 15 *koṭi*, *i.e.* 150,000,000 *yojana*, whilst he fixes the length of the other three sides only at the third of this, *i.e.* 5 *koṭi*. Regarding the four sides of

Meru, he says that on the east are the mountain Mâlava and the ocean, and between them the kingdoms called Bhadrâśva. On the north are Nîla, Sîta, Śriṅgâdri, and the ocean, and between them the kingdoms Ramyaka, Hiraṇmaya, and Kuru. On the west are the mountain Gandhamâdana and the ocean, and between them the kingdom Ketumâla. On the south are Mrâvarta (?), Nishadha, Hemakûṭa, Himagiri, and the ocean, and between them the kingdoms Bhâratavârsha, Kiṁpurusha, and Harivarsha.

This is all I could find of Hindu traditions regarding Meru; and as I have never found a Buddhistic book, and never knew a Buddhist from whom I might have learned their theories on this subject, all I relate of them I can only relate on the authority of Alêrânshahrî, though, according to my mind, his report has no claim to scientific exactness, nor is it the report of a man who has a scientific knowledge of the subject. According to him, the Buddhists believe that Meru lies between four worlds in the four cardinal directions; that it is square at the bottom and round at the top; that it has the length of 80,000 *yojana*, one half of which rises into heaven, whilst the other half goes down into the earth. That side which is next to our world consists of blue sapphires, which is the reason why heaven appears to us blue; the other sides are of rubies, yellow and white gems. Thus Meru is the centre of the earth. Buddhistic views.

The mountain *Ḳâf*, as it is called by our common people, is with the Hindus the Lokâloka. They maintain that the sun revolves from Lokâloka towards Meru, and that he illuminates only its inner northern side. Page 125.

Similar views are held by the Zoroastrians of Sogdiana, viz. that the mountain Ardiyâ surrounds the world; that outside of it is *khôm*, similar to the pupil of the eye, in which there is something of everything, and that behind it there is a *vacuum*. In the centre of the A tradition of the Zoroastrians of Sogdiana.

world is the mountain *Girnagar*, between our *κλίμα* and the six other *κλίματα*, the throne of heaven. Between each two there is burning sand, on which no foot could stand. The spheres revolve in the *climata* like *mills*, but in ours they revolve in an inclined course, because our *clima*, that one inhabited by mankind, is the uppermost.

(Chapter XXIV, pages 251–256, repeats some of the ideas of Chapter XXI. Chapter XXV, pages 257–262, gives lists of Indian rivers and their sources.)

CHAPTER XXVI.

ON THE SHAPE OF HEAVEN AND EARTH ACCORDING TO THE HINDU ASTRONOMERS.

Page 132.

THIS and similar questions have received at the hands of the Hindus a treatment and solution totally different from that which they have received among us Muslims. The sentences of the Koran on these and other subjects necessary for man to know are not such as to require a strained interpretation in order to become positive certainties in the minds of the hearers, and the same may be said regarding the holy codes revealed before the Koran. The sentences of the Koran on all subjects necessary for man to know are in perfect harmony with the other religious codes, and at the same time they are perfectly clear, without any ambiguity. Besides, the Koran does not contain questions which have for ever been subjects of controversy, nor such questions the solution of which has always been despaired of, *e.g.* questions similar to certain puzzles of chronology.

The Koran, a certain and clear basis of all research.

Islam was already in its earliest times exposed to the machinations of people who were opposed to it in the bottom of their heart, people who preached Islam with sectarian tendencies, and who read to simple-minded audiences out of their Koran-copies passages of which not a single word was ever *created* (*i.e.* revealed) by God. But people believed them and copied these things on their authority, beguiled by their hypocrisy; nay, they disregarded the true form of the book which they had had until then, because the vulgar mind is

Islam falsified: I. By a Judaistic party.

always inclined to any kind of delusion. Thus the pure tradition of Islam has been rendered confused by this Judaistic party.

II. By the dualists.

Islam encountered a second mishap at the hands of the Zindîḳs, the followers of Mânî, like Ibn Almuḳaffa', 'Abd-alkarîm Ibn 'Abî-al'aujâ', and others, who, being the fathers of criticism, and declaring one thing as *just*, another as *admissible*, &c., raised doubts in weak-minded people as to the One and First, *i.e.* the Unique and Eternal God, and directed their sympathies towards dualism. At the same time they presented the biography of Mânî to the people in such a beautiful garb that they were gained over to his side. Now this man did not confine himself to the trash of his sectarian theology, but also proclaimed his views about the form of the world, as may be seen from his books, which were intended for deliberate deception. His opinions were far-spread. Together with the inventions of the above-mentioned Judaistic party, they formed a religious system which was declared to be *the Islam*, but with which God has nothing whatever to do. Whoso opposes it and firmly adheres to the orthodox faith in conformity with the Koran is stigmatised by them as an infidel and heretic and condemned to death, and they will not allow him to hear the word of the Koran. All these acts of theirs are more impious than even the words of Pharaoh, "I am your highest lord" (Sura, 79, 24), and "I do not know of any god for you save myself" (Sura, 28, 38). If party spirit of this kind will go on and rule for a long time, we may easily decline from the straight path of honour and duty. We, however, take our refuge with God, who renders firm the foot of every one who seeks *Him*, and who seeks the truth about Him.

Veneration of the Hindus for their astronomers.

The religious books of the Hindus and their codes of tradition, the Purâṇas, contain sentences about the shape of the world which stand in direct opposition to scientific truth as known to their astronomers. By these books people are guided in fulfilling the rites of their religion, and by means of them the great mass of the nation have been wheedled into a predilection for astronomical calculation and astrological predictions and warnings. The consequence is, that they show much affection to their astronomers, declaring that they are excellent men, that it is a good omen to meet them, and firmly believing that all of them come into Paradise and none into hell. For this the astronomers requite them by accepting their popular notions as truth, by conforming themselves to them, however far from truth most of them may be, and by presenting them with such spiritual stuff as they stand in need of. This is the reason why the two theories, the vulgar and the scientific, have become intermingled in the course of time, why the doctrines of the astronomers have been disturbed and confused, in particular the doctrines of those authors—and they are the majority—who simply copy their predecessors, who take the bases of their science from tradition and do not make them the objects of independent scientific research.

Astronomers admit popular notions into their doctrines.

We shall now explain the views of Hindu astronomers regarding the present subject, viz. the shape of heaven and earth. According to them, heaven as well as the whole world is round, and the earth has a globular shape, the northern half being dry land, the southern half being covered with water. The dimension of the earth is larger according to them than it is according to the Greeks and modern observations, and in their calculations to find this dimension they have entirely given up any mention of the traditional seas and *Dvîpas*, and of the enormous sums of *yojana* attributed to each of them. The astronomers follow the theologians in everything which does not encroach upon their science, *e.g.* they adopt the theory of Mount Meru being under the north pole, and that of the island

General observations on the rotundity of the earth, on Meru and Vaḍavâmukha.

Page 133.

Vaḍavâmukha lying under the south pole. Now, it is entirely irrelevant whether Meru is there or not, as it is only required for the explanation of the particular mill-like rotation, which is necessitated by the fact that to each spot on the plane of the earth corresponds a spot in the sky as its zenith. Also the fable of the southern island Vaḍavâmukha does no harm to their science, although it is possible, nay, even likely, that each pair of quarters of the earth forms a coherent, uninterrupted unity, the one as a continent, the other as an ocean (and that in reality there is no such island under the south pole). Such a disposition of the earth is required by the law of gravitation, for according to them the earth is in the centre of the universe, and everything heavy gravitates towards it. Evidently on account of this law of gravitation they consider heaven, too, as having a globular shape.

We shall now exhibit the opinions of the Hindu astronomers on this subject according to our translation of their works. In case, however, one word or other in our translation should be used in a meaning different from that which it generally has in our sciences, we ask the reader to consider only the original meaning of the word (not the technical one), for this only is meant.

Quotation from the *Siddhânta* of Pulisa.

Pulisa says in his *Siddhânta:* "Paulisa the Greek says somewhere that the earth has *a globular shape,* whilst in another place he says that it has *the shape of a cover* (*i.e.* of a flat plane). And in both sentences he is right; for the plane or surface of the earth is *round,* and its diameter is a straight line. That he, however, only believed in the globular shape of the earth, may be proved by many passages of his work. Besides, all scholars agree on this head, as Varâhamihira, Ârya-bhaṭa, Deva, Śrîsheṇa, Vishṇucandra, and Brahman. If the earth were not round, it would not be girded with the latitudes of the different places on earth, day and night would not be different in winter and summer, and the conditions of the planets and of their rotations would be quite different from what they are.

"The position of the earth is central. Half of it is clay, half water. Mount Meru is in the dry half, the home of the Deva, the angels, and above it is the pole. In the other half, which is covered by water, lies Vaḍavâmukha, under the south pole, a continent like an island, inhabited by the Daitya and Nâga, relatives of the Deva on Meru. Therefore it is also called Daityântara.

"The line which divides the two earth-halves, the dry and the wet, from each other, is called *Niraksha, i.e. having no latitude*, being identical with our equator. In the four cardinal directions with relation to this line there are four great cities:—

Yamakoṭi, in the east.	Romaka, in the west.
Laṅkâ, in the south.	Siddhapura, in the north.

"The earth is fastened on the two poles, and held by the axis. When the sun rises over the line which passes both through Meru and Laṅkâ, that moment is noon to Yamakoṭi, midnight to the Greeks, and evening to Siddhapura."

In the same manner things are represented by Âryabhaṭa.

Quotation from the *Brahmasiddhânta* of Brahmagupta.

Brahmagupta, the son of Jishṇu, a native of Bhillamâla, says in his *Brahmasiddhânta*: "Many are the sayings of people about the shape of the earth, specially among those who study the Purâṇas and the religious books. Some say that it is level like a mirror, others say that it is hollow like a bowl. Others maintain that it is level like a mirror, inclosed by a sea, this sea being inclosed by an earth, this earth being inclosed by a sea, &c., all of them being round like collars. Each sea or earth has the double size of that which it incloses. The outside earth is sixty-four times as large as the central earth, and the sea inclosing the outside earth is

Page 134.

sixty-four times as large as the sea inclosing the central earth. Several circumstances, however, compel us to attribute globular shape both to the earth and heaven, viz. the fact that the stars rise and set in different places at different times, so that, *e.g.* a man in Yamakoṭi observes one identical star rising above the western horizon, whilst a man in Rûm at the same time observes it rising above the eastern horizon. Another argument to the same effect is this, that a man on Meru observes one identical star above the horizon in the zenith of Laṅkâ, the country of the demons, whilst a man in Laṅkâ at the same time observes it above his head. Besides, all astronomical calculations are not correct unless we assume the globular figure of heaven and earth. Therefore we must declare that heaven is a globe, because we observe in it all the characteristics of a globe, and the observation of these characteristics of the world would not be correct unless in reality it were a globe. Now, it is evident that all the other theories about the world are futile."

Quotations from various astronomers.

Âryabhaṭa inquires into the nature of the world, and says that it consists of earth, water, fire, and wind, and that each of these elements is round.

Likewise Vasishṭha and Lâṭa say that the five elements, viz. earth, water, fire, wind, and heaven, are round.

Varâhamihira says that all things which are perceived by the senses, are witnesses in favour of the globular shape of the earth, and refute the possibility of its having another shape.

Âryabhaṭa, Pulisa, Vasishṭha, and Lâṭa agree in this, that when it is noon in Yamakoṭi, it is midnight in Rûm, beginning of the day in Laṅkâ, and beginning of the night in Siddhapura, which is not possible if the world is not round. Likewise the periodicity of the eclipses can only be explained by the world's being round.

Lâṭa says: "On each place of the earth only one-half of the globe of heaven is seen. The more northern our latitude is, the more Meru and the pole rise above the horizon; as they sink down below the horizon, the more southern is our latitude. The equator sinks down from the zenith of places, the greater their latitude is both in north and south. A man who is north of the equator only sees the north pole, whilst the south pole is invisible to him, and *vice versâ*."

Considerations regarding the rotundity of the earth, the balance of gravity between the northern and southern halves, and the attraction of gravitation.

These are the words of Hindu astronomers regarding the globular shape of heaven and earth, and what is between them, and regarding the fact that the earth, situated in the centre of the globe, is only of a small size in comparison with the visible part of heaven. These thoughts are the elements of astronomy as contained in the first chapter of Ptolemy's *Almagest*, and of similar books, though they are not worked out in that scientific form in which we are accustomed to give them,

(*Lacuna*,)

for the earth is more heavy than the water, and the water is fluid like the air. The globular form must be to the earth a physical necessity, as long as it does not, by the order of God, take another form. Therefore the earth could not move towards the north, nor the water Page 135. move towards the south, and in consequence one whole half is not *terra firma*, nor the other half water, unless we suppose that the *terra firma* half be hollow. As far as our observation, based on induction, goes, the *terra firma* must be in one of the two northern quarters, and therefore we guess that the same is the case on the adjacent quarter. We admit the possibility of the existence of the island Vaḍavâmukha, but we do not maintain it, since all we know of it and of Meru is exclusively based on tradition.

The equatorial line does not, in the quarter of the earth known to us, represent a boundary between *terra firma* and the ocean. For in certain places the continent protrudes far into the ocean, so as to pass beyond the equator, *e.g.* the plains of the negroes in the west, which protrude far towards the south, even beyond the *mountains of the moon* and the sources of the Nile, in fact, into regions which we do not exactly know. For that continent is desert and impassable, and likewise the sea behind Sufâla of the Zanj is unnavigable. No ship which ventured to go there has ever returned to relate what it had witnessed.

Also a great part of India above the province of Sindh deeply protrudes far towards the south, and seems even to pass beyond the equator.

In the midst between both lie Arabia and Yemen, but they do not go so far south as to cross the equator.

Further, as the *terra firma* stretches far out into the ocean, thus the ocean too penetrates into *terra firma*, breaking into it in various places, and forming bays and gulfs. For instance, the sea extends as a tongue along the west side of Arabia as far as the neighbourhood of Central Syria. It is narrowest near Ḳulzum, whence it is also called *the Sea of Ḳulzum.*

Another and still larger arm of the sea exists east of Arabia, the so-called *Persian Sea.* Between India and China, also, the sea forms a great curve towards the north.

Hence it is evident that the coast-line of these countries does not correspond to the equator, nor keep an invariable distance from it,

(*Lacuna,*)

and the explanation relating to the four cities will follow in its proper place.

The difference of the times which has been remarked is one of the results of the rotundity of the earth, and of its occupying the centre of the globe. And if they attribute to the earth, though it be round, inhabitants—for cities cannot be imagined without inhabitants—the existence of men on earth is accounted for by the attraction of everything heavy towards its centre, *i.e.* the middle of the world.

Much to the same effect are the expressions of *Vâyu-Purâṇa*, viz. that noon in Amarâvatî is sunrise in Vaivasvata, midnight in Sukhâ, and sunset in Vibhâ.

Quotations from the *Vâyu* and *Matsya Puranas.*

Similar, also, are the expressions of *Matsya-Purâṇa*, for this book explains that east of Meru lies the city Amarâvatîpura, the residence of Indra, the ruler, and his wife; south of Meru, the city Saṁyamanîpura, the residence of Yama, the son of the Sun, where he punishes and requites mankind; west of Meru, the city Sukhâpura, the residence of Varuṇa, *i.e.* the water; and north of Meru, the city Vibhâvarîpura, belonging to the Moon. Sun and planets revolve round Meru. When the sun has his noon position in Amarâvatîpura, it is the beginning of the day in Saṁyamanîpura, midnight in Sukhâ, and the beginning of the night in Vibhâvarîpura. And when the sun has his noon position in Saṁyamanîpura, he rises over Sukhâpura, sets over Amaravatîpura, and has his midnight position with relation to Vibhavarîpura.

Page 136.

If the author of the *Matsya-Purâṇa* says that the sun revolves round Meru, he means a mill-like rotation round those who inhabit Meru, who, in consequence of this nature of the rotation, do not know east nor west. The sun does not rise for the inhabitants of Meru in one particular place, but in various places. By the word *east* the author means the zenith of one city, and by *west* the zenith of another. Possibly those four cities of the *Matsya-Purâṇa* are identical with those mentioned by the astronomers. But the author has not mentioned how far they are distant from Meru. What we have besides related as notions of the Hindus is perfectly correct and borne out by scientific methods; however, they are wont never to speak of the pole unless they mention in the same breath also the mountain Meru.

A note of the author on the passage from the *Matsya-Purâṇa.*

In the definition of what is *low* the Hindus agree with us, viz. that it is *the centre of the world*, but their

Brahmagupta and Varâhamihira on the law of gravitation.

expressions on this head are subtle, more particularly as this is one of the great questions which is only handled by the most eminent of their scholars.

So Brahmagupta says: "Scholars have declared that the globe of the earth is in the midst of heaven, and that Mount Meru, the home of the Devas, as well as Vaḍavâmukha below, is the home of their opponents; the Daitya and Dânava belong to it. But this *below* is according to them only a relative one. Disregarding this, we say that the earth on all its sides is the same; all people on earth stand upright, and all heavy things fall down to the earth by a law of nature, for it is the nature of the earth to attract and to keep things, as it is the nature of water to flow, that of fire to burn, and that of the wind to set in motion. If a thing wants to go deeper down than the earth, let it try. The earth is the only *low* thing, and seeds always return to it, in whatever direction you may throw them away, and never rise upwards from the earth."

Varâhamihira says: "Mountains, seas, rivers, trees, cities, men, and angels, all are around the globe of the earth. And if Yamakoṭi and Rûm are opposite to each other, one could not say that the one is *low* in its relation to the other, since the *low* does not exist. How could one say of one place of the earth that it is *low*, as it is in every particular identical with any other place on earth, and one place could as little *fall* as any other. Every one speaks to himself with regard to his own self, '*I* am *above* and the others are *below*,' whilst all of them are around the globe like the blossoms springing on the branches of a Kadamba-tree. They encircle it on all sides, but each individual blossom has the same position as the other, neither the one hanging downward nor the other standing upright. For the earth attracts that which is upon her, for it is the *below* towards all directions, and heaven is the *above* towards all directions."

As the reader will observe, these theories of the

Hindus are based on the correct knowledge of the laws of nature, but, at the same time, they practise a little deceit upon their traditionalists and theologians. So Balabhadra the commentator says: "It is the most correct of the opinions of people, many and different as they are, that the earth and Meru and the zodiacal sphere are round. And the Âpta (?)-purâṇa-kâra, *i.e.* the faithful followers of the Purâṇa, say: 'The earth is like the back of a tortoise; it is not round from below.' They are perfectly right, because the earth is in the midst of the water, and that which appears above the water has the shape of a tortoise-back; and the sea around the earth is not navigable. The fact of the earth being round is proved by eyesight."

Quotations from Balabhadra, and the author's criticisms on them.

Page 137.

Here the reader must notice how Balabhadra declares the theory of the theologians as to the rotundity of the back to be true. He gives himself the air of not knowing that they deny that the womb, *i.e.* the other half of the globe, is round, and he busies himself with a traditional element (as to the earth being like the back of a tortoise), which, in reality, has no connection with the subject.

Further, Balabhadra says: "Human eyesight reaches to a point distant from the earth and its rotundity the 96th part of 5000 *yojana*, *i.e.* 52 *yojana* (exactly $52\frac{1}{12}$). Therefore man does not observe its rotundity, and hence the discrepancy of opinions on the subject."

Those pious men (the Âpta (?)-purâṇa-kâra) do not deny the rotundity of the back of the earth; nay, they maintain it by comparing the earth to the back of a tortoise. Only Balabhadra makes them deny it (by the words, "the earth is not round from below," *supra*), since he understood their words as meaning that the water surrounds the earth. That which rises above the water may either be globular or a plain rising above the water like an inverted drum, *i.e.* like a segment of a round pilaster.

Further, the remark of Balabhadra (v. p. 273), that man, on account of the smallness of his stature, cannot observe the rotundity of the earth, is not true; because even if the human stature were as tall as the plumb-line of the highest mountain, if he were to make his observation only from one single point without going to other places, and without reasoning about the observations made at the different places, even such a height would be of no avail to him, and he would not be able to perceive the rotundity of the earth and its nature.

What, however, is the connection of this remark with the popular theory? If he had concluded from analogy that that side of the earth which is opposed to the *round* one—I mean the lower half—was also round, and if he then had given his theory about the extent of the power of human vision as a result of reflection, not as a result of the perception of the senses, his theory would seem to have a certain foundation.

Calculation on the extent of human vision on the earth.

With regard to Balabhadra's definition of the extent which may be reached by the human eye, we propose the following calculation:—

Let A B round the centre H represent the globe of the earth. B is the standing-point of the observer; his stature is B C. Further, we draw the line C A, so that it touches the earth.

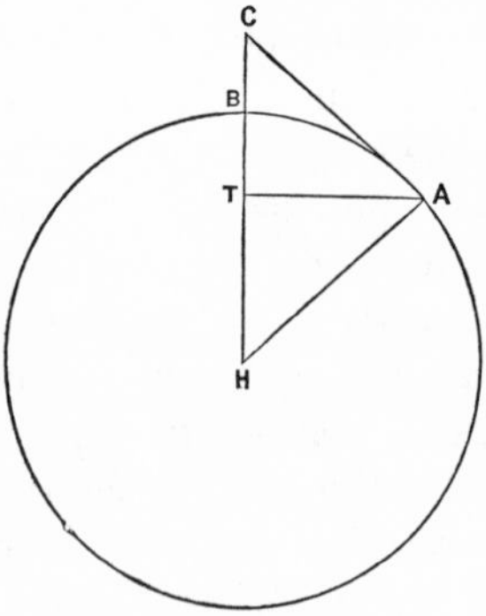

Now it is evident that the field of vision is B A, which we suppose to be equal to $\frac{1}{96}$ of the circle, *i.e.* $3\frac{3}{4}$ degrees, if we divide the circle into 360 degrees.

According to the method followed in the calculation of the mountain Meru (in chap. xxiii.), we divide the square of T A, *i.e.* 50,625, by

H T, *i.e.* 3431′. So we get as quotient T C = 0° 14′ 45″; and B C, the stature of the observer, is 0° 7′ 45″.

Our calculation is based on this, that H B, the *sinus totus*, is 3438′. However, the radius of the earth is, according to the circumference which we have mentioned, 795° 27′ 16″ (*yojana*). If we measure B C by this measure, it is = 1 *yojana*, 6 *krośa*, 1035 yards (= 57,035 yards). If we suppose B C to be equal to four yards, it stands in the same relation to A T, according to the measure of the sine, as 57,035, *i.e.* the yards which we have found as the measure of the stature, to A T according to the measure of the sine, *i.e.* 225. If we now calculate the sine, we find it to be 0° 0′ 1″ 3‴, and its arc has the same measure. However, each degree of the rotundity of the earth represents the measure of 13 *yojana*, 7 *krośa*, and 333⅓ yards (*sic*). Therefore the field of vision on the earth is 291⅔ yards (*sic*). Page 138.

(*For an explanation of this calculation see the notes.*)

The source of this calculation of Balabhadra's is the *Pulisa-siddhânta*, which divides the arc of the quarter of a circle into 24 *kardajât*. He says: "If anybody asks for the reason of this, he must know that each of these *kardajât* is $\frac{1}{96}$ of the circle = 225 minutes (= 3¾ degrees). And if we reckon its sine, we find it also to be = 225 minutes." This shows us that the sines are equal to their arcs in parts which are smaller than this *kardaja*. And because the *sinus totus*, according to Pulisa and Âryabhaṭa, has the relation of the diameter to the circle of 360 degrees, this arithmetical equality brought Balabhadra to think that the arc was perpendicular; and any expanse in which no convexity protrudes preventing the vision from passing, and which is not too small to be seen, is visible.

This, however, is a gross mistake; for the arc is never perpendicular, and the sine, however small it be, never equals the arc. This is admissible only for such degrees as are supposed for the convenience of calculation, but it is never and nowhere true for the degrees of the earth.

The axis of the earth according to Pulisa.

If Pulisa says (v. p. 267) that the earth is held by an axis, he does not mean thereby that in reality there exists such an axis, and that but for it the earth would fall. How could he say such a thing, since he is of opinion that there are four inhabited cities around the world, which is explained by the fact that everything heavy falls from all sides down towards the earth? However, Pulisa holds this view, that the motion of the peripheric parts is the reason why the central parts are motionless, and that the motion of a globe presupposes two poles, and one line connecting them, which in the idea is the axis. It is as if he meant to say, that the motion of heaven keeps the earth in its place, making it the natural place for the earth, outside of which it could never be. And this place lies on the midst of the axis of motion. For the other diameters of the globe may also be imagined to be axes, since *ἐν δυνάμει* they are all axes, and if the earth were not in the midst of an axis, there might be axes which did not pass through the earth. Hence one may say metaphorically that the earth is supported by the axes.

Whether the earth moves or is at rest, according to Brahmagupta and the author.

As regards the resting of the earth, one of the elementary problems of astronomy, which offers many and great difficulties, this, too, is a dogma with the Hindu astronomers. Brahmagupta says in the *Brahmasiddhânta:* "Some people maintain that the *first* motion

Page 139.

(from east to west) does not lie in the meridian, but belongs to the earth. But Varâhamihira refutes them by saying: 'If that were the case, a bird would not return to its nest as soon as it had flown away from it towards the west.' And, in fact, it is precisely as Varâhamihira says."

Brahmagupta says in another place of the same book: "The followers of Âryabhaṭa maintain that the earth is moving and heaven resting. People have tried to refute them by saying that, if such were the case, stones and trees would fall from the earth."

But Brahmagupta does not agree with them, and says that that would not necessarily follow from their theory, apparently because he thought that all heavy things are attracted towards the centre of the earth. He says: "On the contrary, if that were the case, *the earth would not vie in keeping an even and uniform pace with the minutes of heaven, the prâṇas of the times.*"

There seems to be some confusion in this chapter, perhaps by the fault of the translator. For the *minutes of heaven* are 21,600, and are called *prâṇa, i.e.* breaths, because according to them each minute of the meridian revolves in *the time of an ordinary human breath.*

Supposing this to be true, and that the earth makes a complete rotation eastward in so many breaths as heaven does according to his (Brahmagupta's) view, we cannot see what should prevent the earth from keeping an even and uniform pace with heaven.

Besides, the rotation of the earth does in no way impair the value of astronomy, as all appearances of an astronomic character can quite as well be explained according to this theory as to the other. There are, however, other reasons which make it impossible. This question is most difficult to solve. The most prominent of both modern and ancient astronomers have deeply studied the question of the moving of the earth, and tried to refute it. We, too, have composed a book on the subject called *Miftâḥ-'ilm-alhai'a* (*Key of Astronomy*), in which we think we have surpassed our predecessors, if not in the words, at all events in the matter.

(Chapter XXVII, pages 278–288, quotes the *Puranas* on the equinoxes. Chapter XXVIII, pages 289–292, is a discussion of Indian ideas of directions. Chapter XXIX, pages 294–305, is a further discussion of the Hindu understanding of the geography of the world.)

CHAPTER XXX.

ON LAṄKÂ, OR THE CUPOLA OF THE EARTH.

On the meaning of the term *cupola of the earth.*

THE midst of the inhabitable world, of its longitudinal extension from east to west on the equator, is by the astronomers (of the Muslims) called the *cupola of the earth*, and the *great* circle which passes through the pole and this point of the equator is called the *meridian of the cupola.* We must, however, observe that whatever may be the natural form of the earth, there is no place on it which to the exclusion of others deserves the name of a *cupola;* that this term is only a metaphorical one to denote a point from which the two ends of the inhabitable world in east and west are equidistant, comparable to the top of a cupola or a tent, as all things hanging down from this top (tent-ropes or walls) have the same length, and their lower ends the same distances therefrom. But the Hindus never call this point by a term that in our language must be interpreted by *cupola;* they only say that Laṅkâ is between the two ends of the inhabitable world and without latitude.

The story of Râma.

There Râvaṇa, the demon, fortified himself when he had carried off the wife of Râma, the son of Daśaratha. His labyrinthine fortress is called تنكت درو (?), whilst in our (Muslim) countries it is called *Yâvana-koṭi*, which has frequently been explained as Rome.

The following is the plan of the labyrinthine fortress :—

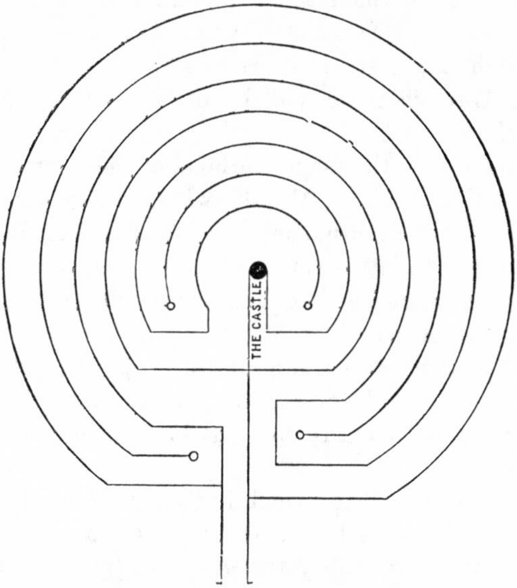

Door of the road leading to the castle.

Râma attacked Râvaṇa after having crossed the ocean on a dyke of the length of 100 *yojana*, which he had constructed from a mountain in a place called *Setubandha, i.e.* bridge of the ocean, east of Ceylon. He fought with him and killed him, and Râma's brother killed the brother of Râvaṇa, as is described in the story of Râma and Râmâyana. Thereupon he broke the dyke in ten different places by arrow-shots. Page 159.

On the island of Laṅkâ.

According to the Hindus, Laṅkâ is the castle of the demons. It is 30 *yojana* above the earth, *i.e.* 80 *farsakh.* Its length from east to west is 100 *yojana*; its breadth from north to south is the same as the height (*i.e.* thirty).

It is on account of Laṅkâ and the island of Vaḍavâmukha that the Hindus consider the south as foreboding evil. In no work of piety do they direct themselves southward or walk southward. The south occurs only in connection with impious actions.

The first meridian.

The line on which the astronomical calculations are based (as 0° of longitude), which passes in a straight line from Lankâ to Meru, passes—

(1.) Through the city of Ujain (Ujjayinî) in Mâlava (Mâlvâ).

(2.) Through the neighbourhood of the fortress Rohitaka in the district of Multân, which is now deserted.

(3.) Through Kurukshetra, *i.e.* the plain of Tâneshar (Sthâneśvara), in the centre of their country.

(4.) Through the river Yamunâ, on which the city of Mathurâ is situated.

(5.) Through the mountains of the Himavant, which are covered with everlasting snow, and where the rivers of their country rise. Behind them lies Mount Meru.

The situation of Ujain.

The city of Ujain, which in the tables of the longitudes of places is mentioned as *Uzain*, and as situated on the sea, is in reality 100 *yojana* distant from the sea. Some undiscriminating Muslim astronomer has uttered the opinion that Ujain lies on the meridian of Al-shabûrkân in Al-jûzajân; but such is not the case, for it lies by many degrees of the equator more to the east than Al-shabûrkân. There is some confusion about the longitude of Ujain, particularly among such (Muslim) astronomers as mix up with each other the different opinions about the first degree of longitude both in east and west, and are unable to distinguish them properly.

The author's conjecture about Lankâ and Langabâlûs.

No sailor who has traversed the ocean round the place which is ascribed to Lankâ, and has travelled in that direction, has ever given such an account of it as tallies with the traditions of the Hindus or resembles them. In fact, there is no tradition which makes the thing appear to us more possible (than it is according to the reports of the Hindus). The name Lankâ, however, makes me think of something entirely different viz. that the clove is called *lavang*, because it is imported from a country called *Langa*. According to the uniform report of all sailors, the ships which are sent to this country land their cargo in boats, viz. ancient Western *denars* and various kinds of merchandise, striped Indian cloth, salt, and other usual articles of trade. These wares are deposited on the shore on leather sheets, each of which is marked with the name of its owner. Thereupon the merchants retire to their ships. On the following day they find the sheets covered with cloves by way of payment, little or much, as the natives happen to own.

The people with whom this trade is carried on are demons according to some, savage men according to others.

A certain wind as the cause of small-pox.

The Hindus who are the neighbours of those regions (of Laṅkâ) believe that the small-pox is a wind blowing from the island of Laṅkâ towards the continent to carry off souls. According to one report, some men warn people beforehand of the blowing of this wind, and can exactly tell at what times it will reach the different parts of the country. After the small-pox has broken out, they recognise from certain signs whether it is virulent or not. Against the virulent small-pox they use a method of treatment by which they destroy only one single limb of the body, but do not kill. They use as medicine cloves, which they give to the patient to drink, together with gold-dust; and, besides, the males tie the cloves, which are similar to date-kernels, to their necks. If these precautions are taken, perhaps nine people out of ten will be proof against this malady.

Page 160.

All this makes me think that the Laṅkâ which the Hindus mention is identical with the clove-country Langa, though their descriptions do not tally. However, there is no communication kept up with the latter, for people say that when perchance a merchant is left behind on this island, there is no more trace found of him. And this my conjecture is strengthened by the fact that, according to the book of Râma and Râmâyana, behind the well-known country of Sindh there are cannibals. And, on the other hand, it is well known among all seamen that cannibalism is the cause of the savagery and bestiality of the inhabitants of the island of Langabâlûs.

CHAPTER XXXI.

ON THAT DIFFERENCE OF VARIOUS PLACES WHICH WE CALL THE DIFFERENCE OF LONGITUDE.

On the Hindu method of determining longitude.

HE who aims at accuracy in this subject must try to determine the distance between the spheres of the meridians of the two places in question. Muslim astronomers reckon by *equatorial times* corresponding to the distance between the two meridians, and begin to count from one (the western one) of the two places. The sum of equatorial minutes which they find is called *the difference between the two longitudes;* for they consider as the *longitude* of each place the distance of its meridian from *the great circle* passing through the pole of the equator, which has been chosen as the limit of the *οἰκουμένη*, and for this first meridian they have chosen the *western* (not the eastern) limit of the *οἰκουμένη*. It is all the same whether these *equatorial times*, whatsoever their number for each meridian may be, are reckoned as 360th parts of a circle, or as its 60th parts, so as to correspond to the *day-minutes*, or as *farsakh* or *yojana*.

The Hindus employ in this subject methods which do not rest on the same principle as ours. They are totally different; and howsoever different they are, it is perfectly clear that none of them hits the right mark. As we (Muslims) note for each place its *longitude*, the Hindus note the number of *yojanas* of its distance from the meridian of Ujain. And the more to the west the position of a place is, the greater is the number of *yojanas;* the more to the east it is, the smaller is this number. They call it *deśântara*, i.e. *the difference between the places.* Further, they multiply the *deśântara* by the mean daily motion of *the planet* (the sun), and divide the product by 4800. Then the quotient represents that amount of the motion of the star which corresponds to the number of *yojana* in question, *i.e.* that which must be added to the mean place of the sun, as it has been found for moon or midnight of Ujain, if you want to find the longitude of the place in question.

On the circumference of the earth.

The number which they use as divisor (4800) is the number of the *yojanas* of the circumference of the earth, for the difference between the spheres of the meridians of the two places stands in the same relation to the whole circumference of the earth as the mean motion of the planet (sun) from one place to the other to its whole daily rotation round the earth.

If the circumference of the earth is 4800 *yojanas*, the diameter is nearly 1527; but Pulisa reckons it as 1600, Brahmagupta as 1581 *yojanas*, each of which is equal to eight miles. The same value is given in the astronomical handbook *Al-arkand* as 1050. This number, however, is, according to Ibn Ṭârik, the radius, whilst the diameter is 2100 *yojanas*, each *yojana* being reckoned as equal to four miles, and the circumference is stated as $6596\frac{9}{25}$ *yojanas*.

Page 161.

Quotations from the *Khaṇḍakhâdyaka* and the *Karaṇatilaka*.

Brahmagupta uses 4800 as the number of *yojanas* of the earth's circumference in his canon *Khaṇḍakhâdyaka*, but in the amended edition he uses, instead of this, the *corrected* circumference, agreeing with Pulisa. The correction he propounds is this, that he multiplies the *yojanas* of the earth's circumference by the *sines* of the complement of the latitude of the place, and divides the product by the *sinus totus;* then the quotient is the *corrected* circumference of the earth, or the number of *yojanas* of the parallel circle of the place in question. Sometimes this number is called *the collar of the meri-*

dian. Hereby people are frequently misled to think that the 4800 *yojanas* are the *corrected* circumference for the city of Ujain. If we calculate it (according to Brahmagupta's correction), we find the latitude of Ujain to be 16¼ degrees, whilst in reality it is 24 degrees.

The author of the canon *Karaṇa-tilaka* makes this correction in the following way. He multiplies the diameter of the earth by 12 and divides the product by the equinoctial shadow of the place. The gnomon stands in the same relation to this shadow as the radius of the parallel circle of the place to the sine of the latitude of the place, not to the *sinus totus.* Evidently the author of this method thinks that we have here the same kind of equation as that which the Hindus call *vyastatrairâśika*, i.e. *the places with the retrograde motion.* An example of it is the following.

The equation *vyastatrairâśika.*

If the price of a harlot of 15 years be, *e.g.* 10 denars, how much will it be when she is 40 years old?

The method is this, that you multiply the first number by the second ($15 \times 10 = 150$), and divide the product by the third number ($150 : 40 = 3\frac{3}{4}$). Then the quotient or fourth number is her price when she has become old, viz. $3\frac{3}{4}$ denars.

Now the author of the *Karaṇa-tilaka*, after having found that the straight shadow *increases* with the latitude, whilst the diameter of the circle *decreases*, thought, according to the analogy of the just mentioned calculation, that between this increase and decrease there is a certain *ratio.* Therefore he maintains that the diameter of the circle *decreases, i.e.* becomes gradually smaller than the diameter of the earth, at the same rate as the straight shadow *increases.* Thereupon he calculates the corrected circumference from the corrected diameter.

After having thus found the longitudinal difference between two places, he observes a lunar eclipse, and fixes in day-minutes the difference between the time of its appearance in the two places. Pulisa multiplies these day-minutes by the circumference of the earth, and divides the product by 60, viz. the minutes (or 60th parts) of the daily revolution. The quotient, then, is the number of the *yojanas* of the distance between the two places.

This calculation is correct. The result refers to the *great circle* on which Laṅkâ lies.

Brahmagupta calculates in the same manner, save that he multiplies by 4800. The other details have already been mentioned.

Calculation of the *deśântara* according to Alfazârî.

As far as this, one clearly recognises what the Hindu astronomers aim at, be their method correct or faulty. However, we cannot say the same of their calculation of the *deśântara* from the latitudes of two different places, which is reported by Alfazârî in his canon in the following manner:—

"Add together the squares of the sines of the latitudes of the two places, and take the root of the sum. This root is the *portio*.

"Further, square the difference of these two sines and add it to the *portio*. Multiply the sum by 8 and divide the product by 377. The quotient, then, is the distance between the two places, that is to say, according to a rough calculation.

"Further, multiply the difference between the two latitudes by the *yojanas* of the circumference of the earth and divide the product by 360."

Evidently this latter calculation is nothing but the transferring of the difference between the two latitudes from the measure of degrees and minutes to the measure of *yojanas*. Then he proceeds:—

"Now the square of the quotient is substracted from the square of the roughly calculated *distance*, and of the remainder you take the root, which represents the *straight yojanas*."

Page 162.

Evidently the latter number represents the distance between the spheres of the *meridians* of the two places on the circle of latitude, whilst the *roughly calculated* number is the distance between the two places in longitude.

The author criticises this method.

This method of calculation is found in the astronomical handbooks of the Hindus in conformity with the account of Alfazârî, save in one particular. The here-mentioned *portio* is the *root* of the difference between the squares of the sines of the two latitudes, not *the sum* of the squares of the sines of the two latitudes.

But whatever this method may be, it does not hit the right mark. We have fully explained it in several of our publications specially devoted to this subject, and there we have shown that it is impossible to determine the distance between two places and the difference of longitude between them by means of their latitudes alone, and that only in case one of these two things is known (the distance between two places or the difference between the longitudes of them), by this and by means of the two latitudes, the third value can be found.

Another calculation of the *deśântara*.

Based on the same principle, the following calculation has been found, there being no indication by whom it was invented :—

"Multiply the *yojanas* of the distance between two places by 9, and divide the product by (*lacuna*); the root of the difference between its square and the square of the difference of the two latitudes. Divide this number by 6. Then you get as quotient the number of day-minutes of the difference of the two longitudes."

It is clear that the author of this calculation first takes the distance (between the two places), then he reduces it to the measure of the circumference of the circle. However, if we invert the calculation and reduce the parts (or degrees) of the great circle to *yojanas* according to his method, we get the number 3200, *i.e.* 100 *yojanas* less then we have given on the authority of

Al-arkand (v. p. 312). The double of it, 6400, comes near the number mentioned by Ibn Ṭârik (*i.e.* $6596\frac{9}{25}$, v. p. 312), being only about 200 *yojanas* smaller.

We shall now give the latitudes of some places, as we hold them to be correct.

A criticism of Âryabhaṭa of Kusumapura on the meridian of Ujain.

All canons of the Hindus agree in this that the line connecting Laṅkâ with Meru divides the οἰκουμένη lengthways in two halves, and that it passes through the city of Ujain, the fortress of Rohitaka, the river Yamunâ, the plain of Tâneshar, and the Cold Mountains. The longitudes of the places are measured by their distance from this line. On this head I know of no difference between them except the following passage in the book of Âryabhaṭa of Kusumapura:—

"People say that Kurukshetra, *i.e.* the plain of Tâneshar, lies on the line which connects Laṅkâ with Meru and passes through Ujain. So they report on the authority of Pulisa. But he was much too intelligent not to have known the subject better. The times of the eclipses prove that statement to be erroneous, and Pṛithusvâmin maintains that the difference between the longitudes of Kurukshetra and Ujain is 120 *yojanas*."

These are the words of Âryabhaṭa.

On the latitude of Ujain.

Ya'ḳûb Ibn Ṭârik says in his book entitled *The Composition of the Spheres*, that the latitude of Ujain is $4\frac{3}{5}$ degrees, but he does not say whether it lies in the north or the south. Besides, he states it, on the authority of the book *Al-Arkand*, to be $4\frac{2}{5}$ degrees. We, however, have found a totally different latitude of Ujain in the same book in a calculation relating to the distance between Ujain and Almanṣûra, which the author calls Brahmaṇavâṭa, *i.e.* Bamhanwâ, viz. latitude of Ujain, 22° 29′; latitude of Almanṣûra, 24° 1′.

According to the same book, the straight shadow in Lohâniyye, *i.e.* Loharânî, is $5\frac{3}{5}$ digits.

On the other hand, however, all the canons of the Hindus agree in this, that the latitude of Ujain is 24 degrees, and that the sun culminates over it at the time of the summer solstice.

Balabhadra, the commentator, gives as the latitude of Kanoj 26° 35′; as that of Tâneshar, 30° 12′. Page 163.

The learned Abû-Aḥmad, the son of Catlaghtagîn, calculated the latitude of the city of Karlî (?), and found it to be 28° 0′, that of Tâneshar 27′, and both places to be distant from each other by three days' marches. What the cause of this difference is I do not know.

According to the book *Karaṇa-sâra*, the latitude of Kashmîr is 34° 9′, and the straight shadow there $8\frac{7}{60}$ digits.

I myself have found the latitude of the fortress Lauhûr to be 34° 10′. The distance from Lauhûr to the capital of Kashmîr is 56 miles, half the way being rugged country, the other half plain. What other latitudes I have been able to observe myself, I shall enumerate in this place:—

Ghazna	33° 35′	Lamghân	34° 43′
Kâbul	33° 47′	Purshâvar	34° 44′
Kandî, the guard-station of the prince	33° 55′	Waihand	34° 30′
Dunpûr	34° 20′	Jailam	33° 20′
		The fortress Nandna	32° 0′

The distance between the latter place and Multân is nearly 200 miles.

Sâlkot	32° 58′
Mandakkakor	31° 50′
Multân	29° 40′

If the latitudes of places are known, and the distances between them have been measured, the difference between their longitudes also may be found according to the methods explained in the books to which we have referred the reader.

We ourselves have (in our travels) in their country not passed beyond the places which we have mentioned, nor have we learned any more longitudes and latitudes (of places in India) from their literature. It is God alone who helps us to reach our objects!

CHAPTER XXXII.

ON THE NOTIONS OF DURATION AND TIME IN GENERAL, AND ON THE CREATION OF THE WORLD AND ITS DESTRUCTION.

On the notion of time according to Alrâzî and other philosophers.

According to the relation of Muḥammad Ibn Zakariyyâ Alrâzî, the most ancient philosophers of the Greeks thought that the following five things existed from all eternity, *the creator, the universal soul, the first ὕλη, space in the abstract,* and *time in the abstract.* On these things Alrâzî has founded that theory of his, which is at the bottom of his whole philosophy. Further, he distinguishes between *time* and *duration* in so far as *number* applies to the former, not to the latter; for a thing which can be numbered is finite, whilst duration is infinite. Similarly, philosophers have explained *time* as duration with a beginning and an end, and *eternity* as duration without beginning and end.

According to Alrâzî, those five things are *necessary postulates* of the actually existing world. For that which the senses perceive in it is the ὕλη acquiring shape by means of combination. Besides, the ὕλη occupies some place, and therefore we must admit the existence of *space.* The changes apparent in the world of sense compel us to assume the existence of time, for some of them are earlier, others later, and the *before* and the *afterwards,* the earlier and the later, and the simultaneous can only be perceived by means of the notion of time, which is a necessary postulate of the existing world.

Further, there are *living beings* in the existing world. Therefore we must assume the existence of *the soul.* Among these living beings there are *intelligent* ones, capable of carrying the arts to the highest perfection; and this compels us to assume the existence of a Creator, who is wise and intelligent, who establishes and arranges everything in the best possible manner, and inspires people with the force of intelligence for the purpose of liberation.

On the other hand, some sophists consider eternity and time as one and the same thing, and declare the motion which serves to measure time alone to be finite.

Another one declares eternity to be the circular motion. No doubt this motion is indissolubly connected with that being which *moves* by it, and which is of the most sublime nature, since it lasts for ever. Thereupon he rises in his argumentation from the moving being to its mover, and from the moving mover to the first mover who is motionless.

This kind of research is very subtle and obscure. But for this, the opinions would not differ to such an extent that some people declare that there is no time at all, while others declare that time is an independent substance. According to Alexander of Aphrodisias, Aristotle gives in his book *φυσικὴ ἀκρόασις* the following argumentation: "Everything moving is moved by a mover;" and Galenus says on the same subject that he could not understand the notion of time, much less prove it.

Page 164.

The notions of Hindu philosophers on time.

The theory of the Hindus on this subject is rather poor in thought and very little developed. Varâhamihira says in the opening of his book *Saṁhitâ,* when speaking of that which existed from all eternity: "It has been said in the ancient books that the first primeval thing was darkness, which is not identical with the black colour, but a kind of non-existence like the state of a sleeping person. Then God created this world for Brahman as a cupola for him. He made it to consist of two parts, a higher and a lower one, and placed the sun and moon in it." Kapila declares: "God has always existed, and with him the world, with all its substances and bodies. He, however, is a cause to the world, and rises by the subtlety of his nature above the gross nature of the world." Kumbhaka says: "The primeval one is *Mahâbhûta, i.e.* the compound of the five elements. Some declare that the primeval thing is *time*, others *nature*, and still others maintain that the director is *karman, i.e.* action."

In the book *Vishṇu-Dharma*, Vajra speaks to Mârkaṇḍeya: "Explain to me the times;" whereupon the latter answers: "Duration is *âtmapurusha*," *i.e. a breath*, and *purusha*, which means *the lord of the universe*. Thereupon, he commenced explaining to him the divisions of time and their dominants, just as we have propounded these things in detail in the proper chapters (chap. xxxiii. *et seq.*)

The Hindus have divided duration into two periods, a period of *motion*, which has been determined as *time*, and a period of *rest*, which can be determined only in an imaginary way according to the analogy of that which has first been determined, the period of motion. The Hindus hold the eternity of the Creator to be *determinable*, not *measurable*, since it is infinite. We, however, cannot refrain from remarking that it is extremely difficult to imagine a thing which is *determinable* but not *measurable*, and that the whole idea is very far-fetched. We shall here communicate so much as will suffice for the reader of the opinions of the Hindus on this subject, as far as we know them.

The Day of Brahman a period of creation, the Night of

The common notion of the Hindus regarding creation is a popular one, for, as we have already mentioned, they believe matter to be eternal. Therefore, they do

Brahman a period of non-creation.

not, by the word *creation*, understand *a formation of something out of nothing.* They mean by creation only the working with a piece of clay, working out various combinations and figures in it, and making such arrangements with it as will lead to certain ends and aims which are potentially in it. For this reason they attribute the creation to angels and demons, nay, even to human beings, who create either because they carry out some legal obligation which afterwards proves beneficial for the creation, or because they intend to allay their passions after having become envious and ambitious. So, for instance, they relate that Viśvâmitra, the Ṛishi, created the buffaloes for this purpose, that mankind should enjoy all the good and useful things which they afford. All this reminds one of the words of Plato in the book *Timæus:* "The θεοί, *i.e.* the gods, who, according to an order of their father, carried out the creation of man, took an immortal soul and made it the beginning; thereupon they fashioned like a turner a mortal body upon it."

Here in this context we meet with a duration of time which Muslim authors, following the example of the Hindus, call *the years of the world.* People think that at their beginnings and endings creation and destruction take place as kinds of new formations. This, however, is not the belief of the people at large. According to them, this duration is a day of Brahman and a consecutive night of Brahman; for Brahman is intrusted with creating. Further, the coming into existence is a motion in that which grows out of something different from itself, and the most apparent of the causes of this motion are the meteoric motors, *i.e.* the stars. These, however, will never exercise regular influences on the world below them unless they move and change their shapes in every direction (= their *aspects*). Therefore the coming into existence is limited to the *day of Brahman,* because in it only, as the

Hindus believe, the stars are moving and their spheres revolving according to their pre-established order, and in consequence the process of coming into existence is developed on the surface of the earth without any interruption. Page 165.

On the contrary, during *the night of Brahman* the spheres rest from their motions, and all the stars, as well as their apsides and nodes, stand still in one particular place.

In consequence all the affairs of the earth are in one and the same unchanging condition, therefore the coming into existence has ceased, because he who makes things come into existence rests. So both the processes of acting and of being acted upon are suspended; the elements rest from entering into new metamorphoses and combinations, as they rest now in (*lacuna; perhaps:* the night), and they prepare themselves to belong to new beings, which will come into existence on the following day of Brahman.

In this way existence circulates during *the life of Brahman*, a subject which we shall propound in its proper place.

Critical remark of the author.

According to these notions of the Hindus, creation and destruction only refer to the surface of the earth. By such a creation, not one piece of clay comes into existence which did not exist before, and by such a destruction not one piece of clay which exists ceases to exist. It is quite impossible that the Hindus should have the notion of a creation as long as they believe that *matter* existed from all eternity.

Brahman's waking and sleeping.

The Hindus represent to their common people the two *durations* here mentioned, the day of Brahman and the night of Brahman, as his *waking* and *sleeping;* and we do not disapprove of these terms, as they denote something which has a beginning and end. Further, the whole of *the life of Brahman*, consisting of a succession of motion and rest in the world during such a period, is considered as applying only to existence, not to non-existence, since during it the piece of clay exists and, besides, also its shape. The *life of Brahman* is only a *day* for that being who is above him, *i.e.* Purusha (*cf.* chap. xxxv.). When he dies all compounds are dissolved during his *night*, and in consequence of the annihilation of the compounds, that also is suspended which kept him (Brahman) within the laws of nature. This, then, is the rest of Purusha, and of all that is under his control (*lit.* and of his vehicles).

Vulgar and scientific notions on the sleep of Brahman.

When common people describe these things, they make the night of Brahman follow after the night of Purusha; and as Purusha is the name for a man, they attribute to him sleeping and waking. They derive destruction from his snoring, in consequence of which all things that hang together break asunder, and everything standing is drowned in the sweat of his forehead. And more of the like they produce, things which the mind declines to accept and the ear refuses to hear.

Therefore the educated Hindus do not share these opinions (regarding the waking and sleeping of Brahman), for they know the real nature of sleep. They know that the body, a compound of antipathetic *humores*, requires sleep for the purpose of resting, and for this purpose that all which nature requires, after being wasted, should be duly replaced. So, in consequence of the constant dissolution, the body requires food in order to replace that which had been lost by emaciation. Further, it requires cohabitation for the purpose of perpetuating the species by the body, as without cohabitation the species would die out. Besides, the body requires other things, evil ones, but necessary, while simple substances can dispense with them, as also He can who is above them, like to whom there is nothing.

Further, the Hindus maintain that the world will perish in consequence of the conjunction of the twelve suns, which appear one after the other in the different months, ruining the earth by burning and calcining it, and by withering and drying up all moist substances. Further, the world perishes in consequence of the union of the four rains which now come down in the different seasons of the year; that which has been calcined attracts the water and is thereby dissolved. Lastly, the world perishes by the cessation of light and by the prevalence of darkness and non-existence. By all this the world will be dissolved into atoms and be scattered.

Notions regarding the end of the world.

The *Matsya-Purâṇa* says that the fire which burns the world has come out of the water; that until then it dwelt on Mount Mahisha in the Kusha-Dvîpa, and was called by the name of this mountain.

The *Vishṇu-Purâṇa* says that "Maharloka lies above the pole, and that the duration of the stay there is one *kalpa*. When the three worlds burn, the fire and smoke injure the inhabitants, and then they rise and emigrate to Janaloka, the dwelling-place of the sons of Brahman, who preceded creation, vîz. Sanaka, Sananda, Sanandanâda (?), Asuras, Kapila, Voḍhu, and Pañća-śikha."

Page 166.

The context of these passages makes it clear that this destruction of the world takes place at the end of a *kalpa*, and hence is derived the theory of Abû-Maʿshar that a deluge takes place at the conjunction of the planets, because, in fact, they stand in conjunction at the end of each *caturyuga* and at the beginning of each *kaliyuga*. If this conjunction is not a complete one, the deluge, too, will evidently not attain the highest degree of its destructive power. The farther we advance in the investigation of these subjects, the more light will be shed on all ideas of this kind, and the better the reader will understand all words and terms occurring in this context.

Abû-Maʿshar uses Indian theories.

Buddhist notions from Alêrânshahrî.

Alêrânshahrî records a tradition, as representing the belief of the Buddhists, which much resembles the silly tales just mentioned. On the sides of Mount Meru there are four worlds, which are alternately civilised or desert. A world becomes desert when it is overpowered by the fire, in consequence of the rising of seven suns, one after the other, over it, when the water of the fountains dries up, and the burning fire becomes so strong as to penetrate into the world. A world becomes civilised when the fire leaves it and migrates to another world; after it has left, a strong wind rises in the world, drives the clouds, and makes them rain, so that the world becomes like an ocean. Out of its foam shells are produced, with which the souls are connected, and out of these human beings originate when the water has sunk into the ground. Some Buddhists think that a man comes by accident from the perishing world to the growing world. Since he feels unhappy on account of his being alone, out of his thought there arises a spouse, and from this couple generation commences.

(Chapters XXXIII–XLII, pages 327–377, are concerned with Hindu calculations of time. This material is summarized elsewhere in the book where it is relevant.)

CHAPTER XLIII.

A DESCRIPTION OF THE FOUR YUGAS, AND OF ALL THAT IS EXPECTED TO TAKE PLACE AT THE END OF THE FOURTH YUGA.

THE ancient Greeks held regarding the earth various opinions, of which we shall relate one for the sake of an example.

On natural cataclysms.

Page 190.

The disasters which from time to time befal the earth, both from above and from below, differ in quality and quantity. Frequently it has experienced one so incommensurable in quality or in quantity, or in both together, that there was no remedy against it, and that no flight or caution was of any avail. The catastrophe comes on like a deluge or an earthquake, bringing destruction either by the breaking in of the surface, or by drowning with water which breaks forth, or by burning with hot stones and ashes that are thrown out, by thunderstorms, by landslips, and typhoons; further, by contagious and other diseases, by pestilence, and more of the like. Thereby a large region is stripped of its inhabitants; but when after a while, after the disaster and its consequences have passed away, the country begins to recover and to show new signs of life, then different people flock there together like wild animals, who formerly were dwelling in hiding-holes and on the tops of the mountains. They become civilised by assisting each other against common foes, wild beasts or men, and furthering each other in the hope for a life in safety and joy. Thus they increase to great numbers; but then ambition, circling round them with the wings of wrath and envy, begins to disturb the serene bliss of their life.

Sometimes a nation of such a kind derives its pedigree from a person who first settled in the place or distinguished himself by something or other, so that he alone continues to live in the recollection of the succeeding generations, whilst all others beside him are forgotten. Plato mentions in the *Book of Laws* Zeus, *i.e.* Jupiter, as the forefather of the Greeks, and to Zeus is traced back the pedigree of Hippocrates, which is mentioned in the last chapters added at the end of the book. We must, however, observe that the pedigree contains only very few generations, not more than fourteen. It is the following:—Hippokrates—Gnosidikos—Nebros—Sostratos—Theodoros—Kleomyttades—Krisamis—Dardanas—Sostratos—ادلوسوس (?)—Hippolochos—Podaleirios—Machaon—Asclepios—Apollo—Zeus—Kronos, *i.e.* Saturn.

Pedigree of Hippocrates.

The Hindus have similar traditions regarding the Caturyuga, for according to them, at the beginning of it, *i.e.* at the beginning of Kṛitayuga, there was happiness and safety, fertility and abundance, health and force, ample knowledge and a great number of Brahmans. The good is complete in this age, like four-fourths of a whole, and life lasted 4000 years alike for all beings during this whole space of time.

Hindu notions regarding the four ages or *yugas*.

Thereupon things began to decrease and to be mixed with opposite elements to such a degree, that at the beginning of Tretâyuga the good was thrice as much as the invading bad, and that bliss was three-quarters of the whole. There were a greater number of Kshatriyas than of Brahmans, and life had the same length as in the preceding age. So it is represented by the *Vishṇu-Dharma*, whilst analogy requires that it should be shorter by the same amount than bliss is smaller, *i.e.* by one-fourth. In this age, when offering to the fire, they begin to kill animals and to tear off plants, practices which before were unknown.

Thus the evil increases till, at the beginning of Dvâpara, evil and good exist in equal proportions, and likewise bliss and misfortune. The climates begin to differ, there is much killing going on, and the religions become different. Life becomes shorter, and lasts only 400 years, according to the *Vishṇu-Dharma*. At the beginning of Tishya, *i.e.* Kaliyuga, evil is thrice as much as the remaining good.

The Hindus have several well-known traditions of events which are said to have occurred in the Tretâ and Dvâpara *yugas*, *e.g.* the story of Râma, who killed Ravaṇa; that of Paraśurâma the Brahman, who killed every Kshatriya he laid hold upon, revenging on them the death of his father. They think that he lives in heaven, that he has already twenty-one times appeared on earth, and that he will again appear. Further, the story of the war of the children of Pâṇḍu with those of Kuru.

Page 191.

In the Kaliyuga evil increases, till at last it results in the destruction of all good. At that time the inhabitants of the earth perish, and a new race rises out of those who are scattered through the mountains and hide themselves in caves, uniting for the purpose of worshipping and flying from the horrid, demoniac human race. Therefore this age is called *Kṛitayuga*, which means "Being ready for going away after having finished the work."

Description of the Kaliyuga.

In the story of Śaunaka which Venus received from Brahman, God speaks to him in the following words: "When the Kaliyuga comes, I send Buddhodana, the son of Śuddhodana the pious, to spread the good in the creation. But then the *Muḥammira*, *i.e.* the red-wearing ones, who derive their origin from him, will change everything that he has brought, and the dignity of the Brahmans will be gone to such a degree that a Śûdra, their servant, will be impudent towards them, and that a Śûdra and Caṇḍâla will share with them the presents and offerings. Men will entirely be occupied with gathering wealth by crimes, with hoarding up, not refraining from committing horrid and sinful crimes. All this will result in a rebellion of the small ones against the great ones, of the children against their parents, of the servants against their masters. The castes will be in uproar against each other, the genealogies will become confused, the four castes will be abolished, and there will be many religions and sects. Many books will be composed, and the communities which formerly were united will on account of them be dissolved into single individuals. The temples will be destroyed and the schools will lie waste. Justice will be gone, and the kings will not know anything but oppression and spoliation, robbing and destroying, as if they wanted to devour the people, foolishly indulging in far-reaching hopes, and not considering how short life is in comparison with the sins (for which they have to atone). The more the mind of people is depraved, the more will pestilential diseases be prevalent. Lastly, people maintain that most of the astrological rules obtained in that age are void and false.

Saying of Mânî.

These ideas have been adopted by Mânî, for he says: "Know ye that the affairs of the world have been changed and altered; also priesthood has been changed since the *σφαῖραι* of heaven, *i.e.* the spheres, have been changed, and the priest can no longer acquire such a knowledge of the stars in the circle of a sphere as their fathers were able to acquire. They lead mankind astray by fraud. What they prophesy may by chance happen, but frequently it does not happen."

Description of the Kṛitayuga according to *Vishṇu-Dharma.*

The description of these things in the *Vishṇu-Dharma* is much more copious than we have given it. People will be ignorant of what is reward and punishment; they will deny that the angels have absolute knowledge. Their lives will be of different length, and none

of them will know how long it is. The one will die as an embryo, the other as a baby or child. The pious will be torn away and will not have a long life, but he who does evil and denies religion will live longer. Śûdras will be kings, and will be like rapacious wolves, robbing the others of all that pleases them. The doings of the Brahmans will be of the same kind, but the majority will be Śûdras and brigands. The laws of the Brahmans will be abolished. People will point with their fingers at those who worry themselves with the practice of frugality and poverty as a curiosity, will despise them, and will wonder at a man worshipping Vishṇu; for all of them have become of the same (wicked) character. Therefore any wish will soon be
Page 192.
granted, little merit receive great reward, and honour and dignity be obtained by little worship and service.

But finally, at the end of the *yuga*, when the evil will have reached its highest pitch, there will come forward Garga, the son of J-Ś-V (?) the Brahman, *i.e.* Kali, after whom this *yuga* is called, gifted with an irresistible force, and more skilled in the use of any weapon than any other. Then he draws his sword to make good all that has become bad; he cleans the surface of the earth of the impurity of people and clears the earth of them. He collects the pure and pious ones for the purpose of procreation. Then the Kṛitayuga lies far behind them, and the time and the world return to purity, and to absolute good and to bliss.

This is the nature of the *yugas* as they circle round through the Caturyuga.

The origin of medicine according to the book *Caraka*.

The book *Caraka*, as quoted by ʿAlî Ibn Zain of Ṭabaristan, says: "In primeval times the earth was always fertile and healthy, and the elements or *mahabhûta* were equally mixed. Men lived with each other in harmony and love, without any lust and ambition, hatred and envy, without anything that makes soul and body ill. But then came envy, and lust followed.

Driven by lust, they strove to hoard up, which was difficult to some, easy to others. All kinds of thoughts, labours, and cares followed, and resulted in war, deceit, and lying. The hearts of men were hardened, the natures were altered and became exposed to diseases, which seized hold of men and made them neglect the worship of God and the furtherance of science. Ignorance became deeply rooted, and the calamity became great. Then the pious met before their anchorite Kṛiśa (?) the son of Âtreya, and deliberated; whereupon the sage ascended the mountain and threw himself on the earth. Thereafter God taught him the science of medicine."

Quotation from Aratus.

All this much resembles the traditions of the Greeks, which we have related (in another place). For Aratus says in his *Φαινόμενα*, and in his intimations referring to the seventh zodiacal sign: "Look under the feet of the Herdsman, *i.e. Al'awwâ*, among the northern figures, and you see the Virgin coming with a blooming ear of corn in her hand, *i.e. Alsimâk Al'a'zal.* She belongs either to the star-race, which are said to be the forefathers of the ancient stars, or she was procreated by another race which we do not know. People say that in primeval times she lived among mankind, but only among women, not visible to men, being called *Justice.* She used to unite the aged men and those who stood in the market-places and in the streets, and exhorted them with a loud voice to adhere to the truth. She presented mankind with innumerable wealth and bestowed rights upon them. At that time the earth was called *golden.* None of its inhabitants knew pernicious hypocrisy in deed or word, and there was no objectionable schism among them. They lived a quiet life, and did not yet navigate the sea in ships. The cows afforded the necessary sustenance.

"Afterwards, when the golden race had expired and the silver race come on, Virgo mixed with them, but without being happy, and concealed herself in the mountains, having no longer intercourse with the women as formerly. Then she went to the large towns, warned their inhabitants, scolded them for their evil doings, Page 193. and blamed them for ruining the race which the *golden fathers* had left behind. She foretold them that there would come a race still worse than they, and that wars, bloodshed, and other great disasters would follow.

"After having finished, she disappeared into the mountains till the silver race expired and a bronze race came up. People invented the sword, the doer of evil; they tasted of the meat of cows, the first who did it. By all this their neighbourhood became odious to Justice, and she flew away to the sphere."

A scholion on Aratus.

The commentator of the book of Aratus says: "This Virgin is the daughter of Zeus. She spoke to the people on the public places and streets, and at that time they were obedient to their rulers, not knowing the bad nor discord. Without any altercation or envy they lived from agriculture, and did not travel on sea for the sake of commerce nor for the lust of plunder. Their nature was as pure as gold.

"But when they gave up these manners and no longer adhered to truth, Justice no longer had intercourse with them, but she observed them, dwelling in the mountains. When, however, she came to their meetings, though unwillingly, she threatened them, for they listened in silence to her words, and therefore she no longer appeared to those who called her, as she had formerly done.

"When, then, after the silver race, the bronze race came up, when wars followed each other and the evil spread in the world, she started off, for she wanted on no account to stay with them, and hated them, and went towards the sphere.

"There are many traditions regarding this Justice.

According to some, she is Demeter, because she has the ear of corn; according to others, she is *Τύχη*."

This is what Aratus says.

The following occurs in the third book of the Laws of Plato:— Quotation from the Laws of Plato.

"The Athenian said, 'There have been deluges, diseases, disasters on earth, from which none has been saved but herdsmen and mountaineers, as the remnants of a race not practised in deceit and in the love of power.'

"The Knossian said, 'At the beginning men loved each other sincerely, feeling lonely in the desert of the world, and because the world had sufficient room for all of them, and did not compel them to any exertion. There was no poverty among them, no possession, no contract. There was no greed among them, and neither silver nor gold. There were no rich people among them and no poor. If we found any of their books, they would afford us numerous proofs for all this.'"

(Chapters XLIV and XLV, pages 386–394, are detailed discussions of Hindu theories of time, with lists of eras.)

CHAPTER XLVI.

ON NÂRÂYAṆA, HIS APPEARANCE AT DIFFERENT TIMES, AND HIS NAMES.

Page 198.

On the nature of Nârâyaṇa.

NÂRÂYAṆA is according to the Hindus a supernatural power, which does not on principle try to bring about the good by the good, nor the bad by the bad, but to prevent the evil and destruction by whatever means happen to be available. For this force the good exists prior to the bad, but if the good does not properly develop nor is available, it uses the bad, this being unavoidable. In so doing, it may be compared to a rider who has got into the midst of a cornfield. When he then comes back to his senses, and wants to avoid evil-doing and to get out of the mischief he has committed, he has no other means but that of turning his horse back and riding out on the same road on which he has entered the field, though in going out he will do as much mischief as he has done in entering, and even more. But there is no other possibility of making amends save this.

The Hindus do not distinguish between this force and the *First Cause* of their philosophy. Its dwelling in the world is of such a nature that people compare it to a material existence, an appearance in body and colour, since they cannot conceive any other kind of appearance.

Besides other times, Nârâyaṇa has appeared at the end of the first *manvantara*, to take away the rule of the worlds from Vâlakhilya (?), who had given it the name, and wanted to take it into his own hands. Nârâyaṇa came and handed it over to Śatakratu, the performer of a hundred sacrifices, and made him Indra.

Story of Bali, the son of Virocana.

Another time he appeared at the end of the sixth *manvantara*, when he killed the King Bali, the son of Virocana, who ruled the whole world and had Venus as his vazîr. On having heard from his mother that the time of his father had been much better than *his* time, since it was nearer the *kṛitayuga*, when people enjoyed more profound bliss and did not know any fatigue, he became ambitious and desirous of vying with his father. Therefore he commenced doing works of piety, giving presents, distributing money, and performing sacrifices, which earn the rule of paradise and earth for him who finishes a hundred of them. When he was near this term, or had nearly finished the ninety-ninth sacrifice, the angels began to feel uneasy and to fear for their dignity, knowing that the tribute which men bring them would cease if they stood no longer in need of them. Now they united and went to Nârâyaṇa, asking him to help them. He granted their wish, and descended to the earth in the shape of Vâmana, *i.e.* a man whose hands and feet are too short in comparison with his body, and in consequence his figure is thought to be hideous.

Nârâyaṇa came to the King Bali whilst he was offering, his Brahmans standing round the fires, and Venus, his vazîr, standing before him. The treasure-houses had been opened and the precious stones had been thrown out in heaps, to be given as presents and alms. Now Vâmana commenced to recite the Veda like the Brahmans from that part which is now called *Sâmaveda*, in a melancholy, impressive kind of melody, persuading the king to grant him liberally what he would wish and demand. Upon this Venus spoke stealthily to him: "This is Nârâyaṇa. He has come to rob thee of thy rule." But the king was so excited that he did not mind the words of Venus, and asked Vâmana what was his desire. Thereupon Vâmana said, "As much as four paces of thy realm, that I may live there." The king answered, "Choose what you wish, and how you wish it;" and according to Hindu custom, he ordered water to be brought to pour it over his hands as a sign of the confirmation of the order he had given. Now Venus, because of her love to the king, brought in the jug, but had corked the spout, so that no water should flow out of it, whilst she closed the hole in the cork with the *kuśa* grass of her ring-finger. But Venus Page 199. had only one eye; she missed the hole, and now the water flowed out. In consequence, Vâmana made a pace towards east, another towards west, and a third towards above as far as Svarloka. As for the fourth pace, there was no more space in the world; he made, by the fourth pace, the king a slave, putting his foot between his shoulders as a sign of making him a slave. He made him sink down into the earth as far as Pâtâla, the lowest of the low. He took the worlds away from him, and handed the rule over to Puraṁdara.

Quotation from *Vishṇu-Purâṇa.*

The following occurs in the *Vishṇu-Purâṇa*:—

"The King Maitreya asked Parâśara about the *yugas*. So the latter answered, 'They exist for the purpose that Vishṇu should occupy himself with something in them. In the Kṛitayuga he comes in the shape of Kapila alone, for the purpose of spreading wisdom; in Tretâyuga, in the shape of Râma alone, for the purpose of spreading fortitude, to conquer the bad, and to preserve the three worlds by force and the prevalence of virtuous action; in Dvâpara, in the shape of Vyâsa, to divide the Veda into four parts, and to derive many branches from it. In the end of Dvâpara he appears in the shape of Vâsudeva to destroy the giants; in the Kaliyuga, in the shape of Kali, the son of *J-sh-v* (?) the Brahman, to kill all, and to make the cycle of the *yugas* commence anew. That is his (Vishṇu's) occupation.'"

In another passage of the same book we read: "Vishṇu, *i.e.* another name for Nârâyaṇa, comes at the end of each *dvâpara* to divide the Veda into four parts, because men are feeble and unable to observe the whole of it. In his face he resembles Vyâsa."

Enumeration of the Vyâsas of the seventh *manvantara*.

We exhibit his names in the following table, though they vary in different sources, enumerating the Vyâsas who have appeared in the *caturyugas* of the present or seventh *manvantara* which have elapsed:—

1	Svayaṁbhû	16	Dhanaṁjaya
2	Prajâpati	17	Kṛitaṁjaya
3	Uśanas	18	Ṛiṇajyeshṭha (?)
4	Bṛihaspati	19	Bharadvâja
5	Savitṛi	20	Gautama
6	Mṛityu	21	Uttama
7	Indra	22	Haryâtman
8	Vasishṭha	23	Veda-vyâsa
9	Sârasvata	24	Vâjaśravas
10	Tridhâman	25	Somaśushma
11	Trivṛisha	26	Bhârgava
12	Bharadvâja	27	Vâlmîki
13	Antariksha	28	Kṛishṇa
14	Vapra (?)	29	Aśvatthâman the son of Droṇa
15	Trayyâruṇa		

Kṛishṇa Dvaipâyana is Vyâsa the son of Parâśara. The twenty-ninth Vyâsa has not yet come, but will appear in future.

Quotation from *Vishṇu-Dharma*.

The book *Vishṇu-Dharma* says: "The names of Hari, *i.e.* Nârâyaṇa, differ in the *yugas*. They are the following: Vâsudeva, Saṁkarshaṇa, Pradyumna, and Aniruddha."

I suppose that the author has not here preserved the proper sequence, for Vâsudeva belongs to the end of the four *yugas*.

The same book says: "Also his colours differ in the *yugas*. In the Kṛitayuga he is white, in the Tretâyuga red, in the Dvâpara yellow, the latter is the first phase of his being embodied in human shape, and in the Kaliyuga he is black."

These colours are something like *the three primary forces* of their philosophy, for they maintain that *Satya* is transparent white, *Rajas* red, and *Tamas* black. We shall in a later part of this book give a description of his last appearance in the world. Page 200.

CHAPTER XLVII.

ON VÂSUDEVA AND THE WARS OF THE BHÂRATA.

Analogies of the course of nature to the history of mankind.

THE life of the world depends upon sowing and procreating. Both processes increase in the course of time, and this increase is unlimited, whilst the world is limited.

When a class of plants or animals does not increase any more in its structure, and its peculiar kind is established as *a species* of its own, when each individual of it does not simply come into existence once and perish, but besides procreates a being like itself or several together, and not only once but several times, then this will as a single species of plants or animals occupy the earth and spread itself and its kind over as much territory as it can find.

The agriculturist selects his corn, letting grow as much as he requires, and tearing out the remainder. The forester leaves those branches which he perceives to be excellent, whilst he cuts away all others. The bees kill those of their kind who only eat, but do not work in their beehive.

Nature proceeds in a similar way; however, it does not distinguish, for its action is under all circumstances one and the same. It allows the leaves and fruit of the trees to perish, thus preventing them from realising that result which they are intended to produce in the economy of nature. It removes them so as to make room for others.

If thus the earth is ruined, or is near to be ruined

by having too many inhabitants, its ruler—for it has a ruler, and his all-embracing care is apparent in every single particle of it—sends it a messenger for the purpose of reducing the too great number and of cutting away all that is evil.

Story of the birth of Vâsudeva.

A messenger of this kind is, according to the belief of the Hindus, Vâsudeva, who was sent the last time in human shape, being called Vâsudeva. It was a time when the giants were numerous on earth and the earth was full of their oppression; it tottered, being hardly able to bear the whole number of them, and it trembled from the vehemence of their treading. Then there was born a child in the city of Mathurâ to Vâsudeva by the sister of Kaṁsa, at that time ruler of the town. They were a Jatt family, cattle-owners, low Śûdra people. Kaṁsa had learned, by a voice which he heard at the wedding of his sister, that he would perish at the hands of her child; therefore he appointed people who were to bring him every child of hers as soon as she gave birth to it, and he killed all her children, both male and female. Finally, she gave birth to Balabhadra, and Yaśodâ, the wife of the herdsman Nanda, took the child to herself, and managed to keep it concealed from the spies of Kaṁsa. Thereupon she became pregnant an eighth time, and gave birth to *Vâsudeva* in a rainy night of the eighth day of the black half of the month Bhâdrapada, whilst the moon was ascending in the station Rohiṇî. As the guards had fallen into deep sleep and neglected the watch, the father stole the child and brought it to *Nandakula*, *i.e.* the stable of the cows of Nanda, the husband of Yaśodâ, near Mathurâ, but separated from this place by the river Yamunâ. Vâsudeva exchanged the child for a daughter of Nanda, which happened to be born at the moment when Vâsudeva arrived with the boy. He brought this female child to the guards instead of his son. Kaṁsa, the ruler, wanted to kill the child, but she flew up into the air and disappeared.

Vâsudeva grew up under the care of his foster-mother Yaśodâ without her knowing that he had been exchanged for her daughter, but Kaṁsa got some inkling of the matter. Now he tried to get the child into his power by cunning plans, but all of them turned out against him. Lastly, Kaṁsa demanded from his parents that they should send him (Vâsudeva) to wrestle in his (Kaṁsa's) presence. Now Vâsudeva began to behave overbearingly towards everybody. On the road he had already roused the wrath of his aunt by hurting a serpent which had been appointed to watch over the lotus flowers of a pond, for he had drawn a cord through its nostrils like a bridle. Further, he had killed his fuller, because the latter had refused to lend him clothes for the wrestling. He had robbed the girl who accom-
Page 201.
panied him of the sandal-wood with which she was ordered to anoint the wrestlers. Lastly, he had killed the rutting elephant which was provided for the purpose of killing him before the door of Kaṁsa. All this heightened the wrath of Kaṁsa to such a degree, that his bile burst, and he died on the spot. Then Vâsudeva, his sister's son, ruled in his stead.

The names of Vâsudeva in the different months.

Vâsudeva has a special name in each month. His followers begin the months with Mârgaśîrsha, and each month they begin with the eleventh day, because on this day Vâsudeva appeared.

The following table contains the names of Vâsudeva in the months:—

The Months.	The Names of Vâsudeva.	The Months.	The Names of Vâsudeva.
Mârgaśîrsha	Keśava	Jyaishṭha	Trivikrama
Pausha	Nârâyaṇa	Âshâḍha	Vâmana
Mâgha	Mâdhava	Śrâvaṇa	Śrîdhara
Phâlguna	Govinda	Bhâdrapada	Hṛishîkeśa
Caitra	Vishṇu	Âśvayuja	Padmanâbhi
Vaiśâkha	Madhusûdana	Kârttika	Dâmodara

Continuation of the story of Vâsudeva.

Now the brother-in-law of the deceased Kaṁsa became angry, went rapidly to Mathurâ, took possession of the realm of Vâsudeva, and banished him to the ocean. Then there appeared near the coast a golden castle called Barodâ, and Vâsudeva made it his residence.

The children of Kaurava (*i.e.* Dhṛitarâshṭra) had the charge of their cousins (the children of Pâṇḍu). Dhṛitarâshṭra received them and played dice with them, the last stake being their whole property. They lost more and more, until he laid upon them the obligation of expatriation for more than ten years, and of concealment in the remotest part of the country, where nobody knew them. If they did not keep this engagement they would be bound to return into banishment for a like number of years. This engagement was carried out, but finally came the time of their coming forward for battle. Now each party began to assemble their whole number and to sue for allies, till at last nearly innumerable hosts had gathered in the plain of Tâneshar. There were eighteen *akshauhiṇî*. Each party tried to gain Vâsudeva as ally, whereupon he offered either himself or his brother Balabhadra together with an army. But the children of Pâṇḍu preferred him. They were five men—Yudhishṭhira, their leader, Arjuna, the bravest of them, Sahadeva, Bhîmasena, and Nakula. They had seven *akshauhiṇî*, whilst their enemies were much stronger. But for the cunning devices of Vâsudeva and his teaching them whereby they might gain victory, they would have been in a less favourable situation than their enemies. But now they conquered; all those hosts were destroyed, and none remained except the five brothers. Thereafter Vâsudeva returned to his residence and died, together with his family, who were called Yâdava. Also the five brothers died before the year had reached its end, at the end of those wars.

End of Vâsudeva and of the five Pâṇḍu brothers.

Vâsudeva had concerted with Arjuna the arrangement that they would consider the quivering of the left arm or left eye as a mysterious intimation that there was something happening to him. At that time there lived a pious Ṛishi called Durvâsas. Now the brothers and relations of Vâsudeva were a rather malicious, inconsiderate set of people. One of them hid under his coat a new frying-pan, went to the anchorite, and asked him what would be the result of his pregnancy, jeering at the pious man. The latter said, "In thy belly there is something which will be the cause of thy death and that of thy whole clan." When Vâsudeva heard this he became sorry, because he knew that these words would be fulfilled. He gave orders that the pan should be filed away and be thrown into the water. This was done. There was only a small part of it left, which the artisan who had done the filing considered as insignificant. Therefore he threw it, as it was, into the water. A fish devoured it; the fish was caught, and the fisherman found it in its belly. He thought it would be a good tip for his arrow.

Page 202.

When the predestined time came, Vâsudeva rested on the coast under the shadow of a tree, one of his feet being crossed over the other; the fisherman took him for a gazelle, shot at him, and hit his right foot. This wound became the cause of the death of Vâsudeva. At the same time the left side of Arjuna began to quiver, and then his arm. Now his brother Sahadeva gave orders that he should never any more embrace anybody, that he might not be bereft of his strength (?). Arjuna went to Vâsudeva, but could not embrace him on account of the state in which he was. Vâsudeva ordered his bow to be brought, and handed it over to Arjuna, who tried his strength at it. Vâsudeva ordered him to burn his body and the bodies of his relations when they had died, and to bring away his wives from the castle, and then he died.

Out of the filings or bits of iron which had fallen off when the pan was filed a *bardî* bush had grown. To this there came the Yâdavas, who tied together some bundles of its twigs to sit upon. Whilst they were drinking there arose a quarrel between them; they beat each other with the *bardî* bundles, and killed each other. All this happened near the mouth of the river Sarsatî, where it flows into the sea, near the situation of Somanâth.

Arjuna had done all he had been ordered by Vâsudeva. When he brought away the women, they were suddenly attacked by robbers. When, now, Arjuna was no longer able to bend his bow, he felt that his strength was going. He whirled the bow in a circle above his head, and all who stood under the bow were saved, while the others were seized by the robbers. Now Arjuna and his brothers saw that life was no more of any use to them, therefore they emigrated to the north and entered the mountains, the snow of which never melts. The cold killed them one after the other, till at last only Yudhishṭhira remained. He obtained the distinction of being admitted to paradise, but before that he was to pass through hell in consequence of the sole lie which he had spoken in his life, at the request of his brothers and of Vâsudeva. These were the words which he had spoken within hearing of the Brahman Droṇa: "Aśvatthâman, the elephant, has died." He had made a pause between *Aśvatthâman* and *the elephant,* by which he had led Droṇa to believe that he meant *his son.* Yudhishṭhira spoke to the angels: "If this must be, may my intercession be accepted on behalf of the people in hell; may they be freed from it." After this desire of his had been granted, he went into paradise.

(Chapter XLVIII, pages 407–408, is an analysis of the meaning of a battle term.)

CHAPTER XLIX.

A SUMMARY DESCRIPTION OF THE ERAS.

THE eras serve to fix certain moments of time which are mentioned in some historical or astronomical connection. The Hindus do not consider it wearisome to reckon with huge numbers, but rather enjoy it. Still, in practical use, they are compelled to replace them by smaller (more handy) ones.

Page 203. Enumeration of some of the eras of the Hindus.

Of their eras we mention—

1. The beginning of the existence of Brahman.
2. The beginning of the day of the present nychthemeron of Brahman, *i.e.* the beginning of the *kalpa*.
3. The beginning of the seventh *manvantara*, in which we are now.
4. The beginning of the twenty-eighth *caturyuga*, in which we are now.
5. The beginning of the fourth *yuga* of the present *caturyuga*, called *kalikâla*, *i.e.* the time of Kali. The whole *yuga* is called after him, though, accurately speaking, *his* time falls only in the last part of the *yuga*. Notwithstanding, the Hindus mean by *kalikâla* the beginning of the *kaliyuga*.
6. *Pâṇḍava-kâla*, *i.e.* the time of the life and the wars of Bhârata.

All these eras vie with each other in antiquity, the

one going back to a still more remote beginning than the other, and the sums of years which they afford go beyond hundreds, thousands, and higher orders of numbers. Therefore not only astronomers, but also other people, think it wearisome and unpractical to use them.

The author adopts the year 400 of Yazdajird as a test-year.

In order to give an idea of these eras, we shall use as a first gauge or point of comparison that Hindu year the great bulk of which coincides with the *year 400 of Yazdajird.* This number consists only of hundreds, not of units and tens, and by this peculiarity it is distinguished from all other years that might possibly be chosen. Besides, it is a memorable time; for the breaking of the strongest pillar of the religion, the decease of the pattern of a prince, Maḥmûd, the lion of the world, the wonder of his time—may God have mercy upon him!—took place only a short time, less than a year, before it. The Hindu year precedes the Naurôz or new year's day of this year only by twelve days, and the death of the prince occurred precisely ten complete Persian months before it.

Page 204.

Now, presupposing this our gauge as known, we shall compute the years for this point of junction, which is the beginning of the corresponding Hindu year, for the end of all years which come into question coincides with it, and the Naurôz of the year 400 of Yazdajird falls only a little latter (viz. twelve days).

How much of the life of Brahman has elapsed according to the *Vishṇu-Dharma.*

The book *Vishṇu-Dharma* says: "Vajra asked Mârkaṇḍeya how much of the life of Brahman had elapsed; whereupon the sage answered: 'That which has elapsed is 8 years, 5 months, 4 days, 6 *manvantaras,* 7 *saṁdhi,* 27 *caturyugas,* and 3 *yugas* of the twenty-eighth *caturyuga,* and 10 *divya-years* up to the time of the *aśvamedha* which thou hast offered.' He who knows the details of this statement and comprehends them duly is a *sage* man, and *the sage* is he who serves the only Lord and strives to reach the neighbourhood of his place, which is called *Paramapada.*"

Presupposing this statement to be known, and referring the reader to our explanation of the various measures of time which we have given in former chapters, we offer the following analysis.

Of the life of Brahman there have elapsed before our gauge 26,215,732,948,132 of our years. Of the nychthemeron of Brahman, *i.e.* of the *kalpa of the day*, there have elapsed 1,972,948,132, and of the seventh *manvantara* 120,532,132.

The latter is also the date of the imprisoning of the King Bali, for it happened in the first *caturyuga* of the seventh *manvantara*.

In all chronological dates which we have mentioned already and shall still mention, we only reckon with *complete* years, for the Hindus are in the habit of disregarding *fractions* of a year.

The time of Râma according to *Vishṇu-Dharma*.

Further, the *Vishṇu-Dharma* says: "Mârkaṇḍeya says, in answer to a question of Vajra, 'I have already lived as long as 6 *kalpas* and 6 *manvantaras* of the seventh *kalpa*, 23 *tretâyugas* of the seventh *manvantara*. In the twenty-fourth *tretâyuga* Râma killed Râvaṇa, and Lakshmaṇa, the brother of Râma, killed Kumbhakarṇa, the brother of Râvaṇa. The two subjugated all the Râkshasas. At that time Vâlmîki, the Ṛishi, composed the story of Râma and Râmâyaṇa and eternalised it in his books. It was I who told it to Yudhishṭhira, the son of Pâṇḍu, in the forest of Kâmyakavana.'"

The author of the *Vishṇu-Dharma* reckons here with *tretâyugas*, first, because the events which he mentions occurred in a certain *tretâyuya*, and secondly, because it is more convenient to reckon with a simple unit than with such a unit as requires to be explained by reference to its single quarters. Besides, the latter part of the *tretâyuga* is a more suitable time for the events mentioned than its beginning, because it is so much nearer to the age of evil-doing (v. i. pp. 379, 380). No doubt, the date of Râma and Râmâyaṇa is known among the

Hindus, but I for my part have not been able to ascertain it.

Twenty-three *caturyugas* are 99,360,000 years, and, together with the time from the beginning of a *caturyuga* till the end of the *tretâyuga,* 102,384,000 years.

If we subtract this number of years from the number of years of the seventh *manvantara* that have elapsed before our gauge-year, viz. 120,532,132 (v. p. 3), we get the remainder of 18,148,132 years, *i.e.* so many years before our gauge-year as the conjectural date of Râma; and this may suffice, as long as it is not supported by a trustworthy tradition. The here-mentioned year corresponds to the 3,892,132d year of the 28th *caturyuga.*

How much time has elapsed before o of the present *kalpa*, according to Pulisa and Brahmagupta.

All these computations rest on the measures adopted by Brahmagupta. He and Pulisa agree in this, that the number of *kalpas* which have elapsed of the life of Brahman before the present *kalpa* is 6068 (equal to 8 years, 5 months, 4 days of Brahman). But they differ from each other in converting this number into *caturyugas.* According to Pulisa, it is equal to 6,116,544; according to Brahmagupta, only to 6,068,000 *caturyugas.* Therefore, if we adopt the system of Pulisa, reckoning 1 *manvantara* as 72 *caturyugas* without *saṁdhi,* 1 *kalpa* as 1008 *caturyugas,* and each *yuga* as the fourth part of a *caturyuga,* that which has elapsed of the life of Brahman before our gauge-year is the sum of 26,425,456,204,132 (!) years, and of the *kalpa*
Page 205.
there have elapsed 1,986,124,132 years, of the *manvantara* 119,884,132 years, and of the *caturyuga* 3,244,132 years.

How much time has elapsed of the current *kaliyuga.*

Regarding the time which has elapsed since the beginning of the *kaliyuga,* there exists no difference amounting to whole years. According to both Brahmagupta and Pulisa, of the *kaliyuga* there have elapsed before our gauge-year 4132 years, and between the wars of Bhârata and our gauge-year there have elapsed 3479 years. The year 4132 before the gauge-year is the epoch of the *kalikâla*, and the year 3479 before the gauge-year is the epoch of the *Pâṇḍavakâla*.

The Hindus have an era called *Kâlayavana*, regarding which I have not been able to obtain full information. They place its epoch in the end of the last *dvâparayuga*. The here-mentioned Yavana (JMN) severely oppressed both their country and their religion. The era Kâlayavana.

To date by the here-mentioned eras requires in any case vast numbers, since their epochs go back to a most remote antiquity. For this reason people have given up using them, and have adopted instead the eras of—

(1.) *Śrî Harsha.*
(2.) *Vikramâditya.*
(3.) *Śaka.*
(4.) *Valabha*, and
(5.) *Gupta.*

The Hindus believe regarding Śrî Harsha that he used to examine the soil in order to see what of hidden treasures was in its interior, as far down as the seventh earth; that, in fact, he found such treasures; and that, in consequence, he could dispense with oppressing his subjects (by taxes, &c.) His era is used in Mathurâ and the country of Kanoj. Between Śrî Harsha and Vikramâditya there is an interval of 400 years, as I have been told by some of the inhabitants of that region. However, in the Kashmîrian calendar I have read that Śrî Harsha was 664 years later than Vikramâditya. In face of this discrepancy I am in perfect uncertainty, which to the present moment has not yet been cleared up by any trustworthy information. Era of Śrî Harsha.

Those who use the era of Vikramâditya live in the southern and western parts of India. It is used in the following way: 342 are multiplied by 3, which gives Era of Vikramâditya.

the product 1026. To this number you add the years which have elapsed of the current *shashṭyabda* or sexagesimal *samvatsara*, and the sum is the corresponding year of the era of Vikramâditya. In the book *Srûdhava* by Mahâdeva I find as his name *Candrabîja*.

As regards this method of calculation, we must first say that it is rather awkward and unnatural, for if they began with 1026 as the basis of the calculation, as they begin—without any apparent necessity—with 342, this would serve the same purpose. And, secondly, admitting that the method is correct as long as there is only *one shashṭyabda* in the date, how are we to reckon if there is a number of *shashṭyabdas?*

The Śakakâla.

The epoch of the era of Śaka or Śakakâla falls 135 years later than that of Vikramâditya. The here-mentioned Śaka tyrannised over their country between the river Sindh and the ocean, after he had made Âryavarta in the midst of this realm his dwelling-place. He interdicted the Hindus from considering and representing themselves as anything but Śakas. Some maintain that he was a Śûdra from the city of Almanṣûra; others maintain that he was not a Hindu at all, and that he had come to India from the west. The Hindus had much to suffer from him, till at last they received help from the east, when Vikramâditya marched against him, put him to flight and killed him in the region of Karûr, between Multân and the castle of Lônî. Now this date became famous, as people rejoiced in the news of the death of the tyrant, and was used as the epoch of an era, especially by the astronomers. They honour the conqueror by adding Śrî to his name, so as to say Śrî Vikramâditya. Since there is a long interval between the era which is called the era of Vikramâditya (v. p. 5) and the killing of Śaka, we think that that Vikramâditya from whom the era has got its name is not identical with that one who killed Śaka, but only a namesake of his.

The era of Valabha is called so from Valabha, the ruler of the town Valabhî, nearly 30 *yojanas* south of Anhilvâra. The epoch of this era falls 241 years later than the epoch of the Śaka era. People use it in this way. They first put down the year of the Śakakâla, and then subtract from it the cube of 6 and the square of 5 (216 + 25 = 241). The remainder is the year of the Valabha era. The history of Valabha is given in its proper place (cf. chap. xvii.) Era of Valabha. Page 206.

As regards the Guptakâla, people say that the Guptas were wicked powerful people, and that when they ceased to exist this date was used as the epoch of an era. It seems that Valabha was the last of them, because the epoch of the era of the Guptas falls, like that of the Valabha era, 241 years later than the Śakakâla. Guptakâla.

The *era of the astronomers* begins 587 years later than the Śakakâla. On this era is based the canon *Khaṇḍakhâdyaka* by Brahmagupta, which among Muhammadans is known as *Al-arkand.* Era of the astronomers.

Now, the year 400 of Yazdajird, which we have chosen as a gauge, corresponds to the following years of the Indian eras:— Comparison of the epochs of the Indian eras with the test-year.

(1) To the year 1488 of the era of Śrî Harsha,
(2) To the year 1088 of the era of Vikramâditya,
(3) To the year 953 of the Śakakâla,
(4) To the year 712 of the Valabha era, which is identical with the Guptakâla,
(5) To the year 366 of the era of the canon *Khaṇḍakhâdyaka,*
(6) To the year 526 of the era of the canon *Pañcasiddhântikâ* by Varâhamihira,
(7) To the year 132 of the era of the canon *Karaṇasâra;* and
(8) To the year 65 of the era of the canon *Karaṇatilaka.*

The eras of the here-mentioned *canones* are such as the authors of them considered the most suitable to be used as cardinal points in astronomical and other calculations, whence calculation may conveniently extend forward or backward. Perhaps the epochs of these eras fall within the time when the authors in question themselves lived, but it is also possible that they fall within a time anterior to their lifetime.

On the popular mode of dating by *centennia* or *samvatsaras*.

Common people in India date by the years of a *centennium*, which they call *samvatsara*. If a *centennium* is finished, they drop it, and simply begin to date by a new one. This era is called *lokakâla*, *i.e.* the era of the nation at large. But of this era people give such totally different accounts, that I have no means of making out the truth. In a similar manner they also differ among themselves regarding the beginning of the year. On the latter subject I shall communicate what I have heard myself, hoping meanwhile that one day we shall be able to discover a rule in this apparent confusion.

Different beginnings of the year.

Those who use the Śaka era, the astronomers, begin the year with the month Caitra, whilst the inhabitants of Kanîr, which is conterminous with Kashmîr, begin it with the month Bhâdrapada. The same people count our gauge-year (400 Yazdajird) as the eighty-fourth year of an era of theirs.

All the people who inhabit the country between Bardarî and Mârîgala begin the year with the month Kârttika, and they count the gauge-year as the 110th year of an era of theirs. The author of the Kashmirian calendar maintains that the latter year corresponds to the sixth year of a new *centennium*, and this, indeed, is the usage of the people of Kashmîr.

The people living in the country Nîrahara, behind Mârîgala, as far as the utmost frontiers of Tâkeshar and Lohâvar, begin the year with the month Mârgaśîrsha, and reckon our gauge-year as the 108th year of their era. The people of *Lanbaga, i.e.* Lamghân, follow their example. I have been told by people of Multân that this system is peculiar to the people of Sindh and Kanoj, and that they used to begin the year with the new moon of Mârgaśîrsha, but that the people of Multân only a few years ago had given up this system, and had adopted the system of the people of Kashmîr, and followed their example in beginning the year with the new moon of Caitra.

Popular mode of dating in use among the Hindus, and criticisms thereon.

I have already before excused myself on account of the imperfection of the information given in this chapter. For we cannot offer a strictly scientific account of the eras to which it is devoted, simply because in them we have to reckon with periods of time far exceeding a *centennium*, (and because all tradition of events farther back than a hundred years is confused (v. p. 8).) So I have myself seen the roundabout way in which they compute the year of the destruction of Somanâth in the year of the Hijra 416, or 947 Śakakâla. First, they write down the number 242, then under it 606, then under this 99. The sum of these numbers is 947, or the year of the Śakakâla.

Now I am inclined to think that the 242 years have elapsed before the beginning of their centennial system, and that they have adopted the latter together with the Guptakâla; further, that the number 606 represents complete *samvatsaras* or centennials, each of which they must reckon as 101 years; lastly, that the 99 years represent that time which has elapsed of the current *centennium*. Page 207.

That this, indeed, is the nature of the calculation is confirmed by a leaf of a canon composed by Durlabha of Multân, which I have found by chance. Here the author says: "First write 848 and add to it the *laukika-kâla, i.e.* the era of the people, and the sum is the Śakakâla."

If we write first the year of the Śakakâla corresponding to our gauge-year, viz. 953, and subtract 848 from it, the remainder, 105, is the year of the *laukika-kâla*, whilst the destruction of Somanâth falls in the ninety-eighth year of the *centennium* or *laukika-kâla*.

Durlabha says, besides, that the year begins with the month Mârgaśîrsha, but that the astronomers of Multân begin it with Caitra.

Origin of the dynasty of the Shâhs of Kâbul.

The Hindus had kings residing in Kâbul, Turks who were said to be of Tibetan origin. The first of them, Barhatakîn, came into the country and entered a cave in Kâbul, which none could enter except by creeping on hands and knees. The cave had water, and besides he deposited there victuals for a certain number of days. It is still known in our time, and is called *Var*. People who consider the name of Barhatakîn as a good omen enter the cave and bring out some of its water with great trouble.

Certain troops of peasants were working before the door of the cave. Tricks of this kind can only be carried out and become notorious, if their author has made a secret arrangement with somebody else — in fact, with confederates. Now these had induced persons to work there continually day and night in turns, so that the place was never empty of people.

Some days after he had entered the cave, he began to creep out of it in the presence of the people, who looked on him as a new-born baby. He wore Turkish dress, a short tunic open in front, a high hat, boots and arms. Now people honoured him as a being of miraculous origin, who had been destined to be king, and in fact he brought those countries under his sway and ruled them under the title of a *shâhiya of Kâbul*. The rule remained among his descendants for generations, the number of which is said to be about sixty.

Unfortunately the Hindus do not pay much attention to the historical order of things, they are very careless in relating the chronological succession of their kings, and when they are pressed for information and are at a loss, not knowing what to say, they invariably take to tale-telling. But for this, we should communicate to the reader the traditions which we have received from some people among them. I have been told that the pedigree of this royal family, written on silk, exists in the fortress *Nagarkot*, and I much desired to make myself acquainted with it, but the thing was impossible for various reasons.

One of this series of kings was Kanik, the same who is said to have built the *vihâra* (Buddhistic monastery) of Purushâvar. It is called, after him, *Kanik-caitya*. People relate that the king of Kanoj had presented to him, among other gifts, a gorgeous and most singular piece of cloth. Now Kanik wanted to have dresses made out of it for himself, but his tailor had not the courage to make them, for he said, "There is (in the embroidery) the figure of a human foot, and whatever trouble I may take, the foot will always lie between the shoulders." And that means the same as we have already mentioned in the story of Bali, the son of Virocana (*i.e.* a sign of subjugation, cf. i. p. 397). Now Kanik felt convinced that the ruler of Kanoj had thereby intended to vilify and disgrace him, and in hot haste he set out with his troops marching against him.

The story of Kanik.

When the *râî* heard this, he was greatly perplexed, for he had no power to resist Kanik. Therefore he consulted his Vazîr, and the latter said, "You have roused a man who was quiet before, and have done unbecoming things. Now cut off my nose and lips, let me be mutilated, that I may find a cunning device; for there is no possibility of an open resistance." The *râî* did with him as he had proposed, and then he went off to the frontiers of the realm.

There he was found by the hostile army, was recognised and brought before Kanik, who asked what was the matter with him. The Vazîr said, "I tried to dissuade *him* from opposing you, and sincerely advised him to be obedient to you. He, however, conceived a suspicion against me and ordered me to be mutilated. Since then he has gone, of his own accord, to a place which a man can only reach by a very long journey when he marches on the highroad, but which he may easily reach by undergoing the trouble of crossing an intervening desert, supposing that he can carry with himself water for so and so many days." Thereupon Kanik answered: "The latter is easily done." He ordered water to be carried along, and engaged the Vazîr to show him the road. The Vazîr marched before the king and led him into a boundless desert. After the number of days had elapsed and the road did not come to an end, the king asked the Vazîr what was now to be done. Then the Vazîr said, "No blame attaches to me that I tried to save my master and to destroy his enemy. The nearest road leading out of this desert is that on which you have come. Now do with me as you like, for none will leave this desert alive."

Then Kanik got on his horse and rode round a depression in the soil. In the centre of it he thrust his spear into the earth, and lo! water poured from it in sufficient quantity for the army to drink from and to draw from for the march back. Upon this the Vazîr said, "I had not directed my cunning scheme against powerful angels, but against feeble men. As things stand thus, accept my intercession for the prince, my benefactor, and pardon him." Kanik answered, "I
Page 208. march back from this place. Thy wish is granted to thee. Thy master has already received what is due to him." Kanik returned out of the desert, and the Vazîr went back to his master, the *râî* of Kanoj. There he

found that on the same day when Kanik had thrust his spear into the earth, both the hands and feet had fallen off the body of the *râî*.

End of the Tibetan dynasty, and origin of the Brahman dynasty.

The last king of this race was *Lagatûrmân*, and his Vazír was Kallar, a Brahman. The latter had been fortunate, in so far as he had found by accident hidden treasures, which gave him much influence and power. In consequence, the last king of this Tibetan house, after it had held the royal power for so long a period, let it by degrees slip from his hands. Besides, Lagatûrmân had bad manners and a worse behaviour, on account of which people complained of him greatly to the Vazîr. Now the Vazîr put him in chains and imprisoned him for correction, but then he himself found ruling sweet, his riches enabled him to carry out his plans, and so he occupied the royal throne. After him ruled the Brahman kings Sâmand (Sâmanta), Kamalû, Bhîm (Bhîma), Jaipâl (Jayapâla), Ânandapâla, Tarojanapâla (Trilocanapâla). The latter was killed A.H. 412 (A.D. 1021), and his son Bhîmapâla five years later (A.D. 1026).

This Hindu Shâhiya dynasty is now extinct, and of the whole house there is no longer the slightest remnant in existence. We must say that, in all their grandeur, they never slackened in the ardent desire of doing that which is good and right, that they were men of noble sentiment and noble bearing. I admire the following passage in a letter of Ânandapâla, which he wrote to the prince Maḥmûd, when the relations between them were already strained to the utmost: "I have learned that the Turks have rebelled against you and are spreading in Khurâsân. If you wish, I shall come to you with 5000 horsemen, 10,000 foot-soldiers, and 100 elephants, or, if you wish, I shall send you my son with double the number. In acting thus, I do not speculate on the impression which this will make on you. I have been conquered by *you*, and therefore I do not wish that another man should conquer you."

The same prince cherished the bitterest hatred against the Muhammadans from the time when his son was made a prisoner, whilst his son Tarojanapâla (Trilocanapâla) was the very opposite of his father.

(Chapters L–LIV, pages 15–61, are concerned with the revolutions of the planets and the meaning of Hindu technical terms.)

CHAPTER LV.

ON THE ORDER OF THE PLANETS, THEIR DISTANCES AND SIZES.

Traditional view on the sun being below the moon.

WHEN speaking of the *lokas*, we have already given a quotation from the *Vishṇu-Purâṇa* and from the commentary of Patañjali, according to which the place of the sun is in the order of the planets below that of the moon. This is the traditional view of the Hindus. Compare in particular the following passage of the *Matsya-Purâṇa*:—

"The distance of heaven from the earth is equal to the radius of the earth. The sun is the lowest of all planets. Above him there is the moon, and above the moon are the lunar stations and their stars. Above them is Mercury, then follow Venus, Mars, Jupiter, Saturn, the Great Bear, and above it the pole. The pole is connected with the heaven. The stars cannot be counted by man. Those who impugn this view maintain that the moon at conjunction becomes hidden by the sun, as the light of the lamp becomes invisible in the light of the sun, and she becomes more visible the more she moves away from the sun."

We shall now give some quotations from the books of this school relating to the sun, the moon, and the stars, and we shall combine herewith the views of the astronomers, although of the latter we have only a very slender knowledge.

Popular notions of astronomy.

Page 232.

The *Vâyu-Purâṇa* says: "The sun has globular shape, fiery nature, and 1000 rays, by which he attracts the water; 400 of these are for the rain, 300 for the snow, and 300 for the air." Quotations from *Vâyu-Purâṇa.*

In another passage it says: "Some of them (*i.e.* the rays) are for this purpose, that the *devas* should live in bliss; others for the purpose that men should live in comfort, whilst others are destined for the fathers."

In another passage the author of the *Vâyu-Purâṇa* divides the rays of the sun over the six seasons of the year, saying: "The sun illuminates the earth in that third of the year which commences with 0° of Pisces by 300 rays; he causes rain in the following third by 400 rays, and he causes cold and snow in the remaining third by 300 rays."

Another passage of the same book runs as follows: "The rays of the sun and the wind raise the water from the sea to the sun. Now, if the water dropped down from the sun, it would be hot. Therefore the sun hands the water over to the moon, that it should drop down from the moon cold, and thus refresh the world."

Another passage: "The heat of the sun and his light are one-fourth of the heat and the light of the fire. In the north, the sun falls into the water during the night; therefore he becomes red."

Another passage: "In the beginning there were the earth, water, wind, and heaven. Then Brahman perceived sparks under the earth. He brought them forth and divided them into three parts. One third of them is the common fire, which requires wood and is extinguished by water. Another third is the sun, and the last third is the lightning. In the animals, too, there is fire, which cannot be extinguished by water. The sun attracts the water, the lightning shines through the rain, but the fire in the animals is distributed over the moist substances by which they nourish themselves."

The Hindus seem to believe that the heavenly bodies nourish themselves by the vapours, which also Aristotle mentions as the theory of certain people. Thus the author of the *Vishṇu-Dharma* explains that "the sun nourishes the moon and the stars. If the sun did not exist, there would not be a star, nor angel, nor man."

On the nature of the stars.

The Hindus believe regarding the bodies of all the stars that they have a globular shape, a watery essence, and that they do not shine, whilst the sun alone is of fiery essence, self-shining, and *per accidens* illuminates other stars when they stand opposite to him. They reckon, according to eyesight, among the stars also such luminous bodies as in reality are not stars, but the lights into which those men have been metamorphosed who have received eternal reward from God, and reside in the height of heaven on thrones of crystal. The *Vishṇu-Dharma* says: "The stars are watery, and the rays of the sun illuminate them in the night. Those who by their pious deeds have obtained a place in the height sit there on their thrones, and, when shining, they are reckoned among the stars."

Quotation from the *Vishṇu-Dharma.*

All the stars are called *târa*, which word is derived from *taraṇa, i.e.* the passage. The idea is that those saints have *passed* through the wicked world and have reached bliss, and that the stars *pass* through heaven in a circular motion. The word *nakshatra* is limited to the stars of the lunar stations. As, however, all of these are called *fixed stars*, the word *nakshatra* also applies to all the fixed stars; for it means *not increasing and not decreasing.* I for my part am inclined to think that this increasing and decreasing refers to their number and to the distances of the one from the other, but the author of the last-mentioned book (*Vishṇu-Dharma*) combines it with their light. For he adds, "as the moon increases and decreases."

Further, there is a passage in the same book where Mârkaṇḍeya says: "The stars which do not perish before the end of the *kalpa* are equal to a *nikharva, i.e.* 100,000,000,000. The number of those which fall down before the end of a *kalpa* is unknown. Only he can know it who dwells in the height during a *kalpa.*"

Vajra spoke: "O Mârkaṇḍeya, thou hast lived during six *kalpas*. This is thy seventh *kalpa*. Therefore why dost thou not know them?"

He answered: "If they always remained in the same condition, not changing as long as they exist, I should not be ignorant of them. However, they perpetually raise some pious man and bring another down to the earth. Therefore I do not keep them in my memory."

On the diameters of the planets.

Regarding the diameters of sun and moon and their shadows the *Matsya-Purâṇa* says: "The diameter of the body of the sun is 9000 *yojanas*; the diameter of the moon is the double of it, and the apsis is as much as the two together."

The same occurs in the *Vâyu-Purâṇa*, except that it says with regard to the apsis that it is equal to the sun when it is with the sun, and that it is equal to the moon when it is with the moon.

Another author says: "The apsis is 50,000 *yojanas*."

Regarding the diameters of the planets the *Matsya-Purâṇa* says: "The circumference of Venus is one-sixteenth of the circumference of the moon, that of Page 233 Jupiter three-fourths of the circumference of Venus, that of Saturn or Mars three-fourths of that of Jupiter, that of Mercury three-fourths of that of Mars."

The same statement is also found in the *Vâyu-Purâṇa*.

On the circumference of the fixed stars.

The same two books fix the circumference of the great fixed stars as equal to that of Mercury. The next smaller class have a circumference of 500 *yojanas*, the following classes 400, 300, and 200. But there are no fixed stars with a smaller circumference than 150 *yojanas*.

Thus the *Vâyu-Purâṇa*. But the *Matsya-Purâṇa* says: "The next following classes have a circumference of 400, 300, 200, and 100 *yojanas*. But there is no fixed star with less circumference than a half *yojana*."

The latter statement, however, looks suspicious to me, and is perhaps a fault in the manuscript.

The author of *Vishṇu-Dharma* says, relating the

words of Mârkaṇḍeya: "*Abhijit*, the Falling Eagle; *Ârdrâ*, the Sirius Yemenicus; *Rohiṇî*, or Aldabarân; *Punarvasu*, *i.e.* the Two Heads of the Twins; *Pushya*, *Revatî*, *Agastya* or Canopus, the Great Bear, the master of *Vâyu*, the master of *Ahirbudhnya*, and the master of *Vasishṭha*, each of these stars has a circumference of five *yojanas*. All the other stars have each only a circumference of four *yojanas*. I do not know those stars, the distance of which is not measurable. They have a circumference between four *yojanas* and two *kuroh*, *i.e.* two miles. Those which have less circumference than two *kuroh* are not seen by men, but only by the *devas*."

The Hindus have the following theory regarding the magnitude of the stars, which is not traced back to any known authority: "The diameters of the sun and moon are each 67 *yojanas*; that of the apsis is 100; that of Venus 10, of Jupiter 9, of Saturn 8, of Mars 7, of Mercury 7."

Views of the Hindu astronomers on the same subjects.

This is all we have been able to learn of the confused notions of the Hindus regarding these subjects. We shall now pass on to the views of the Hindu astronomers with whom we agree regarding the order of the planets and other topics, viz. that the sun is the middle of the planets, Saturn and the moon their two ends, and that the fixed stars are above the planets. Some of these things have already been mentioned in the preceding chapters.

Quotation from the *Saṁhitâ* of Varâhamihira, chap. iv. 1–3.

Varâhamihira says in the book *Saṁhitâ*: "The moon is always below the sun, who throws his rays upon her, and lits up the one half of her body, whilst the other half remains dark and shadowy like a pot which you place in the sunshine. The one half which faces the sun is lit up, whilst the other half which does not face it remains dark. The moon is watery in her essence, therefore the rays which fall on her are reflected, as they are reflected from the water and the mirror towards the wall. If the moon is in conjunction with the sun, the white part of her turns towards the sun, the black part towards us. Then the white part sinks downward towards us slowly, as the sun marches away from the moon."

Every educated man among the Hindu theologians, and much more so among their astronomers, believes indeed that the moon is below the sun, and even below all the planets.

Ya'kub Ibn Târiķ on the distances of the stars.

The only Hindu traditions we have regarding the distances of the stars are those mentioned by Ya'ķub Ibn Ţâriķ in his book, *The Composition of the Spheres*, and he had drawn his information from the well-known Hindu scholar who, A.H. 161, accompanied an embassy to Bagdâd. First, he gives a metrological statement: "A finger is equal to six barleycorns which are put one by the side of the other. An arm (yard) is equal to twenty-four fingers. A *farsakh* is equal to 16,000 yards."

Here, however, we must observe that the Hindus do not know the *farsakh*, that it is, as we have already explained, equal to one half a *yojana*.

Further, Ya'ķûb says: "The diameter of the earth is 2100 *farsakh*, its circumference $6596\frac{9}{25}$ *farsakh*."

On this basis he has computed the distances of the planets as we exhibit them in the following table.

Pulisa and Brahmagupta on the same subject.

However, this statement regarding the size of the earth is by no means generally agreed to by all the Hindus. So, *e.g.* Pulisa reckons its diameter as 1600 *yojanas*, and its circumference as $5026\frac{14}{15}$ *yojanas*, whilst Brahmagupta reckons the former as 1581 *yojanas*, and the latter as 5000 *yojanas*.

If we double thesenumbers, they ought to be equal to the numbers of Ya'ķûb; but this is not the case. Now the yard and the mile are respectively identical according to the measurement both of us and of the Hindus. According to our computation the radius of the earth is 3184 miles. Reckoning, according to the custom of our country, 1 *farsakh* = 3 miles, we get 6728 *farsakh;* and reckoning 1 *farsakh* = 16,000 yards, as is mentioned by Ya'ḳûb, we get 5046 *farsakh.* Reckoning 1 *yojana* = 32,000 yards, we get 2523 *yojanas.*

Page 234.

Distances of the planets from the centre of the earth, and their diameters, according to Ya'ḳûb Ibn Ṭâriḳ.

The following table is borrowed from the book of Ya'ḳûb Ibn Ṭâriḳ:—

The planets.	Their distances from the centre of the earth, and their diameters.	The conventional measures of the distances, differing according to time and place, reckoned in *fársakh*, 1 *farsakh* = 16,000 yards.	Their constant measures, based on the radius of the earth = 1.
	Radius of the earth .	1,050	1
Moon.	The smallest distance .	37,500	$35\frac{5}{7}$
	The middle distance .	48,500	$46\frac{4}{21}$
	The greatest distance .	59,000	$56\frac{4}{21}$
	Diameter of the moon	5,000	$4\frac{16}{21}$
Mercury.	The smallest distance .	64,000	$60\frac{20}{21}$
	The middle distance .	164,000	$156\frac{4}{21}$
	The greatest distance .	264,000	$251\frac{3}{7}$
	Diameter of Mercury	5,000	$4\frac{16}{21}$
Venus.	The smallest distance .	269,000	$256\frac{4}{21}$
	The middle distance .	709,500	$675\frac{5}{7}$
	The greatest distance .	1,150,000	$1,095\frac{5}{21}$
	Diameter of Venus .	20,000	$19\frac{1}{21}$
Sun.	The smallest distance .	1,170,000	$1,114\frac{2}{7}$
	The middle distance .	1,690,000	$1,609\frac{11}{21}$
	The greatest distance .	2,210,000	$2,104\frac{16}{21}$
	Diameter of the Sun .	20,000	$19\frac{1}{21}$
Mars.	The smallest distance .	2,230,000	$2,123\frac{17}{21}$
	The middle distance .	5,315,000	$5,061\frac{19}{21}$
	The greatest distance .	8,400,000	8,000
	Diameter of Mars .	20,000	$19\frac{1}{21}$
Jupiter.	The smallest distance .	8,420,000	$8,019\frac{1}{21}$
	The middle distance .	11,410,000	$10,866\frac{2}{3}$
	The greatest distance .	14,400,000	$13,714\frac{2}{7}$
	Diameter of Jupiter .	20,000	$19\frac{1}{21}$
Saturn.	The smallest distance .	14,420,000	$13,733\frac{1}{3}$
	The middle distance .	16,220,000	$15,447\frac{13}{21}$
	The greatest distance .	18,020,000	$17,161\frac{19}{21}$
	Diameter of Saturn .	20,000	$19\frac{1}{21}$
Zodiacus.	The radius of the outside	20,000,000	$19,047\frac{13}{21}$
	The radius of the inside	19,962,000	$1,866\frac{2}{3}$ (*sic*)
	Its circumference from the outside . .	125,664,000	

Page 235.

Ptolemy on the distances of the planets. Page 236.

This theory differs from that on which Ptolemy has based his computation of the distances of the planets in the *Kitâb-almanshûrât*, and in which he has been followed both by the ancient and the modern astronomers. It is their principle that the greatest distance of a planet is equal to its smallest distance from the next higher planet, and that between the two globes there is not a space void of action.

According to this theory, there is between the two globes a space not occupied by either of them, in which there is something like an axis around which the rotation takes place. It seems that they attributed to the æther a certain gravity, in consequence of which they felt the necessity of adopting something which *keeps* or *holds* the inner globe (the planet) in the midst of the outer globe (the æther).

On occultation and the parallax.

It is well known among all astronomers that there is no possibility of distinguishing between the higher and the lower one of two planets except by means of the *occultation* or the increase of the *parallax*. However, the occultation occurs only very seldom, and only the parallax of a single planet, viz. the moon, can be observed. Now the Hindus believe that the motions are equal, but the distances different. The reason why the higher planet moves more slowly than the lower is the greater extension of its sphere (or orbit); and the reason why the lower planet moves more rapidly is that its sphere or orbit is less extended. Thus, *e.g.* one minute in the sphere of Saturn is equal to 262 minutes in the sphere of the moon. Therefore the times in which Saturn and the moon traverse the same space are different, whilst their motions are equal.

I have never found a Hindu treatise on this subject, but only numbers relating thereto scattered in various books—numbers which are corrupt. Somebody objected to Pulisa that he reckoned the circumference of the sphere of each planet as 21,600, and its radius as 3438, whilst Varâhamihira reckoned the sun's distance from the earth as 2,598,900, and the distance of the fixed stars as 321,362,683. Thereupon Pulisa replied that the former numbers were minutes, the latter *yojanas;* whilst in another passage he says that the distance of the fixed stars from the earth is sixty times larger than the distance of the sun. Accordingly he ought to have reckoned the distance of the fixed stars as 155,934,000.

Hindu method for the computation of the distances of the planets.

The Hindu method of the computation of the distances of the planets which we have above mentioned is based on a principle which is unknown to me in the present stage of my knowledge, and as long as I have no facility in translating the books of the Hindus. The principle is this, that the extension of a minute in the orbit of the moon is equal to fifteen *yojanas.* The nature of this principle is not cleared up by the commentaries of Balabhadra, whatsoever trouble he takes. For he says: "People have tried to fix by observation the time of the moon's passing through the horizon, *i.e.* the time between the shining of the first part of her body and the rising of the whole, or the time between the beginning of her setting and the completion of the act of setting. People have found this process to last thirty-two minutes of the circumference of the sphere." However, if it is difficult to fix by observation the degrees, it is much more so to fix the minutes.

Quotations from Balabhadra.

Further, the Hindus have tried to determine by observation the *yojanas* of the diameter of the moon, and have found them to be 480. If you divide them by the minutes of her body, the quotient is 15 *yojanas,* as corresponding to one minute. If you multiply it by the minutes of the circumference, you get the product 324,000. This is the measure of the sphere of the moon which she traverses in each rotation. If you multiply this number by the cycles of the moon in a *kalpa* or *caturyuga,* the product is the distance which the moon traverses in either of them. According to Brahmagupta, this is in a *kalpa* 18,712,069,200,000,000 *yojanas*. Brahmagupta calls this number *the yojanas of the ecliptic*.

Evidently if you divide this number by the cycles of each planet in a *kalpa*, the quotient represents the *yojanas* of one rotation. However, the motion of the planets is, according to the Hindus, as we have already mentioned, in every distance one and the same. Therefore the quotient represents the measure of the path of the sphere of the planet in question.

As further, according to Brahmagupta, the relation of the diameter to the circumference is nearly equal to that of 12,959 : 40,980, you multiply the measure of the path of the sphere of the planet by 12,959, and divide the product by 81,960. The quotient is the radius, or the distance of the planet from the centre of the earth.

The radii of the planets, or their distances from the centre of the earth, computed according to Brahmagupta.

We have made this computation for all the planets according to the theory of Brahmagupta, and present the results to the reader in the following table :—

Page 237.

The planets.	The circumference of the sphere of each planet, reckoned in *yojanas*.	Their radii, which are identical with their distances from the earth's centre, reckoned in *yojanas*.
Moon	324,000	51,229
Mercury	$1,043,210\frac{1561237670}{2242124873}$	164,947
Venus	$2,664,629\frac{1627580383}{1755597373}$	421,315
Sun	$4,331,497\frac{1}{2}$	684,869
Mars	$8,146,916\frac{82430924}{1148414261}$	1,288,139
Jupiter	$51,374,821\frac{54182089}{72845291}$	8,123,064
Saturn	$127,668,787\frac{25236637}{73283649}$	20,186,186
The Fixed Stars, their distance from the earth's centre being sixty times the distance of the sun from the same	259,889,850	41,092,140

The same computation according to the theory of Pulisa.

As Pulisa reckons by *caturyugas*, not by *kalpas*, he multiplies the distance of the path of the sphere of the moon by the lunar cycles of a *caturyuga*, and gets the product 18,712,080,864,000 *yojanas*, which he calls *the yojanas of heaven.* It is the distance which the moon traverses in each *caturyuga.*

Pulisa reckons the relation of the diameter to the circumference as 1250 : 3927. Now, if you multiply the circumference of each planetary sphere by 625 and divide the product by 3927, the quotient is the distance of the planet from the earth's centre. We have made the same computation as the last one according to the view of Pulisa, and present the results in the following table. In computing the radii we have disregarded the fractions smaller than $\frac{1}{2}$, and have reduced larger fractions to wholes. We have, however, not taken the same liberty in the calculation of the circumferences, but have calculated with the utmost accuracy, because they are required in the computations of the revolutions. For if you divide the *yojanas of heaven* in Page 238. a *kalpa* or *caturyuga* by the civil days of the one or the other, you get the quotient 11,858 *plus* a remainder, which is $\frac{25,498}{35,419}$ according to Brahmagupta, and $\frac{209,554}{292,207}$ according to Pulisa. This is the distance which the moon every day traverses, and as the motion of all planets is the same, it is the distance which every planet in a day traverses. It stands in the same relation to the *yojanas* of the circumference of its sphere as its motion, which we want to find, to the circumference, the latter being divided into 360 equal parts. If you therefore multiply the path common to all the planets by 360 and divide the product by the *yojanas* of the circumference of the planet in question, the quotient represents its mean daily motion.

The planets.	The circumferences of the spheres of the planets, reckoned in *yojanas*.	The distances of the planets from the earth's centre, reckoned in *yojanas*.
Moon	324,000	51,566
Mercury	1,043,211$\frac{573}{1993}$	166,033
Venus	2,664,632$\frac{90232}{585199}$	424,089
Sun	4,331,500$\frac{1}{5}$	690,295 (*sic*)
Mars	8,146,937$\frac{18163}{95701}$	1,296,624 (!)
Jupiter	51,375,764$\frac{4996}{18211}$	8,176,689 (!)
Saturn . . .	127,671,739$\frac{27301}{36641}$	20,319,542 (!)
The Fixed Stars, the sun's distance from the earth's centre being $\frac{1}{60}$th of theirs	259,890,012	41,417,700 (*sic*)

As, now, the minutes of the diameter of the moon stand in the same relation to the minutes of her circumference, *i.e.* 21,600, as the number of *yojanas* of the diameter, *i.e.* 480, to the *yojanas* of the circumference of the whole sphere, exactly the same method of calculation has been applied to the minutes of the diameter of the sun, which we have found to be equal to 6522 *yojanas* according to Brahmagupta, and equal to 6480 according to Pulisa. Since Pulisa reckons the minutes of the body of the moon as 32, *i.e.* a power of 2, he divides this number in order to get the minutes of the bodies of the planets by 2, till he at last gets 1. Thus he attributes to the body of Venus $\frac{1}{2}$ of 32 minutes, *i.e.* 16; to that of Jupiter $\frac{1}{4}$ of 32 minutes, *i.e.* 8; to that of Mercury $\frac{1}{8}$ of 32 minutes, *i.e.* 4; to that of Saturn $\frac{1}{16}$ of 32 minutes, *i.e.* 2; to that of Mars $\frac{1}{32}$ of of 32 minutes, *i.e.* 1.

The diameters of the planets. Page 239.

This precise order seems to have taken his fancy, or he would not have overlooked the fact that the diameter of Venus is, according to observation, not equal to the radius of the moon, nor Mars equal to $\frac{1}{16}$th of Venus.

Method for the computation of the bodies of sun and moon at any given time.

The following is the method of the computation of the bodies of sun and moon at every time, based on their distances from the earth, *i.e.* the true diameter of its orbit, which is found in the computations of the corrections of sun and moon. AB is the diameter of the body of the sun, CD is the diameter of the earth, CDH is the cone of the shadow, HL is its elevation. Further, draw CR parallel to DB. Then is AR the difference between AB and CD, and the normal line CT is the middle distance of the sun, *i.e.* the radius of its orbit derived from *the yojanas of heaven* (v. p. 72). From this the true distance of the sun always differs, sometimes being larger, sometimes smaller. We draw CK, which is of course determined by the parts of the *sine.* It stands in the same relation to CT, this being the *sinus totus* (=radius), as the *yojanas* of CK to the *yojanas* of CT. Hereby the measure of the diameter is reduced to *yojanas.*

The *yojanas* of AB stand in the same relation to the *yojanas* of TC as the minutes of AB to the minutes of TC, the latter being the *sinus totus.* Thereby AB becomes known and determined by the minutes of the sphere, because the *sinus totus* is determined by the measure of the circumference. For this reason Pulisa says: "Multiply the *yojanas* of the radius of the sphere of the sun or the moon by the true distance, and divide the product by the *sinus totus.* By the quotient you get for the sun, divide 22,278,240, and by the quotient you get for the moon, divide 1,650,240. The quotient then represents the minutes of the diameter of the body of either sun or moon."

Quotations from Pulisa, Brahmagupta, and Balabhadra.

The last-mentioned two numbers are products of the multiplication of the *yojanas* of the diameters of sun and moon by 3438, which is the number of the minutes of the *sinus totus.*

Likewise Brahmagupta says: "Multiply the *yojanas* of sun or moon by 3416, *i.e.* the minutes of the *sinus totus,* and divide the product by the *yojanas* of the radius of the sphere of sun or moon." But the latter rule of division is not correct, because, according to it, the measure of the body would not vary (v. p. 74). Therefore the commentator Balabhadra holds the same opinion as Pulisa, viz. that the divisor in this division should be the true distance reduced (to the measure of *yojanas*).

Brahmagupta gives the following rule for the computation of the diameter of the shadow, which in our *canones* is called *the measure of the sphere of the dragon's head and tail*: "Subtract the *yojanas* of the diameter of the earth, *i.e.* 1581, from the *yojanas* of the diameter of the sun, *i.e.* 6522. There remains 4941, which is kept in memory to be used as divisor. It is represented in the figure by AR. Further multiply the diameter of the earth, which is the double *sinus totus*, by the *yojanas* of the true distance of the sun, which is found by the correction of the sun. Divide the product by the divisor kept in memory. The quotient is the true distance of the shadow's end. **Brahmagupta's method for the computation of the diameter of the shadow.**

"Evidently the two triangles ARC and CDH are similar to each other. However, the normal line CT does not vary in size, whilst in consequence of the true distance the *appearance* of AB varies, though its size is constantly the same. Now let *this* distance be CK. Draw the lines AJ and RV parallel to each other, and JKV parallel to AB. Then the latter is equal to the divisor kept in memory.

"Draw the line JCM. Then M is the head of the cone of the shadow for that time. The relation of JV, the divisor kept in memory, to KC, the true distance, is the same as that of CD, the diameter of the earth, to ML, which he (Brahmagupta) calls a true distance (of the shadow's end), and it is determined by the minutes of the *sine* (the earth's radius being the *sinus totus*). For KC——" **Page 240.**

Now, however, I suspect that in the following something has fallen out in the manuscript, for the author continues: "Then multiply it (*i.e.* the quotient of CK, **Lacuna in the manuscript copy of Brahmagupta.**

by the divisor kept in memory) by the diameter of the earth. The product is the distance between the earth's centre and the end of the shadow. Subtract therefrom the true distance of the moon and multiply the remainder by the diameter of the earth. Divide the product by the true distance of the shadow's end. The quotient is the diameter of the shadow in the sphere of the moon. Further, we suppose the true distance of the moon to be LS, and FN is a part of the lunar sphere, the radius of which is LS. Since we have found LM as determined by the minutes of the *sine*, it stands in the same relation to CD, this being the double *sinus totus*, as MS, measured in minutes of the *sine*, to XZ, measured in minutes of the sine."

Here I suppose Brahmagupta wished to reduce LM, the true distance of the shadow's end, to *yojanas*, which is done by multiplying it by the *yojanas* of the diameter of the earth, and by dividing the product by the double *sinus totus*. The mentioning of this division has fallen out in the manuscript; for without it the multiplication of the corrected distance of the shadow's end by the diameter of the earth is perfectly superfluous, and in no way required by the computation.

Further: "If the number of *yojanas* of LM is known, LS, which is the true distance, must also be reduced to *yojanas*, for the purpose that MS should be determined by the same measure. The measure of the diameter of the shadow which is thus found represents *yojanas*.

Further, Brahmagupta says: "Then multiply the shadow which has been found by the *sinus totus*, and divide the product by the true distance of the moon. The quotient represents the minutes of the shadow which we wanted to find."

Criticisms on Brahmagupta's method.

However, if the shadow which he has found were determined by *yojanas*, he ought to have multiplied it by the double *sinus totus*, and to have divided the product by the *yojanas* of the diameter of the earth, in order to find the minutes of the shadow. But as he has not done so, this shows that, in his computation, he limited himself to determining the true diameter in minutes, without reducing it to *yojanas*.

The author uses the true (*sphuṭa*) diameter without its having been reduced to *yojanas*. Thus he finds that the shadow in the circle, the radius of which is LS, is the true diameter, and this is required for the computation of the circle, the radius of which is the *sinus totus*. The relation of ZX, which he has already found, to SL, the true distance, is the same as the relation of ZX in the measure which is sought to SL, this being the *sinus totus*. On the basis of this equation the reduction (to *yojanas*) must be made.

Another method of Brahmagupta's for computing the shadow.

In another passage Brahmagupta says: "The diameter of the earth is 1581, the diameter of the moon 480, the diameter of the sun 6522, the diameter of the shadow 1581. Subtract the *yojanas* of the earth from the *yojanas* of the sun, there remains 4941. Multiply this remainder by the *yojanas* of the true distance of the moon, and divide the product by the *yojanas* of the true distance of the sun. Subtract the quotient you get from 1581, and the remainder is the measure of the shadow in the sphere of the moon. Multiply it by 3416, and divide the product by the *yojanas* of *the middle radius of the sphere of the moon*. The quotient represents the minutes of the diameter of the shadow.

"Evidently if the *yojanas* of the diameter of the earth are subtracted from the *yojanas* of the diameter of the sun, the remainder is AR, *i.e.* JV. Draw the line VCF and let fall the normal line KC on O. Then the relation of the surplus JV to KC, the true distance of the sun, is the same as the relation of ZF to OC, the true distance of the moon. It is indifferent whether these two *mean* diameters are reduced (to *yojanas*) or not, for ZF is, in this case, found as determined by the measure of *yojana*.

"Draw XN as equal to OF. Then ON is necessarily

equal to the diameter of CD, and its sought-for part is ZX. The number which is thus found must be subtracted from the diameter of the earth, and the remainder will be ZX."

The author criticises the corrupt state of his manuscript of Brahmagupta. Page 241.

For such mistakes as occur in this computation, the author, Brahmagupta, is not to be held responsible, but we rather suspect that the fault lies with the manuscript. We, however, cannot go beyond the text we have at our disposal, as we do not know how it may be in a correct copy.

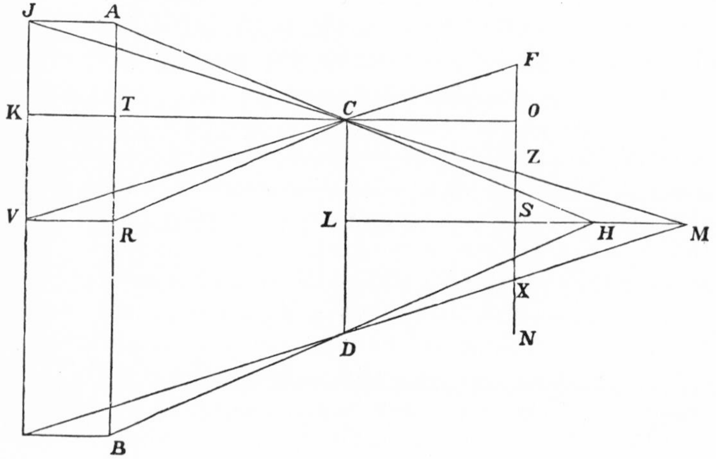

The measure of the shadow adopted by Brahmagupta, from which he orders the reader to subtract, cannot be a *mean* one, for a *mean* measure stands in the midst, between too little and too much. Further, we cannot imagine that this measure should be the greatest of the measures of the shadow, including the *plus* (?); for ZF, which is the *minus*, is the base of a triangle, of which the one side, FC, cuts SL in the direction of the sun, not in the direction of the end of the shadow. Therefore ZF has nothing whatsoever to do with the shadow (conjectural rendering.)

Lastly, there is the possibility that the *minus* belongs to the diameter of the moon. In that case the relation of ZX, which has been determined in *yojanas*, to SL, the *yojanas* of the true distance of the moon, is the same as the relation of ZX reckoned in minutes to SL, this being the *sinus totus* (conjectural rendering.)

By this method is found what Brahmagupta wants to find, quite correctly, without the division by the mean radius of the sphere of the moon, which is derived from the *yojanas of the sphere of heaven* (v. p. 72). (For the last three passages *vide* Notes.)

The computation of the diameters of sun and moon according to other sources.

The methods of the computation of the diameters of sun and moon, as given by the Hindu *canones*, such as the *Khaṇḍakhâdyaka* and *Karaṇasâra*, are the same as are found in the canon of Alkhwârizmî. Also the computation of the diameter of the shadow in the *Khaṇḍakhâdyaka* is similar to that one given by Alkhwârizmî, whilst the *Karaṇasara* has the following method:—"Multiply the *bhukti* of the moon by 4 and the *bhukti* of the sun by 13. Divide the difference between the two products by 30, and the quotient is the diameter of the shadow."

Diameter of the sun and of the shadow according to the *Karaṇatilaka*.

The *Karaṇatilaka* gives the following method for the computation of the diameter of the sun:—"Divide the *bhukti* of the sun by 2, and write down the half in two different places. In the one place divide it by 10, and add the quotient to the number in the second place. The sum is the number of minutes of the diameter of the sun."

In the computation of the diameter of the moon, he first takes the *bhukti* of the moon, adds thereto $\frac{1}{80}$th of it, and divides the number by 25. The quotient is the number of the minutes of the moon's diameter.

In the computation of the diameter of the shadow, he multiplies the *bhukti* of the sun by 3, and from the product he subtracts $\frac{1}{24}$th of it. The remainder he subtracts from the *bhukti* of the moon, and the double of the remainder he divides by 15. The quotient is the number of the minutes of the dragon's head and tail.

If we would indulge in further quotations from the *canones* of the Hindus, we should entirely get away from Page 242. the subject of the present book. Therefore we restrict ourselves to quote from them only subjects more or less connected with the special subject of this book, which either are noteworthy for their strangeness, or which are unknown among our people (the Muslims) and in our (the Muslim) countries.

(Chapters LVI and LVII, pages 81–100, deal with the stations of the moon and the risings of the stars.)

CHAPTER LVIII.

HOW EBB AND FLOW FOLLOW EACH OTHER IN THE OCEAN.

Quotation from the *Matsya-Purâṇa.*

WITH regard to the cause why the water of the ocean always remains as it is, we quote the following passage from the *Matsya-Purâṇa:*—"At the beginning there were sixteen mountains, which had wings and could fly and rise up into the air. However, the rays of Indra, the ruler, burned their wings, so that they fell down, deprived of them, somewhere about the ocean, four of them in each point of the compass—in the east, Ṛishabha, Balâhaka, Cakra, Mainâka; in the north, Candra, Kaṅka, Droṇa, Suhma; in the west, Vakra, Vadhra, Nârada, Parvata; in the south, Jîmûta, Draviṇa, Mainâka, Mahâśaila (?). Between the third and the fourth of the eastern mountains there is the fire *Saṁvartaka,* which drinks the water of the ocean. But for this the ocean would fill up, since the rivers perpetually flow to it.

Story of King Aurva.

"This fire was the fire of one of their kings, called *Aurva.* He had inherited the realm from his father, who was killed while he was still an embryo. When he was born and grew up, and heard the history of his father, he became angry against the angels, and drew his sword to kill them, since they had neglected the guardianship of the world, notwithstanding mankind's worshipping them and notwithstanding their being in close contact with the world. Thereupon the angels humiliated themselves before him and tried to conciliate him, so that he ceased from his wrath. Then he spoke to them: 'But what am I to do with the fire of my wrath?' and they advised him to throw it into the ocean. It is this fire which absorbs the waters of the ocean. Others say: 'The water of the streams does not Page 252. increase the ocean, because Indra, the ruler, takes up the ocean in the shape of the cloud, and sends it down as rains.'"

The man in the moon.

Again the *Matsya-Purâṇa* says: "The black part in the moon which is called *Śaśalaksha, i.e.* the hare's figure, is the image of the figures of the above-mentioned sixteen mountains reflected by the light of the moon on her body."

The *Vishṇu-Dharma* says: "The moon is called Śaśalaksha, for the globe of her body is watery, reflecting the figure of the earth as a mirror reflects. On the earth there are mountains and trees of different shapes, which are reflected in the moon as a hare's figure. It is also called *Mṛigalâñcana, i.e.* the figure of a gazelle, for certain people compare the black part on the moon's face to the figure of a gazelle."

Story of the leprosy of the moon.

The lunar stations they declare to be the daughters of Prajâpati, to whom the moon is married. He was especially attached to Rohiṇî, and preferred her to the others. Now her sisters, urged by jealousy, complained of him to their father Prajâpati. The latter strove to keep peace among them, and admonished him, but without any success. Then he cursed the moon (*Lunus*), in consequence of which his face became leprous. Now the moon repented of his doing, and came penitent to Prajâpati, who spoke to him: "My word is one, and cannot be cancelled; however, I shall cover thy shame for the half of each month." Thereupon the moon spoke to Prajâpati: "But how shall the trace of the sin of the past be wiped off from me?" Prajâpati answered: "By erecting the shape of the *liṅga* of Mahâdeva as an object of thy worship." This he did. The *liṅga* he raised was the stone of Somanâth, for *soma* means the moon and *nâtha* means *master*, so that the whole word means *master of the moon.* The image was destroyed by the Prince Maḥmûd — may God be merciful to him! — A.H. 416. He ordered the upper part to be broken and the remainder to be transported to his residence, Ghaznîn, with all its coverings and trappings of gold, jewels, and embroidered garments. Part of it has been thrown into the hippodrome of the town, together with the *Cakrasvâmin,* an idol of bronze, that had been brought from Tâneshar. Another part of the idol from Somanâth lies before the door of the mosque of Ghaznîn, on which people rub their feet to clean them from dirt and wet.

The idol of Somanâth.

The *liṅga* is an image of the penis of Mahâdeva. I have heard the following story regarding it:—"A Ṛishi, on seeing Mahâdeva with his wife, became suspicious of him, and cursed him that he should lose his penis. At once his penis dropped, and was as if wiped off. But afterwards the Ṛishi was in a position to establish the signs of his innocence and to confirm them by the necessary proofs. The suspicion which had troubled his mind was removed, and he spoke to him: 'Verily, I shall recompense thee by making the image of the limb which thou hast lost the object of worship for men, who thereby will find the road to God, and come near him.'"

Origin of the Liṅga.

Varâhamihira says about the construction of the *liṅga:* "After having chosen a faultless stone for it, take it as long as the image is intended to be. Divide it into three parts. The lowest part of it is quadrangular, as if it were a cube or quadrangular column. The middle part is octagonal, its surface being divided by four pilasters. The upper third is round, rounded off so as to resemble the gland of a penis.

The construction of the Liṅga according to Varâhamihira. *Brihatsaṁhitâ,* chap. lviii. 53.

V. 54.—In erecting the figure, place the quadrangular third within the earth, and for the octagonal third make a cover, which is called *piṇḍa*, quadrangular from without, but so as to fit also on the quadrangular third in the earth. The octagonal form of the inner side is to fit on to the middle third, which projects out

Page 253.] of the earth. The round third alone remains without cover."

Further he says:—

V. 55.—"If you make the round part too small or too thin, it will hurt the country and bring about evil among the inhabitants of the regions who have constructed it. If it does not go deep enough down into the earth, or if it projects too little out of the earth,

Chapter lx. v. 6.

this causes people to fall ill. When it is in the course of construction, and is struck by a peg, the ruler and his family will perish. If on the transport it is hit, and the blow leaves a trace on it, the artist will perish, and destruction and diseases will spread in that country."

The worship of the idol of Somanâth.

In the south-west of the Sindh country this idol is frequently met with in the houses destined for the worship of the Hindus, but Somanâth was the most famous of these places. Every day they brought there a jug of Ganges water and a basket of flowers from Kashmîr. They believed that the *liṅga* of Somanâth would cure persons of every inveterate illness and heal every desperate and incurable disease.

The reason why in particular Somanâth has become so famous is that it was a harbour for seafaring people, and a station for those who went to and fro between Sufâla in the country of the Zanj and China.

Popular belief about the cause of the tides.

Now as regards ebb and flow in the Indian Ocean, of which the former is called *bharṇa* (?), the latter *vuhara* (?), we state that, according to the notions of the common Hindus, there is a fire called *Vaḍavânala* in the ocean, which is always blazing. The flow is caused by the fire's drawing breath and its being blown up by the wind, and the ebb is caused by the fire's exhaling the breath and the cessation of its being blown up by the wind.

Mânî has come to a belief like this, after he had heard from the Hindus that there is a demon in the sea whose drawing breath and exhaling breath causes the flow and the ebb.

The educated Hindus determine the daily phases of the tides by the rising and setting of the moon, the monthly phases by the increase and waning of the moon; but the physical cause of both phenomena is not understood by them.

Origin of the sacredness of Somanâth.

It is flow and ebb to which Somanâth owes its name (*i.e.* master of the moon); for the stone (or *liṅga*) of Somanâth was originally erected on the coast, a little less than three miles west of the mouth of the river Sarsutî, east of the golden fortress Bârôi, which had appeared as a dwelling-place for Vâsudeva, not far from the place where he and his family were killed, and where they were burned. Each time when the moon rises and sets, the water of the ocean rises in the flood so as to cover the place in question. When, then, the moon reaches the meridian of noon and midnight, the water recedes in the ebb, and the place becomes again visible. Thus the moon was perpetually occupied in serving the idol and bathing it. Therefore the place was considered as sacred to the moon. The fortress which contained the idol and its treasures was not ancient, but was built only about a hundred years ago.

Quotation from the *Vishṇu-Purâṇa*.

The *Vishṇu-Purâṇa* says: "The greatest height of the water of the flow is 1500 digits." This statement seems rather exaggerated; for if the waves and the mean height of the ocean rose to between sixty to seventy yards, the shores and the bays would be more overflown than has ever been witnessed. Still this is not entirely improbable, as it is not in itself impossible on account of some law of nature.

The fact that the just-mentioned fortress is said to

have appeared out of the ocean is not astonishing for that particular part of the ocean; for the Dîbajât islands (Maledives and Laccadives) originate in a similar manner, rising out of the ocean as sand-downs. They increase, and rise, and extend themselves, and remain in this condition for a certain time. Then they become decrepit as if from old age; the single parts become dissolved, no longer keep together, and disappear in the water as if melting away. The inhabitants of the islands quit that one which apparently dies away, and migrate to a young and fresh one which is about to rise above the ocean. They take their cocoanut palms along with them, colonise the new island, and dwell on it.

The golden fortress Bârôi. Parallel of the Maledives and Laccadives.

Page 254.

That the fortress in question is called *golden* may only be a conventional epithet. Possibly, however, this object is to be taken literally, for the islands of the Zâbaj are called the *Gold Country* (*Suvarṇadvîpa*), because you obtain much gold as deposit if you wash only a little of the earth of that country.

CHAPTER LIX.

ON THE SOLAR AND LUNAR ECLIPSES.

It is perfectly known to the Hindu astronomers that the moon is eclipsed by the shadow of the earth, and the sun is eclipsed by the moon. Hereon they have based their computations in the astronomical handbooks and other works.

Varâhamihira says in the *Saṁhitâ*:—

Quotation from Varâhamihira's *Saṁhitâ*, ch. v.

V. 1.—"Some scholars maintain that the *Head* belonged to the Daityas, and that his mother was Siṁhikâ. After the angels had fetched the *amṛita* out of the ocean, they asked Vishṇu to distribute it among them. When he did so, the Head also came, resembling the angels in shape, and associated himself with them. When Vishṇu handed him a portion of the *amṛita*, he took and drank it. But then Vishṇu perceived who it was, hit him with his round *cakra*, and cut off his head. However, the head remained alive on account of the *amṛita* in its mouth, whilst the body died, since it had not yet partaken of the *amṛita*, and the force of the latter had not yet spread through it. Then the Head, humbling itself, spoke: 'For what sin has this been done?' Thereupon he was recompensed by being raised to heaven and by being made one of its inhabitants.

V. 2.—Others say that the Head has a body like sun and moon, but that it is black and dark, and cannot therefore be seen in heaven. Brahman, the first father, ordered that he should never appear in heaven except at the time of an eclipse.

V. 3.—Others say that he has a head like that of a serpent, and a tail like that of a serpent, whilst others say that he has no other body besides the black colour which is seen."

After having finished the relation of these absurdities, Varâhamihira continues:—

V. 4.—"If the Head had a body, it would act by immediate contact, whilst we find that he eclipses from a distance, when between him and the moon there is an interval of six zodiacal signs. Besides, his motion does not increase nor decrease, so that we cannot imagine an eclipse to be caused by his body reaching the spot of the lunar eclipse.

V. 5.—And if a man commits himself to such a view, let him tell us for what purpose the cycles of the Head's rotation have been calculated, and what is the use of their being correct in consequence of the fact that his rotation is a regular one. If the Head is imagined to be a serpent with head and tail, why does it not eclipse from a distance less or more than six zodiacal signs?

V. 6.—His body is there present between head and tail; both hang together by means of the body. Still it does not eclipse sun nor moon nor the fixed stars of the lunar stations, there being an eclipse only if there are two heads opposed to each other.

V. 7.—If the latter were the case, and the moon rose, being eclipsed by one of the two, the sun would necessarily set, being eclipsed by the other. Likewise,
Page 255. if the moon should set eclipsed, the sun would rise eclipsed. And nothing of the kind ever occurs.

V. 8.—As has been mentioned by scholars who enjoy the help of God, an eclipse of the moon is her entering the shadow of the earth, and an eclipse of the sun consists in this that the moon covers and hides the sun from us. Therefore the lunar eclipse will never revolve from the west nor the solar eclipse from the east.

V. 9.—A long shadow stretches away from the earth, in like manner as the shadow of a tree.

V. 10.—When the moon has only little latitude, standing in the seventh sign of its distance from the sun, and if it does not stand too far north or south, in that case the moon enters the shadow of the earth and is eclipsed thereby. The first contact takes place on the side of the east.

V. 11.—When the sun is reached by the moon from the west, the moon covers the sun, as if a portion of a cloud covered him. The amount of the covering differs in different regions.

V. 12.—Because that which covers the moon is large, her light wanes when one-half of it is eclipsed; and because that which covers the sun is not large, the rays are powerful notwithstanding the eclipse.

V. 13.—The nature of the Head has nothing whatever to do with the lunar and solar eclipses. On this subject the scholars in their books agree."

After having described the nature of the two eclipses, as *he* understands them, he complains of those who do not know this, and says: "However, common people are always very loud in proclaiming the Head to be the cause of an eclipse, and they say, 'If the Head did not appear and did not bring about the eclipse, the Brahmans would not at that moment undergo an obligatory washing.'"

Varâhamihira says:—

V. 14.—"The reason of this is that the head humiliated itself after it had been cut off, and received from Brahman a portion of the offering which the Brahmans offer to the fire at the moment of an eclipse.

V. 15.—Therefore he is near the spot of the eclipse, searching for his portion. Therefore at that time people mention him frequently, and consider him as the cause of the eclipse, although he has nothing whatsoever to do with it; for the eclipse depends entirely upon the uniformity and the declination of the orbit of the moon."

Praise of Varâhamihira.

The latter words of Varâhamihira, who, in passages quoted previously, has already revealed himself to us as a man who accurately knows the shape of the world, are odd and surprising. However, he seems sometimes to side with the Brahmans, to whom he belonged, and from whom he could not separate himself. Still he does not deserve to be blamed, as, on the whole, his foot stands firmly on the basis of the truth, and he clearly speaks out the truth. Compare, *e.g.* his statement regarding the *Saṁdhi*, which we have mentioned above (v. i. 366).

Strictures on Brahmagupta's want of sincerity.

Would to God that all distinguished men followed his example! But look, for instance, at Brahmagupta, who is certainly the most distinguished of their astronomers. For as he was one of the Brahmans who read in their Purâṇas that the sun is lower than the moon, and who therefore require a head biting the sun in order that he should be eclipsed, he shirks the truth and lends his support to imposture, if he did not—and this we think by no means impossible—from intense disgust at them, speak as he spoke simply in order to mock them, or under the compulsion of some mental derangement, like a man whom death is about to rob of his consciousness. The words in question are found in the first chapter of his *Brahmasiddhânta*:—

Quotation from the *Brahmasiddhânta.*

"Some people think that the eclipse is not caused by the Head. This, however, is a foolish idea, for it is *he* in fact who eclipses, and the generality of the inhabitants of the world say that it is the Head who eclipses. The *Veda*, which is the word of God from the mouth of Brahman, says that the Head eclipses, likewise the book *Smṛiti*, composed by Manu, and the *Saṁhitâ*, composed by Garga the son of Brahman. On the contrary, Varâ-

Page 256.

hamihira, Śrîsheṇa, Âryabhaṭa, and Vishṇucandra maintain that the eclipse is not caused by the Head, but by the moon and the shadow of the earth, in direct opposition to all (to the generality of men), and from enmity against the just-mentioned dogma. For if the Head does not cause the eclipse, all the usages of the Brahmans which they practise at the moment of an eclipse, viz. their rubbing themselves with warm oil, and other works of prescribed worship, would be illusory and not be rewarded by heavenly bliss. If a man declares these things to be illusory, he stands outside of the generally acknowledged dogma, and that is not allowed. Manu says in the *Smṛiti:* 'When the Head keeps the sun or moon in eclipse, all waters on earth become pure, and in purity like the water of the Ganges.' The *Veda* says: 'The Head is the son of a woman of the daughters of the Daityas, called *Sainakâ*' (? Siṁhikâ ?). Therefore people practise the well-known works of piety, and therefore those authors must cease to oppose the generality, for everything which is in the *Veda, Smṛiti,* and *Saṁhitâ* is true."

If Brahmagupta, in this respect, is one of those of whom God says (*Koran,* Sûra xxvii. 14), "*They have denied our signs, although their hearts knew them clearly, from wickedness and haughtiness,*" we shall not argue with him, but only whisper into his ear: If people must under circumstances give up opposing the religious codes (as seems to be your case), why then do you order people to be pious if you forget to be so yourself? Why do you, after having spoken such words, then begin to calculate the diameter of the moon in order to explain her eclipsing the sun, and the diameter of the shadow of the earth in order to explain its eclipsing the moon? Why do you compute both eclipses in agreement with the theory of those heretics, and not according to the views of those with whom you think it proper to agree? If the Brahmans are ordered to practise some act of worship or something else at the occurrence of an eclipse, the eclipse is only *the date* of these things, not *their cause.* Thus we Muslims are bound to say certain prayers, and prohibited from saying others, at certain times of the revolution of the sun and his light. These things are simply chronological dates for those acts, nothing more, for the sun has nothing whatever to do with our (Muslim) worship.

Brahmagupta says (ii. 110), "The generality thinks thus." If he thereby means the totality of the inhabitants of the inhabitable world, we can only say that he would be very little able to investigate *their* opinions either by exact research or by means of historical tradition. For India itself is, in comparison to the whole inhabitable world, only a small matter, and the number of those who differ from the Hindus, both in religion and law, is larger than the number of those who agree with them.

Possible excuses for Brahmagupta.

Or if Brahmagupta means *the generality of the Hindus,* we agree that the uneducated among them are much more numerous than the educated; but we also point out that in all our religious codes of divine revelation the uneducated crowd is blamed as being ignorant, always doubting, and ungrateful.

I, for my part, am inclined to the belief that that which made Brahmagupta speak the above-mentioned words (which involve a sin against conscience) was something of a calamitous fate, like that of Socrates, which had befallen him, notwithstanding the abundance of his knowledge and the sharpness of his intel-
Page 257. lect, and notwithstanding his extreme youth at the time. For he wrote the *Brahmasiddhânta* when he was only thirty years of age. If this indeed is his excuse, we accept it, and herewith drop the matter.

As for the above-mentioned people (the Hindu theologians), from whom you must take care not to differ, how should they be able to understand the astronomical theory regarding the moon's eclipsing the sun, as they, in their Purâṇas, place the moon *above* the sun, and that which is higher cannot cover that which is lower in the sight of those who stand lower than both. Therefore they required some being which devours moon and sun, as the fish devours the bait, and causes them to appear in those shapes in which the eclipsed parts of them in reality appear. However, in each nation there are ignorant people, and leaders still more ignorant than they themselves, who (as the Koran, Sura xxix. 12, says) "*bear their own burdens and other burdens besides them,*" and who think they can increase the light of their minds; the fact being that the masters are as ignorant as the pupils.

Quotations from Varâhamihira's *Saṁhitâ*, chap. v. 17, 16, 63.

Very odd is that which Varâhamihira relates of certain ancient writers, to whom we must pay no attention if we do not want to oppose them, viz. that they tried to prognosticate the occurrence of an eclipse by pouring a small amount of water together with the same amount of oil into a large vase with a flat bottom on the eighth of the lunar days. Then they examined the spots where the oil was united and dispersed. The united portion they considered as a prognostication for the beginning of the eclipse, the dispersed portion as a prognostication for its end.

Further, Varâhamihira says that somebody used to think that the conjunction of the planets is the cause of the eclipse (V. 16), whilst others tried to prognosticate an eclipse from unlucky phenomena, as, *e.g.* the falling of stars, comets, halo, darkness, hurricane, landslip, and earthquake. "These things," so he says, "are not always contemporary with an eclipse, nor are they its cause; the nature of an unlucky event is the only thing which these occurrences have in common with an eclipse. A reasonable explanation is totally different from such absurdities."

The same man, knowing only too well the character

of his countrymen, who like to mix up peas with wolf's beans, pearls with dung, says, without quoting any authority for his words (V. 63): "If at the time of an eclipse a violent wind blows, the next eclipse will be six months later. If a star falls down, the next eclipse will be twelve months later. If the air is dusty, it will be eighteen months later. If there is an earthquake, it will be twenty-four months later. If the air is dark, it will be thirty months later. If hail falls, it will be thirty-six months later."

To such things silence is the only proper answer.

On the colours of the eclipses.

I shall not omit to mention that the different kinds of eclipses described in the canon of Alkhwârizmî, though correctly represented, do not agree with the results of actual observation. More correct is a similar view of the Hindus, viz. that the eclipse has the colour of smoke if it covers less than half the body of the moon; that it is coal-black if it completely covers one half of her; that it has a colour between black and red if the eclipse covers more than half of her body; and, lastly, that it is yellow-brown if it covers the whole body of the moon.

(Chapters LX–LXII, pages 115–129, deal with technical astrological terms.)

CHAPTER LXIII.

ON THAT WHICH ESPECIALLY CONCERNS THE BRAHMANS, AND WHAT THEY ARE OBLIGED TO DO DURING THEIR WHOLE LIFE.

First period in the Brahman's life.

THE life of the Brahman, after seven years of it have passed, is divided into four parts. The first part begins with the eighth year, when the Brahmans come to him to instruct him, to teach him his duties, and to enjoin him to adhere to them and to embrace them as long as he lives. Then they bind a girdle round his waist and invest him with a pair of *yajnopavîtas*, *i.e.* one strong cord consisting of nine single cords which are twisted together, and with a third *yajnopavîta*, a single one made from cloth. This girdle runs from the left shoulder to the right hip. Further, he is presented with a stick which he has to wear, and with a seal-ring of a certain grass, called *darbha*, which he wears on the ring-finger of the right hand. This seal-ring is also called *pavitra*. The object of his wearing the ring on the ring-finger of his right hand is this, that it should be a good omen and a blessing for all those who receive gifts from that hand. The obligation of wearing the ring is not quite so stringent as that of wearing the *yajnopavîta*, for from the latter he is not to separate himself under any circumstances whatever. If he takes it off while eating or fulfilling some want of nature, he thereby commits a sin which cannot be
Page 268.
wiped off save by some work of expiation, fasting, or almsgiving.

This first period of the Brahman's life extends till the twenty-fifth year of his age, or, according to the *Vishṇu-Purâṇa,* till his forty-eighth year. His duty is to practise abstinence, to make the earth his bed, to begin with the learning of the Veda and of its explanation, of the science of theology and law, all this being taught to him by a master whom he serves day and night. He washes himself thrice a day, and performs a sacrifice to the fire both at the beginning and end of the day. After the sacrifice he worships his master. He fasts a day and he breaks fast a day, but he is never allowed to eat meat. He dwells in the house of the master, which he only leaves in order to ask for a gift and to beg in not more than five houses once a day, either at noon or in the evening. Whatever alms he receives he places before his master to choose from it what he likes. Then the master allows him to take the remainder. Thus the pupil nourishes himself from the remains of the dishes of his master. Further, he fetches the wood for the fire, wood of two kinds of trees, *palâśa* (*Butea frondosa*) and *darbha,* in order to perform the sacrifice; for the Hindus highly venerate the fire, and offer flowers to it. It is the same case with all other nations. They always thought that the sacrifice was accepted by the deity if the fire came down upon it, and no other worship has been able to draw them away from it, neither the worship of idols nor that of stars, cows, asses, or images. Therefore Bashshâr Ibn Burd says: "Since there is fire, it is worshipped."

Second period in the Brahman's life.

The second period of their life extends from the twenty-fifth year till the fiftieth, or, according to the *Vishṇu-Purâṇa,* till the seventieth. The master allows him to marry. He marries, establishes a household, and intends to have descendants, but he cohabits with his wife only once in a month after she has become clean of the menstruation. He is not allowed to marry a woman above twelve years of age. He gains his sustenance *either* by the fee he

obtains for teaching Brahmans and Kshatriyas, not as a payment, but as a present, *or* by presents which he receives from some one because he performs for him the sacrifices to the fire, *or* by asking a gift from the kings and nobles, there being no importunate pressing on his part, and no unwillingness on the part of the giver. There is always a Brahman in the houses of those people, who there administers the affairs of religion and the works of piety. He is called *purohita*. Lastly, the Brahman lives from what he gathers on the earth or from the trees. He may try his fortune in the trade of clothes and betel-nuts, but it is preferable that he should not trade himself, and that a Vaiśya should do the business for him, because originally trade is forbidden on account of the deceiving and lying which are mixed up with it. Trading is permitted to him only in case of dire necessity, when he has no other means of sustenance. The Brahmans are not, like the other castes, bound to pay taxes and to perform services to the kings. Further, he is not allowed continually to busy himself with horses and cows, with the care for the cattle, nor with gaining by usury. The blue colour
Page 269. is impure for him, so that if it touches his body, he is obliged to wash himself. Lastly, he must always beat the drum before the fire, and recite for it the prescribed holy texts.

The third period.

The third period of the life of the Brahman extends from the fiftieth year to the seventy-fifth, or, according to the *Vishṇu-Purâṇa*, till the ninetieth. He practises abstinence, leaves his household, and hands it as well as his wife over to his children, if the latter does not prefer to accompany him into the life in the wilderness. He dwells outside civilisation, and leads the same life again which he led in the first period. He does not take shelter under a roof, nor wear any other dress but some bark of a tree, simply sufficient to cover his loins. He sleeps on the earth without any bed, and only nourishes himself by fruit, vegetables, and roots. He lets the hair grow long, and does not anoint himself with oil.

The fourth period.

The fourth period extends till the end of life. He wears a red garment and holds a stick in his hand. He is always given to meditation; he strips the mind of friendship and enmity, and roots out desire, and lust, and wrath. He does not converse with anybody at all. When walking to a place of a particular merit, in order to gain a heavenly reward, he does not stop on the road in a village longer than a day, nor in a city longer than five days. If any one gives him something, he does not leave a remainder of it for the following day. He has no other business but that of caring for the path which leads to salvation, and for reaching *moksha*, whence there is no return to this world.

The duties of Brahmans in general.

The universal duties of the Brahman throughout his whole life are works of piety, giving alms and receiving them. For that which the Brahmans give reverts to the *pitaras* (is in reality a benefit to the *Fathers*). He must continually read, perform the sacrifices, take care of the fire which he lights, offer before it, worship it, and preserve it from being extinguished, that he may be burned by it after his death. It is called *homa*.

Every day he must wash himself thrice: at the *saṁdhi* of rising, *i.e.* morning dawn, at the *saṁdhi* of setting, *i.e.* evening twilight, and between them in the middle of the day. The first washing is on account of sleep, because the openings of the body have become lax during it. Washing is a cleansing from accidental impurity and a preparation for prayer.

Their prayer consists of praise, glorification, and prostration according to their peculiar manner, viz. prostrating themselves on the two thumbs, whilst the two palms of the hands are joined, and they turn their faces towards the sun. For the sun is their *kibla*, wherever he may be, except when in the south. For they do not perform any work of piety with the face turned southward; only when occupied with something evil and unlucky they turn themselves towards the south.

The time when the sun declines from the meridian (the afternoon) is well suited for acquiring in it a heavenly reward. Therefore at this time the Brahman must be clean.

The evening is the time of supper and of prayer. The Brahman may take his supper and pray without having previously washed himself. Therefore, evidently, the rule as to the third washing is not as stringent as that relating to the first and second washings.

A nightly washing is obligatory for the Brahman only at the times of eclipses, that he should be prepared to perform the rules and sacrifices prescribed for that occasion.

The Brahman, as long as he lives, eats only twice a day, at noon and at nightfall; and when he wants to take his meal, he begins by putting aside as much as
Page 270. is sufficient for one or two men as alms, especially for strange Brahmans who happen to come at evening-time asking for something. To neglect *their* maintenance would be a great sin. Further, he puts something aside for the cattle, the birds, and the fire. Over the remainder he says prayers and eats it. The remainder of his dish he places outside his house, and does not any more come near it, as it is no longer allowable for him, being destined for the chance passer-by who wants it, be he a man, bird, dog, or something else.

The Brahman must have a water-vessel for himself. If another one uses it, it is broken. The same remark applies to his eating-instruments. I have seen Brahmans who allowed their relatives to eat with them from the same plate, but most of them disapprove of this.

He is obliged to dwell between the river Sindh in the north and the river Carmaṇvatî in the south. He is not allowed to cross either of these frontiers so as to enter the country of the Turks or of the Karṇâṭa. Further, he must live between the ocean in the east and west. People say that he is not allowed to stay in a country in which the grass which he wears on the ring-finger does not grow, nor the black-haired gazelles graze. This is a description for the whole country within the just-mentioned boundaries. If he passes beyond them he commits a sin.

In a country where not the whole spot in the house which is prepared for people to eat upon it is plastered with clay, where they, on the contrary, prepare a separate tablecloth for each person eating by pouring water over a spot and plastering it with the dung of cows, the shape of the Brahman's tablecloth must be square. Those who have the custom of preparing such tablecloths give the following as the cause of this custom:—The spot of eating is soiled by the eating. If the eating is finished, the spot is washed and plastered to become clean again. If, now, the soiled spot is not distinguished by a separate mark, you would suppose also the other spots to be soiled, since they are similar to and cannot be distinguished from each other.

Five vegetables are forbidden to them by the religious code:—Onions, garlic, a kind of gourd, the root of a plant like the carrots called *krncn* (?), and another vegetable which grows round their tanks called *nâlî*.

CHAPTER LXIV.

ON THE RITES AND CUSTOMS WHICH THE OTHER CASTES, BESIDES THE BRAHMANS, PRACTISE DURING THEIR LIFETIME.

Duties of the single castes.

THE Kshatriya reads the Veda and learns it, but does not teach it. He offers to the fire and acts according to the rules of the Purâṇas. In places where, as we have mentioned (v. p. 135), a tablecloth is prepared for eating, he makes it angular. He rules the people and defends them, for he is created for this task. He girds himself with a single cord of the threefold *yajnopavîta*, and a single other cord of cotton. This takes place after he has finished the twelfth year of his life.

It is the duty of the Vaiśya to practise agriculture and to cultivate the land, to tend the cattle and to remove the needs of the Brahmans. He is only allowed to gird himself with a single *yajnopavîta*, which is made of two cords.

The Śûdra is like a servant to the Brahman, taking care of his affairs and serving him. If, though being poor in the extreme, he still desires not to be without a *yajnopavîta*, he girds himself only with the linen one. Every action which is considered as the privilege of a Brahman, such as saying prayers, the recitation of the Veda, and offering sacrifices to the fire, is forbidden to him, to such a degree that when, *e.g.* a Śûdra or a Vaiśya is proved to have recited the Veda, he is accused by the Brahmans before the ruler, and the latter will order his tongue to be cut off. However, the meditation on God,

Page 271.

works of piety, and almsgiving are not forbidden to him.

Every man who takes to some occupation which is not allowed to his caste, as, *e.g.* a Brahman to trade, a Śûdra to agriculture, commits a sin or crime, which they consider only a little less than the crime of theft.

The following is one of the traditions of the Hindus: —In the days of King Râma human life was very long, always of a well-defined and well-known length. Thus a child never died before its father. Then, however, it happened that the son of a Brahman died while the father was still alive. Now the Brahman brought his child to the door of the king and spoke to him: "This innovation has sprung up in thy days for no other reason but this, that there is something rotten in the state of the country, and because a certain Vazîr commits in thy realm what he commits." Then Râma began to inquire into the cause of this, and finally they pointed out to him a Caṇḍâla who took the greatest pains in performing worship and in self-torment. The king rode to him and found him on the banks of the Ganges, hanging on something with his head downward. The king bent his bow, shot at him, and pierced his bowels. Then he spoke: "That is it! I kill thee on account of a good action which thou art not allowed to do." When he returned home, he found the son of the Brahman, who had been deposited before his door, alive.

Story of King Râma, the *Caṇḍâla* and the Brahman.

All other men except the Caṇḍâla, as far as they are not Hindus, are called *mleccha*, *i.e.* unclean, all those who kill men and slaughter animals and eat the flesh of cows.

All these things originate in the difference of the classes or castes, one set of people treating the others as fools. This apart, all men are equal to each other, as Vâsudeva says regarding him who seeks salvation: "In the judgment of the intelligent man, the Brahman

Philosophic opinion about all things being equal.

and the Caṇḍâla are equal, the friend and the foe, the faithful and the deceitful, nay, even the serpent and the weasel. If to the eyes of intelligence all things are equal, to ignorance they appear as separated and different."

Vâsudeva speaks to Arjuṇa: "If the civilisation of the world is that which is intended, and if the direction of it cannot proceed without our fighting for the purpose of suppressing evil, it is the duty of us who are the intelligent to act and to fight, not in order to bring to an end that which is deficient within us, but because it is necessary for the purpose of healing what is ill and banishing destructive elements. Then the ignorant imitate us in acting, as the children imitate their elders, without their knowing the real aim and purport of actions. For their nature has an aversion to intellectual methods, and they use force only in order to act in accordance with the influences of lust and passion on their senses. In all this, the intelligent and educated man is directly the contrary of them."

CHAPTER LXV.

ON THE SACRIFICES.

MOST of the Veda treats of the sacrifices to the fire, and describes each one of them. They are different in extent, so that certain of them can only be performed by the greatest of their kings. So, *e.g.* the *aśvamedha*. Aśvamedha. A mare is let freely to wander about in the country grazing, without anybody's hindering her. Soldiers follow her, drive her, and cry out before her: "She is the king of the world. He who does not agree, let him come forward." The Brahmans walk behind her and perform sacrifices to the fire where she casts dung. When she thus has wandered about through all parts Page 272. of the world, she becomes food for the Brahmans and for him whose property she is.

Further, the sacrifices differ in duration, so that only he could perform certain of them who lives a very long life; and such long lives do no longer occur in this our age. Therefore most of them have been abolished, and only few of them remain and are practised nowadays.

According to the Hindus, the fire eats everything. On fire-offerings in general. Therefore it becomes defiled, if anything unclean is mixed up with it, as, *e.g.* water. Accordingly they are very punctilious regarding fire and water if they are in the hands of non-Hindus, because they are defiled by being touched by them.

That which the fire eats for its share, reverts to the Devas, because the fire comes out of their mouths.

What the Brahmans present to the fire to eat is oil and different cereals—wheat, barley, and rice—which they throw into the fire. Further, they recite the prescribed texts of the Veda in case they offer on their own behalf. However, if they offer in the name of somebody else, they do not recite anything.

Story of the fire becoming leprous from *Vishṇu-Dharma*.

The *Vishṇu-Dharma* mentions the following tradition:—Once upon a time there was a man of the class of the Daityas, powerful and brave, the ruler of a wide realm called Hiraṇyâksha. He had a daughter of the name of Dkîsh (?), who was always bent upon worship and trying herself by fasting and abstinence. Thereby she had earned as reward a place in heaven. She was married to Mahâdeva. When he, then, was alone with her and did with her according to the custom of the Devas, *i.e.* cohabiting very long and transferring the *semen* very slowly, the fire became aware of it and became jealous, fearing lest the two might procreate a fire similar to themselves. Therefore it determined to defile and to ruin them.

When Mahâdeva saw the fire, his forehead became covered with sweat from the violence of his wrath, so that some of it dropped down to the earth. The earth drank it, and became in consequence pregnant with Mars, *i.e. Skanda*, the commander of the army of the Devas.

Rudra, the destroyer, seized a drop of the *semen* of Mahâdeva and threw it away. It was scattered in the interior of the earth, and represents all atom-like substances (?).

The fire, however, became leprous, and felt so much ashamed and confounded that it plunged down into *pâtâla*, *i.e.* the lowest earth. As, now, the Devas missed the fire, they went out to search for it.

First, the frogs pointed it out to them. The fire, on seeing the Devas, left its place and concealed itself in the tree *aśvattha*, laying a curse on the frogs, that they should have a horrid croaking and be odious to all others.

Next, the parrots betrayed to the Devas the hiding-place of the fire. Thereupon the fire cursed them, that their tongues should be turned topsy-turvy, that their root should be where its tip ought to be. But the Devas spoke to them: "If your tongue is turned topsy-turvy, you shall speak in human dwellings and eat delicate things."

The fire fled from the *aśvattha* tree to the tree *śamî*. Thereupon the elephant gave a hint to the Devas regarding its hiding-place. Now it cursed the elephant that his tongue should be turned topsy-turvy. But then the Devas spoke to him: "If your tongue is turned topsy-turvy, you shall participate with man in his victuals and understand his speech."

At last they hit upon the fire, but the fire refused to stay with them because it was leprous. Now the Devas restored it to health, and freed it from the leprosy. The Devas brought back to them the fire with all honour and made it a mediator between themselves and mankind, receiving from the latter the shares which they offer to the Devas, and making these shares reach them.

CHAPTER LXVI.

ON PILGRIMAGE AND THE VISITING OF SACRED PLACES.

Page 273.

PILGRIMAGES are not obligatory to the Hindus, but facultative and meritorious. A man sets off to wander to some holy region, to some much venerated idol or to some of the holy rivers. He worships in them, worships the idol, makes presents to it, recites many hymns and prayers, fasts, and gives alms to the Brahmans, the priests, and others. He shaves the hair of his head and beard, and returns home.

The holy much venerated ponds are in the cold mountains round Meru. The following information regarding them is found in both the *Vâyu* and the *Matsya Purâṇas*:—

An extract on holy ponds from the *Vâyu* and *Matsya Purâṇas*.

"At the foot of Meru there is Arhata (?), a very great pond, described as shining like the moon. In it originates the river Zanba (? Jambu), which is very pure, flowing over the purest gold.

"Near the mountain Śveta there is the pond Uttaramânasa, and around it twelve other ponds, each of them like a lake. Thence come the two rivers Sâṇḍî (?) and Maddhyandâ (?), which flow to Kiṁpurusha.

"Near the mountain Nîla there is the pond *pyvd* (pitanda ?) adorned with lotuses.

"Near the mountain Nishadha there is the pond Vishṇupada, whence comes the river Sarasvatî, *i.e.*, Sarsuti. Besides, the river Gandharvî comes from there.

"In the mountain Kailâsa there is the pond Manda, as large as a sea, whence comes the river Mandâkinî.

"North-east of Kailâsa there is the mountain Candraparvata, and at its foot the pond Âcûd (?), whence comes the river Âcûd.

"South-east of Kailâsa there is the mountain Lohita, and at its foot a pond called Lohita. Thence comes the river Lohitanadî.

"South of Kailâsa there is the mountain Sarayuśatî (?), and at its foot the pond Mânasa. Thence comes the river Sarayû.

"West of Kailâsa there is the mountain Aruṇa, always covered with snow, which cannot be ascended. At its foot is the pond Śailôdâ, whence comes the river Śailôdâ.

"North of Kailâsa there is the mountain Gaura (?), and at its foot the pond C-n-d-sara (?), *i.e.* having golden sand. Near this pond the King Bhagîratha led his anchorite life.

"His story is as follows:—A king of the Hindus called Sagara had 60,000 sons, all of them bad, mean fellows. Once they happened to lose a horse. They at once searched for it, and in searching they continually ran about so violently that in consequence the surface of the earth broke in. They found the horse in the interior of the earth standing before a man who was looking down with deep-sunken eyes. When they came near him he smote them with his look, in consequence of which they were burned on the spot and went to hell on account of their wicked actions. Story of Bhagîratha.

"The collapsed part of the earth became a sea, the great ocean. A king of the descendants of that king, called Bhagîratha, on hearing the history of his ancestors, was much affected thereby. He went to the above-mentioned pond, the bottom of which was polished gold, and stayed there, fasting all day and worshipping during the nights. Finally, Mahâdeva asked him what he wanted; upon which he answered, Page 284.

'I want the river Ganges which flows in Paradise,' knowing that to any one over whom its water flows all his sins are pardoned. Mahâdeva granted him his desire. However, the Milky Way was the bed of the Ganges, and the Ganges was very haughty, for nobody had ever been able to stand against it. Now Mahâdeva took the Ganges and put it on his head. When the Ganges could not move away, he became very angry and made a great uproar. However, Mahâdeva held him firmly, so that it was not possible for anybody to plunge into it. Then he took part of the Ganges and gave it to Bhagîratha, and this king made the middle one of its seven branches flow over the bones of his ancestors, whereby they became liberated from punishment. Therefore the Hindus throw the burned bones of their dead into the Ganges. The Ganges was also called by the name of that king who brought him to earth, *i.e.* Bhagîratha."

On the construction of holy ponds.

We have already quoted Hindu traditions to the effect that in the Dvîpas there are rivers as holy as the Ganges. In every place to which some particular holiness is ascribed, the Hindus construct ponds intended for the ablutions. In this they have attained to a very high degree of art, so that our people (the Muslims), when they see them, wonder at them, and are unable to describe them, much less to construct anything like them. They build them of great stones of an enormous bulk, joined to each other by sharp and strong cramp-irons, in the form of steps (or terraces) like so many ledges; and these terraces run all around the pond, reaching to a height of more than a man's stature. On the surface of the stones between two terraces they construct staircases rising like pinnacles. Thus the first steps or terraces are like roads (leading round the pond), and the pinnacles are steps (leading up and down). If ever so many people descend to the pond whilst others ascend, they do not meet each other, and the road is never blocked up, because there are so many terraces, and the ascending person can always turn aside to another terrace than that on which the descending people go. By this arrangement all troublesome thronging is avoided.

On single holy ponds.

In Multân there is a pond in which the Hindus worship by bathing themselves, if they are not prevented.

The *Saṁhitâ* of Varâhamihira relates that in Tâneshar there is a pond which the Hindus visit from afar to bathe in its water. Regarding the cause of this custom they relate the following:—The waters of all the other holy ponds visit this particular pond at the time of an eclipse. Therefore, if a man washes in it, it is as if he had washed in every single one of all of them. Then Varâhamihira continues: "People say, if it were not the head (apsis) which causes the eclipse of sun and moon, the other ponds would not visit this pond."

The ponds become particularly famous for holiness either because some important event has happened at them, or because there is some passage in the holy text or tradition which refers to them. We have already quoted words spoken by Śaunaka. Venus had related them to him on the authority of Brahman, to whom they had originally been addressed. In this text King Bali also is mentioned, and what he would do till the time when Nârâyaṇa would plunge him down to the lowest earth. In the same text occurs the following passage:—"I do that to him only for this purpose that the equality between men, which he desires to realise, shall be done away with, that men shall be different in their conditions of life, and that on this difference the order of the world is to be based; further, that people shall turn away from *his* worship and worship *me* and believe in *me*. The mutual assistance of civilised people presupposes a certain difference

On the inequality of created beings and the origin of patriotism. A tradition from Śaunaka.

Page 275.

among them, in consequence of which the one requires the other. According to the same principle, God has created the world as containing many differences in itself. So the single countries differ from each other, one being cold, the other warm; one having good soil, water, and air, the other having bitter salt soil, dirty and bad smelling water, and unhealthy air. There are still more differences of this kind; in some cases advantages of all kinds being numerous, in others few. In some parts there are periodically returning physical disasters; in others they are entirely unknown. All these things induce civilised people carefully to select the places where they want to build towns.

That which makes people do these things is usage and custom. However, religious commands are much more powerful, and influence much more the nature of man than usages and customs. The bases of the latter are investigated, explored, and accordingly either kept or abandoned, whilst the bases of the religious commands are left as they are, not inquired into, adhered to by the majority simply on *trust*. They do not argue over them, as the inhabitants of some sterile region do not argue over it, since they are born in it and do not know anything else, for they love the country as their fatherland, and find it difficult to leave it. If, now, besides physical differences, the countries differ from each other also in law and religion, there is so much attachment to it in the hearts of those who live in them that it can never be rooted out."

On Benares as an asylum.

The Hindus have some places which are venerated for reasons connected with their law and religion, *e.g.* Benares (Bârânasî). For their anchorites wander to it and stay there for ever, as the dwellers of the Kaʿba stay for ever in Mekka. They want to live there to the end of their lives, that their reward after death should be the better for it. They say that a murderer is held responsible for his crime and punished with a punishment due to his guilt, except in case he enters the city of Benares, where he obtains pardon. Regarding the cause of the holiness of this asylum they relate the following story:—

"Brahman was in shape four-headed. Now there happened some quarrel between him and Śaṁkara, *i.e.* Mahâdeva, and the succeeding fight had this result, that one of the heads of Brahman was torn off. At that time it was the custom that the victor took the head of the slain adversary in his hand and let it hang down from his hand as an act of ignominy to the dead and as a sign of his own bravery. Further, a bridle was put into the mouth (?). Thus the head of Brahman was dishonoured by the hand of Mahâdeva, who took it always with him wherever he went and whatever he did. He never once separated himself from it when he entered the towns, till at last he came to Benares. After he had entered Benares the head dropped from his hand and disappeared."

On the holy ponds of Pûkara, Tâneshar, Mâhûra, Kashmîr, and Multân.

A similar place is Pûkara, the story of which is this: Brahman once was occupied in offering there to the fire, when a pig came out of the fire. Therefore they represent his image there as that of a pig. Outside the town, in three places, they have constructed ponds which stand in high veneration, and are places of worship.

Another place of the kind is Tâneshar, also called *Kurukshetra, i.e.* the land of Kuru, who was a peasant, a pious, holy man, who worked miracles by divine power. Therefore the country was called after him, and venerated for his sake. Besides, Tâneshar is the theatre of the exploits of Vâsudeva in the wars of Bhârata and of the destruction of the evil-doers. It is for this reason that people visit the place.

Mâhûra, too, is a holy place, crowded with Brahmans.

Page 276. It is venerated because Vâsudeva was there born and brought up, in a place in the neighbourhood called *Nandagola*.

Nowadays the Hindus also visit Kashmîr. Lastly, they used to visit Mûltân before its idol-temple was destroyed.

CHAPTER LXVII.

ON ALMS, AND HOW A MAN MUST SPEND WHAT HE EARNS.

It is obligatory with them every day to give alms as much as possible. They do not let money become a year or even a month old, for this would be a draft on an unknown future, of which a man does not know whether he reaches it or not.

With regard to that which he earns by the crops or from the cattle, he is bound first to pay to the ruler of the country the tax which attaches to the soil or the pasture-ground. Further, he pays him one-sixth of the income in recognition of the protection which he affords to the subjects, their property, and their families. The same obligation rests also on the common people, but they will always lie and cheat in the declarations about their property. Further, trading businesses, too, pay a tribute for the same reason. Only the Brahmans are exempt from all these taxes.

As to the way in which the remainder of the income, after the taxes have been deducted, is to be employed, there are different opinions. Some destine one-ninth of it for alms. For they divide it into three parts. One of them is kept in reserve to guarantee the heart against anxiety. The second is spent on trade to bring profit, and one-third of the third portion (*i.e.* one-ninth of the whole) is spent on alms, whilst the two other thirds are spent according to the same rule.

Others divide this income into four portions. One-fourth is destined for common expenses, the second for liberal works of a noble mind, the third for alms, and the fourth for being kept in reserve, *i.e.* not more of it than the common expenses for three years. If the quarter which is to be reserved exceeds this amount, only this amount is reserved, whilst the remainder is spent as alms.

Usury or taking percentages is forbidden. The sin which a man commits thereby corresponds to the amount by which the percentages have increased the capital stock. Only to the Śûdra is it allowed to take percentages, as long as his profit is not more than one-fiftieth of the capital (*i.e.* he is not to take more than two per cent.).

CHAPTER LXVIII.

ON WHAT IS ALLOWED AND FORBIDDEN IN EATING AND DRINKING.

ORIGINALLY killing in general was forbidden to them, as it is to the Christians and Manichæans. People, however, have the desire for meat, and will always fling aside every order to the contrary. Therefore the here-mentioned law applies in particular only to the Brahmans, because they are the guardians of the religion, and because it forbids them to give way to their lusts. The same rule applies to those members of the Christian clergy who are in rank above the bishops, viz. the metropolitans, the *catholici*, and the patriarchs, not to the lower grades, such as presbyter and deacon, except in the case that a man who holds one of these degrees is at the same time a monk.

List of animals lawful and unlawful to be eaten.

As matters stand thus, it is allowed to kill animals by means of strangulation, but only certain animals, others being excluded. The meat of such animals, the killing of which is allowed, is forbidden in case they die a sudden death. Animals the killing of which is allowed are sheep, goats, gazelles, hares, rhinoceroses (*gandha*), the buffaloes, fish, water and land birds, as sparrows, ring-doves, francolins, doves, peacocks, and other animals which are not loathsome to man nor noxious. Page 277.

That which is forbidden are cows, horses, mules, asses, camels, elephants, tame poultry, crows, parrots, nightingales, all kinds of eggs and wine. The latter is allowed to the Śûdra. He may drink it, but dare not sell it, as he is not allowed to sell meat.

Why the meat of cows was forbidden.

Some Hindus say that in the time before Bhârata it was allowed to eat the meat of cows, and that there then existed sacrifices part of which was the killing of cows. After that time, however, it had been forbidden on account of the weakness of men, who were too weak to fulfil their duties, as also the Veda, which originally was only one, was afterwards divided into four parts, simply for the purpose of facilitating the study of it to men. This theory, however, is very little substantiated, as the prohibition of the meat of cows is not an alleviating and less strict measure, but, on the contrary, one which is more severe and more restrictive than the former law.

Other Hindus told me that the Brahmans used to suffer from the eating of cows' meat. For their country is hot, the inner parts of the bodies are cold, the natural warmth becomes feeble in them, and the power of digestion is so weak that they must strengthen it by eating the leaves of *betel* after dinner, and by chewing the betel-nut. The hot betel inflames the heat of the body, the chalk on the betel-leaves dries up everything wet, and the betel-nut acts as an astringent on the teeth, the gums, and the stomach. As this is the case, they forbade eating cows' meat, because it is essentially thick and cold.

I, for my part, am uncertain, and hesitate in the question of the origin of this custom between two different views.

(*Lacuna in the manuscript.*)

As for the economical reason, we must keep in mind that the cow is the animal which serves man in travelling by carrying his loads, in agriculture in the works of ploughing and sowing, in the household by the milk and the product made thereof. Further, man makes use of its dung, and in winter-time even of its breath.

Therefore it was forbidden to eat cows' meat; as also Alḥajjâj forbade it, when people complained to him that Babylonia became more and more desert.

That all things are equal from a philosophical point of view.

I have been told the following passage is from an Indian book: "All things are one, and whether allowed or forbidden, equal. They differ only in weakness and power. The wolf has the power to tear the sheep; therefore the sheep is the wolf's food, for the former cannot oppose the latter, and is his prey." I have found in Hindu books passages to the same effect. However, such views come to the intelligent man only by knowledge, when in it he has attained to such a degree that a Brahman and a Caṇḍâla are equal to him. If he is in this state, all other things also are equal to him, in so far as he abstains from them. It is the same if they are all allowed to him, for he can dispense with them, or if they are forbidden to him, for he does not desire them. As to those, however, who require these things, being in the yoke of ignorance, something is allowed to them, something forbidden, and thereby a wall is erected between the two kinds of things.

CHAPTER LXIX.

ON MATRIMONY, THE MENSTRUAL COURSES, EMBRYOS, AND CHILDBED.

Necessity of matrimony.

No nation can exist without a regular married life, for it prevents the uproar of passions abhorred by the cultivated mind, and it removes all those causes which excite the animal to a fury always leading to harm. Considering the life of the animals by pairs, how the one member of the pair helps the other, and how the lust of other animals of the same species is kept aloof from them, you cannot help declaring matrimony to be a necessary institution; whilst disorderly cohabitation or harlotry on the part of man is a shameful proceeding, that does not even attain to the standing of the development of animals, which in every other respect stand far below him.

Page 278.

Law of marriage.

Every nation has particular customs of marriage, and especially those who claim to have a religion and law of divine origin. The Hindus marry at a very young age; therefore the parents arrange the marriage for their sons. On that occasion the Brahmans perform the rites of the sacrifices, and they as well as others receive alms. The implements of the wedding rejoicings are brought forward. No gift is settled between them. The man gives only a present to the wife, as he thinks fit, and a marriage gift in advance, which he has no right to claim back, but the wife may give it back to him of her own will. Husband and wife can only be separated by death, as they have no divorce.

A man may marry one to four wives. He is not allowed to take more than four; but if one of his wives die, he may take another one to complete the legitimate number. However, he must not go beyond it.

If a wife loses her husband by death, she cannot marry another man. She has only to chose between two things—either to remain a widow as long as she lives or to burn herself; and the latter eventuality is considered the preferable, because as a widow she is ill-treated as long as she lives. As regards the wives of the kings, they are in the habit of burning them, whether they wish it or not, by which they desire to prevent any of them by chance committing something unworthy of the illustrious husband. They make an exception only for women of advanced years and for those who have children; for the son is the responsible protector of his mother. The widow.

According to their marriage law it is better to marry a stranger than a relative. The more distant the relationship of a woman with regard to her husband the better. It is absolutely forbidden to marry related women both of the direct *descending* line, viz. a granddaughter or great-granddaughter, and of the direct *ascending* line, viz. a mother, grandmother, or great-grandmother. It is also forbidden to marry collateral relations, viz. a sister, a niece, a maternal or paternal aunt and their daughters, except in case the couple of relations who want to marry each other be removed from each other by five consecutive generations. In that case the prohibition is waived, but, notwithstanding, such a marriage is an object of dislike to them. Forbidden degrees of marriage.

Some Hindus think that the number of the wives depends upon the caste; that, accordingly, a Brahman may take four, a Kshatriya three, a Vaisya two wives, and a Śûdra one. Every man of a caste may marry a woman of his own caste or one of the castes or caste Number of wives.

below his; but nobody is allowed to marry a woman of a caste superior to his own.

Partus sequitur ventrem.

The child belongs to the caste of the mother, not to that of the father. Thus, *e.g.* if the wife of a Brahman is a Brahman, her child also is a Brahman; if she is a Śûdra, her child is a Śûdra. In our time, however, the Brahmans, although it is allowed to them, never marry any woman except one of their own caste.

Duration of the menstrual courses.

The longest duration of the menstrual courses which has been observed is sixteen days, but in reality they last only during the first four days, and then the husband is not allowed to cohabit with his wife, nor even to come near her in the house, because during this time she is impure. After the four days have elapsed and she has washed, she is pure again, and the husband may cohabit with her, even if the blood has not yet entirely disappeared; for this blood is not considered as that of the menstrual courses, but as the same substance-matter of which the embryos consist.

On pregnancy and childbed. Page 279.

It is the duty (of the Brahman), if he wants to cohabit with a wife to get a child, to perform a sacrifice to the fire called *garbhâdhâna;* but he does not perform it, because it requires the presence of the woman, and therefore he feels ashamed to do so. In consequence he postpones the sacrifice and unites it with the next following one, which is due in the fourth month of the pregnancy, called *sîmaṁtonnayanam.* After the wife has given birth to the child, a third sacrifice is performed between the birth and the moment when the mother begins to nourish the child. It is called *jâtakarman.*

The child receives a name after the days of the childbed have elapsed. The sacrifice for the occasion of the name-giving is called *nâmakarman.*

As long as the woman is in childbed, she does not touch any vessel, and nothing is eaten in her house, nor does the Brahman light there a fire. These days are eight for the Brahman, twelve for the Kshatriya, fifteen for the Vaiśya, and thirty for the Śûdra. For the low-caste people which are not reckoned among any caste, no term is fixed.

The longest duration of the suckling of the child is three years, but there is no obligation in this matter. The sacrifice on the occasion of the first cutting of the child's hair is offered in the third, the perforation of the ear takes place in the seventh and eighth years.

On the causes of prostitution.

People think with regard to harlotry that it is allowed with them. Thus, when Kâbul was conquered by the Muslims and the Ispahbad of Kâbul adopted Islâm, he stipulated that he should not be bound to eat cows' meat nor to commit sodomy (which proves that he abhorred the one as much as the other). In reality, the matter is not as people think, but it is rather this, that the Hindus are not very severe in punishing whoredom. The fault, however, in this lies with the kings, not with the nation. But for this, no Brahman or priest would suffer in their idol-temples the women who sing, dance, and play. The kings make them an attraction for their cities, a bait of pleasure for their subjects, for no other but financial reasons. By the revenues which they derive from the business both as fines and taxes, they want to recover the expenses which their treasury has to spend on the army.

In a similar way the Buyide prince ʿAḍud-aldaula acted, who besides also had a second aim in view, viz. that of protecting his subjects against the passions of his unmarried soldiers.

CHAPTER LXX.

ON LAWSUITS.

On procedure.

THE judge demands from the suitor a document written against the accused person in a well-known writing which is thought suitable for writs of the kind, and in the document the well-established proof of the justice of his suit. In case there is no written document, the contest is settled by means of witnesses without a written document.

Number of witnesses.

The witnesses must not be less than four, but there may be more. Only in case the justice of the deposition of a witness is perfectly established and certain before the judge, he may admit it, and decide the question alone on the basis of the deposition of this sole witness. However, he does not admit prying about in secret, deriving arguments from mere signs or indications in public, concluding by analogy from one thing which seems established about another, and using all sorts of tricks to elicit the truth, as 'Iyâs Ibn Mu'âwiya used to do.

If the suitor is not able to prove his claim, the defendant must swear, but he may also tender the oath to the suitor by saying, "Swear thou that thy claim is true, and I will give thee what thou claimest."

Different kinds of oaths and ordeals.

There are many kinds of the oath, in accordance with the value of the object of the claim. If the object is of no great importance, and the suitor agrees that the accused person shall swear, the latter simply swears before five learned Brahmans in the following words:

"If I lie, he shall have as recompense as much of my goods as is equal to the eightfold of the amount of his claim."

A higher sort of oath is this: The accused person is invited to drink the *bísh* (*visha*?) called *brahmaṇa* (?). It is one of the worst kinds; but if he speaks the truth, the drink does not do him any harm.

A still higher sort of ordeal is this: They bring the Page 280. man to a deep and rapidly flowing river, or to a deep well with much water. Then he speaks to the water: "Since thou belongest to the pure angels, and knowest both what is secret and public, kill me if I lie, and preserve me if I speak the truth." Then five men take him between them and throw him into the water. If he has spoken the truth, he will not drown and die.

A still higher sort is the following: The judge sends both claimant and defendant to the temple of the most venerated idol of the town or realm. There the defendant has to fast during that day. On the following day he dresses in new garments, and posts himself together with the claimant in that temple. Then the priests pour water over the idol and give it him to drink. If he, then, has not spoken the truth, he at once vomits blood.

A still higher sort is the following: The defendant is placed on the scale of a balance, and is weighed; whereupon he is taken off the scale, and the scale is left as it is. Then he invokes as witnesses for the truth of his deposition the spiritual beings, the angels, the heavenly beings, one after the other, and all which he speaks he writes down on a piece of paper, and fastens it to his head. He is a second time placed in the scale of the balance. In case he has spoken the truth, he now weighs more than the first time.

There is also a still higher sort. It is the following: They take butter and sesame-oil in equal quantities, and boil them in a kettle. Then they throw a leaf into it, which by getting flaccid and burned is to them a sign of the boiling of the mixture. When the boiling is at its height, they throw a piece of gold into the kettle and order the defendant to fetch it out with his hand. If he has spoken the truth, he fetches it out.

The highest kind of ordeal is the following: They make a piece of iron so hot that it is near melting, and put it with a pair of tongs on the hand of the defendant, there being nothing between his hand and the iron save a broad leaf of some plant, and under it some few and scattered corns of rice in the husks. They order him to carry it seven paces, and then he may throw it to the ground.

CHAPTER LXXI.

ON PUNISHMENTS AND EXPIATIONS.

In this regard the manners and customs of the Hindus resemble those of the Christians, for they are, like those of the latter, based on the principles of virtue and abstinence from wickedness, such as never to kill under any circumstance whatsoever, to give to him who has stripped you of your coat also your shirt, to offer to him who has beaten your cheek the other cheek also, to bless your enemy and to pray for him. Upon my life, this is a noble philosophy; but the people of this world are not all philosophers. Most of them are ignorant and erring, who cannot be kept on the straight road save by the sword and the whip. And, indeed, ever since Constantine the Victorious became a Christian, both sword and whip have ever been employed, for without them it would be impossible to rule.

The Brahmans originally the rulers of the nation.

India has developed in a similar way. For the Hindus relate that originally the affairs of government and war were in the hands of the Brahmans, but the country became disorganised, since they ruled according to the philosophic principles of their religious codes, which proved impossible when opposed to the mischievous and perverse elements of the populace. They were even near losing also the administration of their religious affairs. Therefore they humiliated themselves before the lord of their religion. Whereupon Brahman intrusted them exclusively with the functions which they now have, whilst he intrusted the Kshatriyas with the

Page 281.

duties of ruling and fighting. Ever since the Brahmans live by asking and begging, and the penal code is exercised under the control of the kings, not under that of the scholars.

Law of murder.

The law about murder is this: If the murderer is a Brahman, and the murdered person a member of another caste, he is only bound to do expiation consisting of fasting, prayers, and almsgiving.

If the murdered person is a Brahman, the Brahman murderer has to answer for it in a future life; for he is not allowed to do expiation, because expiation wipes off the sin from the sinner, whilst nothing can wipe off any of the mortal crimes from a Brahman, of which the greatest are: the murder of a Brahman, called *vajra-brahmahatyâ*; further, the killing of a cow, the drinking of wine, whoredom, especially with the wife of one's own father and teacher. However, the kings do not for any of these crimes kill a Brahman or Kshatriya, but they confiscate his property and banish him from their country.

If a man of a caste under those of the Brahman and Kshatriya kills a man of the same caste, he has to do expiation, but besides the kings inflict upon him a punishment in order to establish an example.

Law of theft.

The law of theft directs that the punishment of the thief should be in accordance with the value of the stolen object. Accordingly, sometimes a punishment of extreme or of middling severity is necessary, sometimes a course of correction and imposing a payment, sometimes only exposing to public shame and ridicule. If the object is very great, the kings blind a Brahman and mutilate him, cutting off his left hand and right foot, or the right hand and left foot, whilst they mutilate a Kshatriya without blinding him, and kill thieves of the other castes.

Punishment of an adulteress.

An adulteress is driven out of the house of the husband and banished.

I have repeatedly been told that when Hindu slaves

(in Muslim countries) escape and return to their country and religion, the Hindus order that they should fast by way of expiation, then they bury them in the dung, stale, and milk of cows for a certain number of days, till they get into a state of fermentation. Then they drag them out of the dirt and give them similar dirt to eat, and more of the like.

Hindu prisoners of war, how treated after returning to their country.

I have asked the Brahmans if this is true, but they deny it, and maintain that there is no expiation possible for such an individual, and that he is never allowed to return into those conditions of life in which he was before he was carried off as a prisoner. And how should that be possible? If a Brahman eats in the house of a Śûdra for sundry days, he is expelled from his caste and can never regain it.

CHAPTER LXXII.

ON INHERITANCE, AND WHAT CLAIM THE DECEASED PERSON HAS ON IT.

Law of inheritance.

THE chief rule of their law of inheritance is this, that the women do not inherit, except the daughter. She gets the fourth part of the share of a son, according to a passage in the book *Manu*. If she is not married, the money is spent on her till the time of her marriage, and her dowry is bought by means of her share. Afterwards she has no more income from the house of her father.

If a widow does not burn herself, but prefers to remain alive, the heir of her deceased husband has to provide her with nourishment and clothing as long as she lives.

The debts of the deceased must be paid by his heir, either out of his share or of the stock of his own property, no regard being had whether the deceased has left any property or not. Likewise he must bear the just-mentioned expenses for the widow in any case whatsoever.

As regards the rule about the male heirs, evidently the descendants, *i.e.* the son and grandson, have a nearer claim to the inheritance than the ascendants, *i.e.* the
Page 282.
father and grandfather. Further, as regards the single relatives among the descendants as well as the ascendants, the nearer a man is related, the more claim he has on inheriting. Thus a son has a nearer claim than a grandson, a father than a grandfather.

The collateral relations, as, *e.g.* the brothers, have less claim, and inherit only in case there is nobody who has a better claim. Hence it is evident that the son of a daughter has more claim than the son of a sister, and that the son of a brother has more claim than either of them.

If there are several claimants of the same degree of relationship, as, *e.g.*, sons or brothers, they all get equal shares. A hermaphrodite is reckoned as a male being.

If the deceased leaves no heir, the inheritance falls to the treasury of the king, except in the case that the deceased person was a Brahman. In that case the king has no right to meddle with the inheritance, but it is exclusively spent on almsgiving.

Duties of the heir towards the deceased.

The duty of the heir towards the deceased in the first year consists in his giving sixteen banquets, where every guest in addition to his food receives alms also, viz. on the fifteenth and sixteenth days after death; further, once a month during the whole year. The banquet in the sixth month must be more rich and more liberal than the others. Further, on the last but one day of the year, which banquet is devoted to the deceased and his ancestors; and finally, on the last day of the year. With the end of the year the duties towards the deceased have been fulfilled.

If the heir is a son, he must during the whole year wear mourning dress; he must mourn and have no intercourse with women, if he is a legitimate child and of a good stock. Besides, you must know that nourishment is forbidden to the heirs for one single day in the first part of the mourning-year.

Besides the almsgiving at the just-mentioned sixteen banquets, the heirs must make, above the door of the house, something like a shelf projecting from the wall in the open air, on which they have every day to place a dish of something cooked and a vessel of water, till the end of ten days after the death. For possibly the spirit of the deceased has not yet found its rest, but moves still to and fro around the house, hungry and thirsty.

Parallel from Plato.

A similar view is indicated by Plato in *Phaedo*, where he speaks of the soul circling round the graves, because possibly it still retains some vestiges of the love for the body. Further he says: "People have said regarding the soul that it is its habit to combine something coherent out of the single limbs of the body, which is its dwelling in this as well as in the future world, when it leaves the body, and is by the death of the body separated from it."

On the tenth of the last-mentioned days, the heir spends, in the name of the deceased, much food and cold water. After the eleventh day, the heir sends every day sufficient food for a single person and a *dirham* to the house of the Brahman, and continues doing this during all the days of the mourning-year without any interruption until its end.

CHAPTER LXXIII.

ABOUT WHAT IS DUE TO THE BODIES OF THE DEAD AND OF THE LIVING (*i.e.* ABOUT BURYING AND SUICIDE).

Primitive burial-customs.

IN the most ancient times the bodies of the dead were exposed to the air by being thrown on the fields without any covering; also sick people were exposed on the fields and in the mountains, and were left there. If they died there, they had the fate just mentioned; but if they recovered, they returned to their dwellings.

Page 283.

Thereupon there appeared a legislator who ordered people to expose their dead to the wind. In consequence they constructed roofed buildings with walls of rails, through which the wind blew, passing over the dead, as something similar is the case in the grave-towers of the Zoroastrians.

After they had practised this custom for a long time, Nârâyaṇa prescribed to them to hand the dead over to the fire, and ever since they are in the habit of burning them, so that nothing remains of them, and every defilement, dirt, and smell is annihilated at once, so as scarcely to leave any trace behind.

Greek parallels.

Nowadays the Slavonians, too, burn their dead, whilst the ancient Greeks seem to have had both customs, that of burning and that of burying. Socrates speaks in the book *Phaedo*, after Crito had asked him in what manner he wanted to be buried: "As you wish, when you make arrangements for me. I shall not flee from you." Then he spoke to those around him: "Give to Crito regarding myself the opposite guarantee of that which he has given to the judges regarding myself; for he guaranteed to them that I should stay, whilst you now must guarantee that I shall not stay after death. I shall go away, that the look of my body may be tolerable to Crito when it is *burned* or *buried*, that he may not be in agony, and not say: 'Socrates is carried away, or is burned or buried.' Thou, O Crito, be at ease about the burial of my body. Do as thou likest, and specially in accordance with the laws."

Galenus says in his commentary to the apothegms of Hippocrates: "It is generally known that Asclepius was raised to the angels in a column of fire, the like of which is also related with regard to Dionysos, Heracles, and others, who laboured for the benefit of mankind. People say that God did thus with them in order to destroy the mortal and earthly part of them by the fire, and afterwards to attract to himself the immortal part of them, and to raise their souls to heaven."

In these words, too, there is a reference to the burning as a Greek custom, but it seems to have been in use only for the great men among them.

In a similar way the Hindus express themselves. There is a point in man by which he is what he is. This point becomes free when the mixed elements of the body are dissolved and scattered by combustion.

Fire and the sunbeam as the nearest roads to God.

Regarding this return (of the immortal soul to God), the Hindus think that partly it is effected by the rays of the sun, the soul attaching itself to them and ascending with them, partly by the flame of the fire, which raises it (to God). Some Hindu used to pray that God would make his road to himself as a straight line, because this is the nearest road, and that there is no other road upwards save the fire or the ray.

Similar to this is the practice of the Ghuzz Turks with reference to a drowned person; for they place the body on a bier in the river, and make a cord hang down from his foot, throwing the end of the cord into the water. By means of this cord the spirit of the deceased is to raise himself for resurrection.

The belief of the Hindus on this head was confirmed by the words of Vâsudeva, which he spoke regarding the sign of him who is liberated from the fetters (of bodily existence). "His death takes place during *uttarâyana* (*i.e.* the northern revolution of the sun from the winter solstice to the summer solstice), during the white half of the month, *between lighted lamps, i.e.* between conjunction and opposition (new moon and full moon), in the seasons of winter and spring."

Quotation from Mânî. Page 284.

A similar view is recognised in the following words of Mânî: "The other religious bodies blame us because we worship sun and moon, and represent them as an image. But they do not know their real natures; they do not know that sun and moon are our path, the door whence we march forth into the world of our existence (into heaven), as this has been declared by Jesus." So he maintains.

People relate that Buddha had ordered the bodies of the dead to be thrown into flowing water. Therefore his followers, the Shamanians, throw their dead into the rivers.

Hindu manner of burial.

According to the Hindus, the body of the dead has the claim upon his heirs that they are to wash, embalm, wrap it in a shroud, and then to burn it with as much sandal and other wood as they can get. Part of his burned bones are brought to the Ganges and thrown into it, that the Ganges should flow over them, as it has flowed over the burned bones of the children of Sagara, thereby forcing them from hell and bringing them into paradise. The remainder of the ashes is thrown into some brook of running water. On the spot where the body has been burned they raise a monument similar to a milestone, plastered with gypsum.

The bodies of children under three years are not burned.

Those who fulfil these duties towards the dead afterwards wash themselves as well as their dresses during two days, because they have become unclean by touching the dead.

Those who cannot afford to burn their dead will either throw them somewhere on the open field or into running water.

Modes of suicide.

Now as regards the right of the body of the living, the Hindus would not think of burning it save in the case of a widow who chooses to follow her husband, or in the case of those who are tired of their life, who are distressed over some incurable disease of their body, some irremovable bodily defect, or old age and infirmity. This, however, no man of distinction does, but only Vaiśyas and Śûdras, especially at those times which are prized as the most suitable for a man to acquire in them, for a future repetition of life, a better form and condition than that in which he happens to have been born and to live. Burning oneself is forbidden to Brahmans and Kshatriyas by a special law. Therefore these, if they want to kill themselves, do so at the time of an eclipse in some other manner, or they hire somebody to drown them in the Ganges, keeping them under water till they are dead.

The tree of Prayâga.

At the junction of the two rivers, Yamunâ and Ganges, there is a great tree called *Prayâga*, a tree of the species called *vaṭa*. It is peculiar to this kind of tree that its branches send forth two species of twigs, some directed upward, as is the case with all other trees, and others directed downward like roots, but without leaves. If such a twig enters into the soil, it is like a supporting column to the branch whence it has grown. Nature has arranged this on purpose, since the branches of this tree are of an enormous extent (and require to be supported). Here the Brahmans and Kshatriyas are in the habit of committing suicide by climbing up the tree and throwing themselves into the Ganges.

Johannes Grammaticus relates that certain people in ancient Greek heathendom, "whom I call the *worshippers of the devil*"—so he says—used to beat their limbs with swords, and to throw themselves into the fire, without feeling any pain therefrom. Greek parallels.

As we have related this as a view of the Hindus not to commit suicide, so also Socrates speaks: "Likewise it does not become a man to kill himself before the gods give him a cause in the shape of some compulsion or *dire necessity*, like that in which we now are."

Further he says: "We human beings are, as it were, in a prison. It does not behove us to flee nor to free ourselves from it, because the gods take notice of us, since we, the human beings, are servants to them."

CHAPTER LXXIV.

ON FASTING, AND THE VARIOUS KINDS OF IT.

FASTING is with the Hindus voluntary and supererogatory. Fasting is abstaining from food for a certain length of time, which may be different in duration and
Page 285.
in the manner in which it is carried out.

Various methods of fasting.

The ordinary middle process, by which all the conditions of fasting are realised, is this: A man determines the day on which he will fast, and keeps in mind the name of that being whose benevolence he wishes to gain thereby and for whose sake he will fast, be it a god, or an angel, or some other being. Then he proceeds, prepares (and takes) his food on the day before the fast-day at noon, cleans his teeth by rubbing, and fixes his thoughts on the fasting of the following day. From that moment he abstains from food. On the morning of the fast-day he again rubs his teeth, washes himself, and performs the duties of the day. He takes water in his hand, and sprinkles it into all four directions, he pronounces with his tongue the name of the deity for whom he fasts, and remains in this condition till the day after the fast-day. After the sun has risen, he is at liberty to break the fast at that moment if he likes, or, if he prefers, he may postpone it till noon.

This kind is called *upavâsa, i.e.* the fasting; for the not-eating from one noon to the following is called *ekanakta*, not fasting.

Another kind, called *kṛicchra*, is this: A man takes his food on some day at noon, and on the following day in the evening. On the third day he eats nothing except what by chance is given him without his asking for it. On the fourth day he fasts.

Another kind, called *parâka,* is this: A man takes his food at noon on three consecutive days. Then he transfers his eating-hour to the evening during three further consecutive days. Then he fasts uninterruptedly during three consecutive days without breaking fast.

Another kind, called *candrâyaṇa,* is this: A man fasts on the day of full moon; on the following day he takes only a mouthful, on the third day he takes double this amount, on the fourth day the threefold of it, &c., &c., going on thus till the day of new moon. On that day he fasts; on the following days he again diminishes his food by one mouthful a day, till he again fasts on the day of full moon.

Another kind, called *mâsavâsa* (*mâsopavâsa*), is this: A man uninterruptedly fasts all the days of a month without ever breaking fast.

Reward of the fasting in the single months.

The Hindus explain accurately what reward the latter fasting in every single month will bring to a man for a new life of his after he has died. They say:

If a man fasts all the days of Caitra, he obtains wealth and joy over the nobility of his children.

If he fasts Vaiśâkha, he will be a lord over his tribe and great in his army.

If he fasts Jyaishṭha, he will be a favourite of the women.

If he fasts Âshâḍha, he will obtain wealth.

If he fasts Śrâvaṇa, he obtains wisdom.

If he fasts Bhâdrapada, he obtains health and valour, riches and cattle.

If he fasts Âśvayuja, he will always be victorious over his enemies.

If he fasts Kârttika, he will be grand in the eyes of people and will obtain his wishes.

If he fasts Mârgaśîrsha, he will be born in the most beautiful and fertile country.

If he fasts Pausha, he obtains a high reputation.

If he fasts Mâgha, he obtains innumerable wealth.

If he fasts Phâlguna, he will be beloved.

He, however, who fasts during all the months of the year, only twelve times breaking the fast, will reside in paradise 10,000 years, and will thence return to life as the member of a noble, high, and respected family.

The book *Vishṇu-Dharma* relates that Maitreyî, the
Page 286. wife of Yâjnavalkya, asked her husband what man is to do in order to save his children from calamities and bodily defects, upon which he answered: "If a man begins on the day Duvê, in the month Pausha, *i.e.* the second day of each of the two halves of the month, and fasts four consecutive days, washing himself on the first with water, on the second with sesame oil, on the third with galangale, and on the fourth with a mixture of various balms; if he further on each day gives alms and recites praises over the names of the angels; if he continue to do all this during each month till the end of the year, his children will in the following life be free from calamities and defects, and he will obtain what he wishes; for also *Dilîpa, Dushyanta,* and *Yayâti* obtained their wishes for having acted thus."

(Chapters LXXV–LXXIX, pages 175–210, contain technical discussions on Hindu methods for determining fast-days and other ceremonial occasions by the sun, moon, and stars.)

CHAPTER LXXX.

ON THE INTRODUCTORY PRINCIPLES OF HINDU ASTROLOGY, WITH A SHORT DESCRIPTION OF THEIR METHODS OF ASTROLOGICAL CALCULATIONS.

Indian astrology unknown among Muhammadans.

OUR fellow-believers in these (Muslim) countries are not acquainted with the Hindu methods of astrology, and have never had an opportunity of studying an Indian book on the subject. In consequence, they imagine that Hindu astrology is the same as theirs and relate all sorts of things as being of Indian origin, of which we have not found a single trace with the Hindus themselves. As in the preceding part of this our book we have given something of everything, we shall also give as much of their astrological doctrine as will enable the reader to discuss questions of a similar nature with them. If we were to give an exhaustive representation of the subject, this task would detain us Page 302. very long, even if we limited ourselves to delineate only the leading principles and avoided all details.

First, the reader must know that in most of their prognostics they simply rely on means like auguring from the flight of birds and physiognomy, that they do not—as they ought to do—draw conclusions, regarding the affairs of the sublunary world, from the seconds (*sic*) of the stars, which are the events of the celestial sphere.

On the planets.

Regarding the number seven as that of the planets, there is no difference between us and them. They call them *graha*. Some of them are throughout lucky, viz.

Jupiter, Venus and the Moon, which are called *saumyagraha.* Other three are throughout unlucky, viz. Saturn, Mars, and the Sun, which are called *krûragraha.* Among the latter, they also count the dragon's head, though in reality it is not a star. The nature of one planet is variable and depends upon the nature of that planet with which it is combined, whether it be lucky or unlucky. This is Mercury. However, alone by itself, it is lucky.

The following table represents the natures of the seven planets and everything else concerning them:—

Names of the planets.	*Sun.*	*Moon.*	*Mars.*	*Mercury.*	*Jupiter.*	*Venus.*	*Saturn.*
Whether they are lucky or unlucky.	Unlucky.	Lucky, but depending upon the planet near her. Middling in the first, lucky in the second, and unlucky in the last ten days of the month.	Unlucky.	Lucky, when it is alone. Else depending upon the nature of the planet near it.	Lucky.	Lucky.	Unlucky.
What elements they indicate.	...	...	Fire.	Earth.	Heaven.	Water.	Wind.
Whether they indicate male or female beings.	Male.	Female.	Male.	Neither male nor female.	Male.	Female.	Neither male nor female.
Whether they indicate day or night.	Day.	Night.	Night.	Day and night together.	Day.	Day.	Night.
What point of the compass they indicate.	East.	North-west.	South.	North.	North-east.	Between east and west.	West.
What colour they indicate.	Bronze-colour.	White.	Light red.	Pistachio-green.	Gold-colour.	Many colours.	Black.
What time they indicate.	Ayana.	Muhûrta.	Day.	*Ṛitu, i.e.* a sixth part of the year.	Month.	*Pǎksha, i.e.* half a month.	Year.

Page 303.

Names of the planets.	*Sun.*	*Moon.*	*Mars.*	*Mercury.*	*Jupiter.*	*Venus.*	*Saturn.*
What season they indicate.	o	Varsha.	Grîshma.	Śarad.	Hemanta.	Vasanta.	Śiśira.
What taste they indicate.	Bitter.	Saltish.	...	A mixture of all tastes.	Sweet.	...	...
What material they indicate.	Bronze.	Crystal.	Gold.	Small pearls.	Silver, or if the constellation is very strong, gold.	Pearl.	Iron.
What dress and clothes they indicate.	Thick.	New.	Burned.	Wet from water.	Between new and shabby.	Whole.	Burned.
What angel they indicate.	Nema (?).	Ambu, the water.	Agni, the fire.	Brahman.	Mahâdeva.	Indra.	...
What caste they indicate.	Kshatriyas and commanders.	Vaiśyas and commanders.	Kshatriyas and generals.	Śûdras and princes.	Brahmans and ministers.	Brahmans and ministers.	...
Which Veda they indicate.	o	o	Sâmaveda.	Atharvaṇaveda.	Ṛigveda.	Yajurveda.	o
The months of pregnancy.	The fourth month, in which the bones become hard.	The fifth month, in which the skin appears.	The second month, in which the embyro attains consistency.	The seventh month, in which the child becomes complete, and receives the memory	The third month, in which the limbs begin to branch off.	The first month, in which the semen and the menstrual blood become mixed	The sixth month, when the hair grows.

Character as based on the three primary forces.	Satya.	Satya.	Tamas.	Rajas.	Satya.	Rajas.	Tamas.
Mitra. { Friendly planets.	Jupiter, Mars, Moon.	Sun, Mercury.	Jupiter, Sun, Moon.	Sun, Venus.	Sun, Moon, Mars.	Saturn, Mercury.	Venus, Mercury.
Śatru. { Hostile planets.	Saturn, Venus.	There is no planet hostile to her.	Mercury.	Moon.	Venus, Mercury.	Sun, Moon.	Mars, Sun, Moon.
Vi-miśra. { Indifferent planets.	Mercury.	Saturn, Jupiter, Mars, Venus.	Venus, Saturn.	Saturn, Jupiter, Mars.	Saturn.	Jupiter, Mars.	Jupiter.
What parts of the body they indicate.	The breath and the bones.	The root of the tongue and the blood.	The flesh and brain.	Voice and skin.	Intellect and fat.	Semen.	Sinews, flesh, and pain.
The scale of their magnitude.	1	2	6	5	4	25 (!)	7
Years of *shaḍâya*.	19	25	15	12	15	21	20
Years of *nai-s argka*.	20	1	2	9	18	20	50

Explanatory notes to the preceding table.

The column of this table which indicates the order of the size and power of the planets, serves for the following purpose:—Sometimes two planets indicate exactly the same thing, exercise the same influence, and stand in the same relation to the event in question. In this case, the preference is given to that planet which, in the column in question, is described as the larger or the more powerful of the two.

The months of pregnancy.

The column relating to the months of pregnancy is to be completed by the remark that they consider the eighth month as standing under the influence of a horoscope which causes abortion. According to them, the embryo takes, in this month, the fine substances of the food. If it takes all of them and is then born, it will remain alive; but if it is born before that, it will die from some deficiency in its formation. The ninth month stands under the influence of the moon, the tenth under that of the sun. They do not speak of a longer duration of pregnancy, but if it happens to last longer, they believe that, during this time, some injury is brought about by the wind. At the time of the horoscope of abortion, which they determine by tradition, not by calculation,
Page 304.
they observe the conditions and influences of the planets and give their decision accordingly as this or that planet happens to preside over the month in question.

Friendship and enmity of the planets.

The question as to the friendship and enmity of the planets among each other, as well as the influence of the *dominus domûs*, is of great importance in their astrology. Sometimes it may happen that, at a particular moment of time, this *dominium* entirely loses its original character. Further on we shall give a rule as to the computation of the *dominium* and its single years.

The zodiacal signs.

There is no difference between us and the Hindus regarding the number twelve as the number of the signs of the ecliptic, nor regarding the manner in which the *dominium* of the planets is distributed over them.

The following table shows what qualities are peculiar to each zodiacal sign as a whole:—

The Zodiacal Signs.	*Aries.*	*Taurus.*	*Gemini.*	*Cancer.*	*Leo.*	*Virgo.*	*Libra.*	*Scorpio.*	*Arcitenens.*	*Capricornus.*	*Amphora.*	*Pisces.*
Their dominants.	Mars.	Venus.	Mercury.	Moon.	Sun.	Mercury.	Venus.	Mars.	Jupiter.	Saturn.	Saturn.	Jupiter.
Altitudes: Degrees.	10	3	0	0	0	15	20	0	0	28	0	27
Altitudes: Altitude.	Sun.	Moon.	0	Jupiter.	0	Mercury.	Saturn.	0	0	Mars.	0	Venus.
Dominants of the *mûlatrikoṇa*.	Mars.	Moon.	0	0	Sun.	Mercury.	Venus.	0	Jupiter.	0	Saturn.	0
Whether male or female.	Male.	Female.	Male.	Female.	Male.	Female.	Male.	Female.	Male.	Female.	Male.	Female.
Whether lucky or unlucky.	Unlucky.	Lucky.	Unlucky.	Lucky.	Unlucky.	Lucky.	Unlucky.	Lucky.	Unlucky.	Lucky.	Unlucky.	Lucky.
The colours.	Reddish.	White.	Green.	Yellowish.	Gray.	Many coloured.	Black.	Golden.	...	Striped white and black.	Brown.	Dust-coloured.
The directions.	Due east.	S.S.E.	W.S.W.	N.N.W.	E.N.E.	Due south.	Due west.	Due north.	E.S.E.	S.S.W.	W.N.W.	N.N.E.
In what manner they rise.	Stretched on the ground.	Stretched on the ground.	Lying on the side.	Stretched on the ground.	Standing erect.	Standing erect.	Standing erect.	Standing erect.	Stretched on the ground.	Stretched on the ground.	Standing erect.	Standing erect.

Page 305.

The Zodiacal Signs.	*Aries.*	*Taurus.*	*Gemini.*	*Cancer.*	*Leo.*	*Virgo.*	*Libra.*	*Scorpio.*	*Arcitenens.*	*Capricornus.*	*Amphora.*	*Pisces.*
Whether turning, fixed or double-bodied.	Moving.	Resting.	Moving and resting together.	Moving.	Resting.	Moving and resting together.	Moving.	Resting.	Moving and resting together.	Moving.	Resting.	Moving and resting together.
Whether at night, or during day, according to some people.	At night.	At night.	At night.	At night.	During day.	During day.	During day.	During day.	At night.	At night.	During day.	During day.
What parts of the body they indicate.	Head.	Face.	Shoulders and hands.	Breast.	Belly.	Hip.	Under the navel.	Male and female genitals.	The loins.	The knees.	The calves.	The two feet.
Seasons.	Vasanta.	Grîshma.	Grîshma.	Varsha.	Varsha.	Śarad.	Śarad.	Hemanta.	Hemanta.	Śiśira.	Śiśira	Vasanta.
Their figures.	A ram.	An ox.	A man with a lyre, and a club in his hand.	Crab.	Lion.	A girl with an ear of corn in her hand.	A scale.	A scorpion.	A horse, the head and upper half of which have human shape.	A being with the face of a goat. There is much water in its figure.	A kind of boat or barge.	Two fishes.

What kinds of beings they are.	Quadruped.	Quadruped.	Human biped.	Amphibious.	Quadruped.	Biped.	Biped.	Amphibious.	The upper half a biped, the lower half a quadruped.	The first half a biped, the latter half watery.	The first half a biped, the other half watery, or the whole a human being.	Watery.
The times of their strongest influence according to the different kinds.	At night.	At night.	During the day.	During the saṁdhi.	At night.	During the day.	During the day.	During the saṁdhi.	The human part during the day, the other at night.	During the saṁdhi.	The human part in daytime, the other at night.	During the saṁdhi.

Explanation of some technical terms of astrology.

The *height* or *altitudo* of a planet is called, in the Indian language, *uccastha*, its particular degree *paramoccastha*. The *depth* or *dejectio* of a planet is called *nîcastha*, its particular degree *paramanîcastha*. *Mûlatrikoṇa* is a powerful influence, attributed to a planet, when it is in the *gaudium* in one of its two houses (cf. ii. 225).

They do not refer the *aspectus trigoni* to the elements and the elementary natures, as it is our custom to do, but refer them to the points of the compass in general, as has been specified in the table.

They call the *turning* zodiacal sign (τροπικόν) *cararâśi*, *i.e.* moving, the *fixed* one (στερεόν) *sthirarâśi*, *i.e.* the *resting* one, and the *double-bodied* one (δίσωμα) *dvisvabhâva*, *i.e.* both together.

The houses.

As we have given a table of the zodiacal signs, we next give a table of the *houses* (*domus*), showing the qualities of each of them. The one half of them above

Page 306.

the earth they call *chatra*, *i.e.* parasol, and the half under the earth they call *nau*, *i.e.* ship. Further, they call the half ascending to the midst of heaven and the other half descending to the *cardo* of the earth, *dhanu*, *i.e.* the bow. The *cardines* they call *kendra* (κέντρον), the next following houses *paṇaphara* (ἐπαναφορά), and the *inclining* houses *âpoklima* (ἀπόκλιμα):—

The Houses.	What they indicate.	On the *aspects*, the *ascendens* being taken as basis.	Which zodiacal signs exercise the greatest influence in them.	Which planets exercise the greatest influence in them.	How much is to be subtracted from the unlucky years of the House.	How much is to be subtracted from the lucky years of the House.	How they are divided according to the horizon.	Into what classes they are divided according to the shadow of noon.
Ascendens.	Head and soul.	Basis for the calculation.	The human signs.	Mercury and Jupiter.	0	0	Ship.	Ascending bow.
II.	Face and property.	Two stand in aspect with the *ascendens.*	0	0	0	0		
III.	The two arms and brothers.	The *ascendens* looks towards it, but it does not look towards the *ascendens.*	0	0	0	0		
IV.	Heart, parents, friends, house, and joy.	Two stand in aspect with the *ascendens.*	The watery signs.	Venus and Moon.	0	0		Descending bow.
V.	Belly, child, and cleverness.	Two stand in aspect with the *ascendens.*	0	0	0	0		
VI.	The two sides, the enemy and riding animals.	It looks towards the *ascendens*, but the *ascendens* does not look towards it.	0	0	0	0		
VII.	Under the navel and women.	Two stand in aspect with the *ascendens.*	...	Saturn.	$\frac{1}{6}$ of them.	$\frac{1}{12}$ of them.	Parasol.	
VIII.	Return and death.	The *ascendens* looks towards it, but it does not look towards the *ascendens.*	...	0	$\frac{1}{5}$	$\frac{1}{10}$		
IX.	The two loins, journey and debt.	Two stand in aspect with the *ascendens.*	...	0	$\frac{1}{4}$	$\frac{1}{8}$		

The Houses.	What they indicate.	On the *aspects*, the *ascendens* being taken as basis.	Which zodiacal signs exercise the greatest influence in them.	Which planets exercise the greatest influence in them.	How much is to be subtracted from the unlucky years of the House.	How much is to be subtracted from the lucky years of the House.	How they are divided according to the horizon.	Into what classes they are divided according to the shadow of noon.
X.	The two knees and action.	Two stand in aspect with the *ascendens*.	The quadrupeds.	Mars.	⅓	⅙	Parasol.	Ascending bow.
XI.	The two calves and income.	It looks towards the *ascendens*, but the *ascendens* does not look towards it.	o	o	½	¼		
XII.	The two feet and expenses.	Two do not stand in aspect with the *ascendens*.	o	o	The whole.	½		

Page 307. The hitherto mentioned details are in reality the cardinal-points of Hindu astrology, viz. the planets, zodiacal signs, and *houses*. He who knows how to find out what each of them means or portends deserves the title of a clever adept and of a master in this art.

On the division of a zodiacal sign in *nîmbahras*. Next follows the division of the zodiacal signs in minor portions, first that in *nîmbahras*, which are called *horâ*, *i.e.* hour, because half a sign rises in about an hour's time. The first half of each *male* sign is unlucky as standing under the influence of the sun, because he produces male beings, whilst the second half is lucky as standing under the influence of the moon, because she produces female beings. On the contrary, in the *female* signs the first half is lucky, and the second unlucky.

2. In *drekkâṇas*. Further, there are the triangles, called *drekkâṇa*. There is no use in enlarging on them, as they are simply identical with the so-called *draijânât* of our system.

3. In *nuhbahras*. Further, the *nuhbahrât* (Persian, "*the nine parts*"),

called *navâṁśaka*. As our books of introduction to the art of astrology mention two kinds of them, we shall here explain the Hindu theory regarding them, for the information of Indophiles. You reduce the distance between 0° of the sign and that minute, the *nuhbahr* of which you want to find, to minutes, and divide the number by 200. The quotient represents complete *nuhbahras* or ninth-parts, beginning with the *turning* sign, which is in the triangle of the sign in question; you count the number off on the consecutive signs, so that one sign corresponds to one *nuhbahr*. That sign which corresponds to the last of the ninth-parts which you have is the dominant of the *nuhbahr* we want to find.

The first *nuhbahr* of each *turning* sign, the fifth of each *fixed* sign, and the ninth of each *double-bodied* sign is called *vargottama*, *i.e.* the greatest portion.

4. In twelfth-parts.

Further, the *twelfth-parts*, called *the twelve rulers*. For a certain place within a sign they are found in the following manner:—Reduce the distance between 0° of the sign and the place in question to minutes, and divide the number by 150. The quotient represents complete *twelfth-parts*, which you count off on the following signs, beginning with the sign in question, so that one twelfth-part corresponds to one sign. The dominant of the sign, to which the last twelfth-part corresponds, is at the same time the dominant of the twelfth-part of the place in question.

5. In 30 degrees or ὅρια.

Further, *the degrees* called *triṅśâṁśaka*, *i.e.* the thirty degrees, which correspond to our *limits* (or ὅρια). Their order is this: The first five *degrees* of each *male* sign belong to Mars, the next following five to Saturn, the next eight to Jupiter, the next seven to Mercury, and the last five to Venus. Just the reverse order takes place in the *female* signs, viz. the first five *degrees* belong to Venus, the next seven to Mercury, the next eight to Jupiter, the next five to Saturn, and the last five to Mercury.

These are the elements on which every astrological calculation is based.

On the different kinds of the *aspect*.

The nature of the aspect of every sign depends upon the nature of the *ascendens* which at a given moment rises above the horizon. Regarding the *aspects* they have the following rule:—

A sign does not look at, *i.e.* does not stand *in aspectu* with the two signs immediately before and after it. On the contrary, each pair of signs, the beginnings of which are distant from each other by one-fourth or one-third or one-half of the circle, stand in aspect with each other. If the distance between two signs is one-sixth of the circle, the signs forming this *aspect* are counted in their original order; but if the distance is five-twelfths of the circle, the signs forming the *aspect* are counted in the inverse order.

There are various degrees of *aspects*, viz.:—

The aspect between one sign and the fourth or eleventh following one is a *fourth-part* of an aspect;

The aspect between one sign and the fifth or ninth following one is *half* an aspect;

The aspect between a sign and the sixth or tenth following one is *three-quarters* of an aspect;

The aspect between a sign and the seventh following one is a *whole* aspect.

The Hindus do not speak of an *aspect* between two planets which stand in one and the same sign.

Friendship and enmity of certain planets in relation to each other.

With reference to the change between the friendship and enmity of single planets with regard to each other, the Hindus have the following rule:—

Page 308.

If a planet comes to stand in signs which, in relation to its rising, are the tenth, eleventh, twelfth, first, second, third, and fourth signs, its nature undergoes a change for the better. If it is most inimical, it becomes moderated; if it is moderated, it becomes friendly; if it is friendly, it becomes most friendly. If the planet comes to stand in all the other signs, its nature undergoes a change for the worse. If originally it is friendly, it becomes moderate; if it is moderate, it becomes inimical; if it is inimical, it becomes even worse. Under such circumstances, the nature of a planet is an accidental one for the time being, associating itself with its original nature.

After having explained these things, we now proceed to mention *the four forces* which are peculiar to each planet:— **The four forces of each planet.**

I. The habitual force, called *sthânabala,* which the planet exercises, when it stands in its *altitudo,* its *house,* or the house of its friend, or in the *nuhbahr* of its house, or its *altitudo,* or its *mûlatrikoṇa, i.e.* its *gaudium* in the line of the lucky planets. This force is peculiar to sun and moon when they are in the lucky signs, as it is peculiar to the other planets when they are in the unlucky signs. Especially this force is peculiar to the moon in the first third of her lunation, when it helps every planet which stands *in aspect* with her to acquire the same force. Lastly, it is peculiar to the *ascendens* if it is a sign representing a biped. **Laghujâtakam, ch. ii. 8.**

II. The force called *dṛishṭibala, i.e.* the lateral one, also called *dṛigbala,* which the planet exercises when standing in the *cardo* in which it is strong, and, according to some people, also when standing in the two houses immediately before and after the *cardo.* It is peculiar to the *ascendens* in the day, if it is a sign representing a biped, and in the night, if it is a four-footed sign, and in both the *saṁdhis* (periods of twilight at the beginning and end) of the other signs. This in particular refers to the astrology of nativities. In the other parts of astrology this force is peculiar, as they maintain, to the tenth sign if it represents a quadruped, to the seventh sign if it is Scorpio and Cancer, and to the fourth sign if it is Amphora and Cancer. **Lagh. ii. 11.**

III. *The conquering force,* called *ceshṭâbala,* which a planet exercises, when it is in retrograde motion, **Lagh. ii. 5.**

when it emerges from concealment, marching as a visible star till the end of four signs, and when in the north it meets one of the planets except Venus. For to Venus the south is the same as the north is to the other planets. If the two (——— ? illegible) stand in it (the south), it is peculiar to them that they stand in the ascending half (of the sun's annual rotation), proceeding towards the summer solstice, and that the moon in particular stands near the other planets—except the sun—which afford her something of this force.

The force is, further, peculiar to the *ascendens*, if its dominant is in it, if the two stand in aspect with Jupiter and Mercury, if the *ascendens* is free from an aspect of the unlucky planets, and none of them—except the dominant—is in the *ascendens*. For if an unlucky planet is in it, this weakens the aspect of Jupiter and Mercury, so that their dwelling in this force loses its effect.

Laghujâtakam, ii. 6.

IV. The fourth force is called *kâlabala*, *i.e.* the temporal one, which the daily planets exercise in the day, the nightly planets during the night. It is peculiar to Mercury in the *saṁdhi* of its rotation, whilst others maintain that Mercury always has this force, because he stands in the same relation to both day and night.

Further, this force is peculiar to the lucky planets in the white half of the month, and to the unlucky stars in the black half. It is always peculiar to the *ascendens*.

Other astrologers also mention years, months, days, and hours among the conditions, under which the one or other of the four forces is peculiar to a planet.

These, now, are the forces which are calculated for the planets and for the *ascendens*.

If several planets own, each of them, several forces, that one is preponderant which has the most of them. If two planets have the same number of *balas* or forces, that one has the preponderance the magnitude of which is the larger. This kind of magnitude is in the table of

Page 309.

ii. 215, called *naisargikabala*. This is the order of the planets in magnitude or force. Lagh. ii. 7

The years of life which the single planets bestow. Three species of these years.

The middle years which are computed for the planets are of three different species, two of which are computed according to the distance from the *altitudo*. The measures of the first and second species we exhibit in the table (ii. 215).

The *shaḍâya* and *naisargika* are reckoned as the degree of *altitudo*. The first species is computed when the above-mentioned forces of the sun are preponderating over the forces of the moon and the *ascendens* separately.

The second species is computed if the forces of the moon are preponderating over those of the sun and those of the *ascendens*.

The third species is called *aṁśâya*, and is computed if the forces of the *ascendens* are preponderating over those of sun and moon.

The first species.

The computation of the years of the first species for each planet, if it does not stand in the degree of its *altitudo*, is the following:—

You take the distance of the star from the degree of its *altitudo* if this distance is more than six signs, or the difference between this distance and twelve signs, in case it is less than six signs. This number is multiplied by the number of the years, indicated by the table on page 812. Thus the signs sum up to months, the degrees to days, the minutes to day-minutes, and these values are reduced, each sixty minutes to one day, each thirty days to one month, and each twelve months to one year. Lagh. vi. 1.

The computation of these years for the *ascendens* is this:—

Take the distance of the degree of the star from 0° of Aries, one year for each sign, one month for each 2½ degrees, one day for each five minutes, one day-minute for each five seconds. Lagh. vi. 2.

The second species.

The computation of the years of the second species for the planets is the following:—

Take the distance of the star from the degree of its *altitudo* according to the just-mentioned rule (ii. 227). This number is multiplied by the corresponding number of years which is indicated by the table, and the remainder of the computation proceeds in the same way as in the case of the first species.

The computation of this species of years for the *ascendens* is this:—

Take the distance of its degree from 0° of Aries, a year for each *nuhbahr;* months and days, &c., in the same way as in the preceding computation. The number you get is divided by 12, and the remainder being less than 12, represents the number of years of the *ascendens.*

The third species.

The computation of the years of the third species is the same for the planets as for the *ascendens,* and is similar to the computation of the years of the *ascendens* of the second species. It is this:—

Take the distance of the star from 0° of Aries, one year for each *nuhbahr,* multiplying the whole distance by 108. Then the signs sum up to months, the degrees to days, the minutes to day-minutes, the smaller measure being reduced to the larger one. The years are divided by 12, and the remainder which you get by this division is the number of years which you want to find.

Laghujâtakam, ch. vi. 1.

All the years of this kind are called by the common name *âyurdâya.* Before they undergo the equation they are called *madhyamâya,* and after they have passed it they are called *sphuṭâya, i.e.* the *corrected* ones.

The years of life bestowed by the *ascendens.*

The years of the *ascendens* in all three species are *corrected* ones, which do not require an equation by means of two kinds of subtraction, one according to the position of the *ascendens* in the æther, and a second according to its position in relation to the horizon.

To the third kind of years is peculiar an equation by means of an addition, which always proceeds in the same manner. It is this:— Various computations for the duration of life.

If a planet stands in its largest portion or in its house, the *drekkâṇa* of its house or the *drekkâṇa* of its *altitudo*, in the *nuhbahr* of its house or the *nuhbahr* of its *altitudo*, or, at the same time, in most of these positions together, its years will be the double of the middle number of years. But if the planet is in retrograde motion or in its *altitudo*, or in both together, its years are the threefold of the middle number of years. Page 310.

Regarding the equation by means of the subtraction (*vide* ii. 228) according to the first method, we observe that the years of the planet, which is in its *dejectio*, are reduced to two-thirds of them if they are of the first or second species, and to one-half if they belong to the third species. The standing of a planet in the house of its opponent does not impair the number of its years.

The years of a planet which is concealed by the rays of the sun, and thus prevented from exercising an influence, are reduced to one-half in the case of all three species of years. Only Venus and Saturn are excepted, for the fact of their being concealed by the rays of the sun does not in any way decrease the numbers of their years.

As regards the equation by means of subtraction according to the second method, we have already stated in the table (ii. 221, 222) how much is subtracted from the unlucky and lucky stars, when they stand in the houses above the earth. If two or more planets come together in one house, you examine which of them is the larger and stronger one. The subtraction is added to the years of the stronger planet and the remainder is left as it is.

If to the years of a single planet, years of the third

species, two additions from different sides are to be made, only one addition, viz., the longer one, is taken into account. The same is the case when two subtractions are to be made. However, if an addition as well as a subtraction is to be made, you do the one first and then the other, because in this case the sequence is different.

By these methods the years become *adjusted*, and the sum of them is the duration of the life of that man who is born at the moment in question.

The single elements of the computation of the duration of life.

It now remains for us to explain the method of the Hindus regarding the *periods* (*sic*). Life is divided in the above-mentioned three species of years, and immediately after the birth, into years of sun and moon. That one is preponderating which has the most forces and *balas* (*vide* ii. 225); if they equal each other, that one is preponderating which has the greatest *portio* (*sic*) in its place, then the next one, &c. The companion of these years is either the *ascendens* or that planet which stands in the *cardines* with many forces and *portiones*. The several planets come together in the *cardines*, their influence and sequence are determined by their forces and shares. After them follow those planets which stand near the *cardines*, then those which stand in the *inclined* signs, their order being determined in the same way as in the preceding case. Thus becomes known in what part of the whole human life the years of every single planet fall.

However, the single parts of life are not computed exclusively in the years of the one planet, but according to the influences which companion-stars exercise upon it, *i.e.* the planets which stand in aspect with it. For they make it partake in their rule and make it share in their division of the years. A planet which stands in the same sign with the planet ruling over the part of life in question, shares with it one-half. That which stands in the fifth and ninth signs, shares with it one-third. That which stands in the fourth and eighth signs, shares with it one-fourth. That which stands in the seventh sign, shares with it one-seventh. If, therefore, several planets come together in one position, all of them have in common that share which is necessitated by the position in question.

How one planet is affected by the nature of another one.

The method for the computation of the years of such a companionship (if the ruling planet stands in aspect with other planets) is the following:—

Take for the master of the years (*i.e.* that planet which rules over a certain part of the life of a man) one as numerator and one as denominator, *i.e.* $\frac{1}{1}$, one whole, because it rules over the whole. Further, take for each companion (*i.e.* each planet which stands in aspect with the former) only the numerator of its denominator (not the entire fraction). You multiply each denominator by all the numerators and their sum, in which operation the original planet and its fraction are disregarded. Thereby all the fractions are reduced to one and the same denominator. The equal denominator is disregarded. Each numerator is multiplied by the sum of the year and the product divided by the sum of the numerators. The quotient represents the years *kâlambûka* (*kâla-bhâga* ?) of a planet.

As regards the order of the planets, after the question as to the preponderance of their influence has been decided (? *text in disorder*), in so far as each of them exercises its individual influence. In the same way as has already been explained (*vide* ii. 230), the preponderating planets are those standing in the *cardines*, first the strongest, then the less strong, &c., then those standing near the *cardines*, and lastly those standing in the *inclined* signs. Page 311.

Special methods of inquiry of the Hindu astrologers.

From the description given in the preceding pages, the reader learns how the Hindus compute the duration of human life. He learns from the positions of the planets, which they occupy on the origin (*i.e.* at the moment of birth) and at every given moment of life in what way the years of the different planets are distributed over it. To these things Hindu astrologers join certain methods of the astrology of nativities, which other nations do not take into account. They try, *e.g.*, to find out if, at the birth of a human being, its father was present, and conclude that he was absent, if the moon does not stand in aspect with the *ascendens*, or if the sign in which the moon stands is enclosed between the signs of Venus and Mercury, or if Saturn is in the *ascendens*, or if Mars stands in the seventh sign.

Laghujâtakam, ch. iii. 3.

Chap. iii. 4 (?).—Further, they try to find out if the child will attain full age by examining sun and moon. If sun and moon stand in the same sign, and with them an unlucky planet, or if the moon and Jupiter just quit the aspect with the *ascendens*, or if Jupiter just quits the aspect with the united sun and moon, the child will not live to full age.

Further, they examine the station in which the sun stands, in a certain connection with the circumstances of a lamp. If the sign is a *turning* one, the light of the lamp, when it is transferred from one place to the other, moves. If the sign is a *fixed* one, the light of the lamp is motionless; and if the sign is a *double-bodied* one, it moves one time and is motionless another.

Further, they examine in what relation the degrees of the *ascendens* stand to 30. Corresponding to it is the amount of the wick of the lamp which is consumed by burning. If the moon is full moon, the lamp is full of oil; at other times the decrease or increase of the oil corresponds to the wane and increase of the moonlight.

Chap. iv. 5.—From the strongest planet in the *cardines* they draw a conclusion relating to the door of the house, for its direction is identical with the direction of this planet or with the direction of the sign of the *ascendens*, in case there is no planet in the *cardines*.

Chap. iv. 6.—Further, they consider which is the

light-giving body, the sun or moon. If it is the sun, the house will be destroyed. The moon is beneficent, Mars burning, Mercury bow-shaped, Jupiter constant, and Saturn old.

Chap. iv. 7.—If Jupiter stands in its *altitudo* in the tenth sign, the house will consist of two wings or three. If its *indicium* is strong in Arcitenens, the house will have three wings; if it is in the other double-bodied signs, the house will have two wings.

Chap. iv. 8.—In order to find prognostics for the throne and its feet they examine the third sign, its squares and its length from the twelfth till the third signs. If there are unlucky planets in it, either the foot or the side will perish in the way that the unlucky planet prognosticates. If it is Mars, it will be turned; if it is the sun, it will be broken; and if it is Saturn, it will be destroyed by old age.

Chap. iv. 10.—The number of women who will be present in a house corresponds to the number of stars which are in the signs of the *ascendens* and of the moon. Their qualities correspond to the images of these constellations.

Those stars of these constellations which stand above the earth refer to those women who go away from the house, and those which stand under the earth prognosticate the women who will come *to* the house and enter it.

Laghujâtakam, ch. xii. 3, 4.

Further, they inquire into the coming of the spirit of life in man from the dominant of the *drekkâṇa* of the stronger planet of either sun or moon. If Jupiter is the drekkâṇa, it comes from Devaloka; if it is Venus or the moon, the spirit comes from Pitṛiloka; if it is Mars or the sun, the spirit comes from Vṛiścikaloka; and if it is Saturn or Mercury, the spirit comes from Bhṛiguloka.

Likewise they inquire into the departing of the soul after the death of the body, when it departs to that planet which is stronger than the dominant of the drekkâṇa of the sixth or eighth houses, according to a similar rule to that which has just been laid down. Page 412. However, if Jupiter stands in its *altitudo*, in the sixth house, or in the eighth, or in one of the *cardines*, or if the *ascendens* is Pisces, and Jupiter is the strongest of the planets, and if the constellation of the moment of death is the same as that of the moment of birth, in that case the spirit (or soul) is liberated and no longer wanders about.

On comets.

I mention these things in order to show the reader the difference between the astrological methods of our people and those of the Hindus. Their theories and methods regarding aerial and cosmic phenomena are very lengthy and very subtle at the same time. As we have limited ourselves to mentioning, in their astrology of nativities, only the theory of the determination of the length of life, we shall in this department of science limit ourselves to the species of the comets, according to the statements of those among them who are supposed to know the subject thoroughly. The analogy of the comets shall afterwards be extended to other more remote subjects.

The head of the Dragon is called *râhu*, the tail *ketu*. The Hindus seldom speak of the tail, they only use the head. In general, all comets which appear on heaven are also called *ketu*.

Quotations from the *Saṁhitâ* of Varâhamihira.

Varâhamihira says (chap. iii. 7–12):—

"The Head has thirty-three sons who are called *tâmasakîlaka*. They are the different kinds of the comets, there being no difference whether the head extends away from them or not. Their prognostics correspond to their shapes, colours, sizes, and positions. V. 8.—The worst are those which have the shape of a crow or the shape of a beheaded man, those which have the shape of a sword, dagger, bow and arrow. V. 9, 10.—They are always in the neighbourhood of sun and moon, exciting the waters so that they become thick, and exciting the air that it becomes glowing red. They bring the air into such an uproar that the tornadoes tear out the largest trees, that flying pebbles beat against the calves and knees of the people. They change the nature of the time, so that the seasons seem to have changed their places. When unlucky and calamitous events become numerous, such as earthquakes, landslips, burning heat, red glow of heaven, uninterrupted howling of the wild beasts and screaming of the birds, then know that all this comes from the children of the Head. V. 11.—And if these occurrences take place together with an eclipse or the effulgence of a comet, then recognise in this what thou hast predicted, and do not try to gain prognostics from other beings but the Sons of the Head. V. 12.—In the place of the calamity, point towards their (the comets) region, to all eight sides with relation to the body of the sun."

Varâhamihira says in the *Saṁhitâ* (chap. xi. 1–7):—

"I have spoken of the comets not before having exhausted what is in the books of Garga, Parâśara, Asita and Devala, and in the other books, however numerous they may be.

"It is impossible to comprehend their computation, if the reader does not previously acquire the knowledge of their appearing and disappearing, because they are not of one kind, but of many kinds.

"Some are high and distant from the earth, appearing between the stars of the lunar stations. They are called *divya*.

"Others have a middle distance from the earth, appearing between heaven and earth. They are called *ântarikshya*.

"Others are near to the earth, falling down upon the earth, on the mountains, houses and trees.

"Sometimes you see a light falling down to the earth, which people think to be a fire. If it is not fire, it is *keturûpa*, *i.e.* having the shape of a comet.

"Those animals which, when flying in the air, look

like sparks or like fires which remain in the houses of the *piśâcas*, the devils, and of the demons, efflorescent substances and others do not belong to the genus of the comets.

"Therefore, ere you can tell the prognostics of the comets, you must know their nature, for the prognostics
Page 313. are in agreement with it. That category of lights which is in the air, falling on the banners, weapons, houses, trees, on horses and elephants, and that category coming from a Lord which is observed among the stars of the lunar stations—if a phenomenon does not belong to either of these two categories nor to the above-mentioned phantoms, it is a telluric *ketu*.

V. 5.—"Scholars differ among each other regarding the number of the comets. According to some there are 101, according to others 1000. According to Nârada, the sage, they are only one, which appears in a multitude of different forms, always divesting itself of one form and arraying itself in another.

V. 7.—"Their influence lasts for as many months as their appearance lasts days. If the appearance of a comet lasts longer than one and a half month, subtract from it forty-five days. The remainder represents the months of its influence. If the appearance lasts longer than two months, in that case state the years of its influence to be equal to the number of the months of its appearance. The number of comets does not exceed the number 1000."

We give the contents of the following table in order to facilitate the study of the subject, although we have not been able to fill out all the single fields of the diagram, because the manuscript tradition of the single paragraphs of the book either in the original or in the copy which we have at our disposal is corrupt. The author intends by his explanations to confirm the theory of the ancient scholars regarding the two numbers of comets which he mentions on their authority, and he endeavours to complete the number 1000.

Page 314.

Their names.	Their descent.	How many stars each comet has.	Sum total.	Their qualities.	From what direction they appear.	Their prognostics.
...	The children of Kiraṇa.	25	25	Similar to pearls in rivulets of crystal or gold-coloured.	Only in east and west.	It bodes the fighting of the kings with each other.
...	The children of the Fire (?).	25	50	Green, or of the colour of fire or of lac, or of blood, or of the blossom of the tree.	S.E.	It bodes pestilence.
...	The children of Death.	25	75	With crooked tails, their colour inclining to black and dark.	S.	It bodes hunger and pestilence.
...	The children of the Earth.	22	97	Round, radiant, of the colour of water or sesame oil, without tails.	N.E.	It bodes fertility and wealth.
...	The children of the Moon.	3	100	Like roses, or white lotus, or silver, or polished iron or gold. It shines like the moon.	N.	It bodes evil, in consequence of which the world will be turned topsy-turvy.
Brahmadaṇḍa.	Son of Brahman.	1	101	Having three colours and three tails.	In all directions.	It bodes wickedness and destruction.
...	The children of Venus.	84	185	White, large, brilliant.	N. and N.E.	It bodes evil and fear.
Kanaka.	The children of Saturn.	...	...	Radiant, as if they were horns.	In all directions.	It bodes misfortune and death.
Vikaca.	The children of Jupiter.	65	...	Brilliant, white, without any tails.	S.	It bodes destruction and misfortune.

Their names.	Their descent.	How many stars each comet has.	Sum total.	Their qualities.	From what direction they appear.	Their prognostics.
Taskara, *i.e.* the thief.	The children of Mercury.	51	...	White, thin, long. The eye is dazzled by them.	In all directions.	It bodes nisfortune.
Kauṅkuma.	The children of Mars.	60	...	It has three tails, and the colour of the flame.	N.	It bodes the extremity of evil.
Tâmasa-kîlaka.	The children of the Head.	36	...	Of different shapes.	About the sun and moon.	It bodes fire.
Viśvarûpa.	The children of the Fire.	120	...	Of a blazing light like the flame.	...	It bodes evil.
Aruṇa.	The children of the Wind.	77	...	They have no body, that you could see a star in them. Only their rays are united, so that these appear as rivulets. Their colour is reddish or greenish.	...	It bodes general destruction.
			...			
Gaṇaka.	The children of Prajâpati.	204	...	Square comets, eight in appearance, and 304 in number.	...	It bodes much evil and destruction.
Kaṅka.	The children of the Water.	32	...	Its (?) are united, and it is shining like the moon.	...	It bodes much fear and evil in Puṇḍra.
Kabandha.	The children of the Time.	...	...	Like the cut-off head of a man.	...	It bodes much destruction.
...	...	9	...	One in appearance, nine in number. White, large.	In all directions.	It bodes pestilence.

The author (Varâhamihira) had divided the comets into three classes: the *high* ones near the stars; the *flowing* ones near the earth; the *middle* ones in the air, and he mentions each one of the *high* and *middle* classes of them in our table separately.

Page 315. Further quotations from the *Saṁhitâ* of Varâhamihira.

He further says (chap. xi. 42):—

"If the light of the middle class of comets shines on the instruments of the kings, the banners, parasols, fans, and fly-flaps, this bodes destruction to the rulers. If it shines on a house, or tree, or mountain, this bodes destruction to the empire. If it shines on the furniture of the house, its inhabitants will perish. If it shines on the sweepings of the house, its owner will perish."

Further Varâhamihira says (chap. xi. 6):—

"If a shooting-star falls down opposite to the tail of a comet, health and wellbeing cease, the rains lose their beneficial effects, and likewise the trees which are holy to Mahâdeva—there is no use in enumerating them, since their names and their essences are unknown among us Muslims—and the conditions in the realm of Cola, Sita, the Huns and Chinese are troubled."

Further he says (chap. xi. 62):—

"Examine the direction of the tail of the comet, it being indifferent whether the tail hangs down or stands erect or is inclined, and examine the lunar station, the edge of which is touched by it. In that case predict destruction to the place and that its inhabitants will be attacked by armies which will devour them as the peacock devours the snakes.

"From these comets you must except those which bode something good.

"As regards the other comets, you must investigate in what lunar stations they appear, or in what station their tails lie or to what station their tails reach. In that case you must predict destruction to the princes of those countries which are indicated by the lunar stations in question, and other events which are indicated by those stations."

The Jews hold the same opinion regarding the comets as we hold regarding the stone of the Kaʿba (viz. that they all are stones which have fallen down from heaven). According to the same book of Varâhamihira, comets are such beings as have been on account of their merits raised to heaven, whose period of dwelling in heaven has elapsed and who are then redescending to the earth.

The following two tables embody the Hindu theories of the comets:—

Page 316.

TABLE OF COMETS OF THE GREATEST HEIGHT IN THE ÆTHER.

1	Vasâ.	West.	It is flashing and thick, and extends itself from the north.	It bodes death and excessive wealth and fertility.
2	Asthi.	West.	Less bright than the first.	It bodes hunger and pestilence.
3	Śastra.	West.	Similar to the first.	It bodes the fighting of the kings with each other.
4	Kapâlaketu.	East.	Its tail extends till nearly the midst of heaven. It has a smoke-colour and appears on the day of new-moon.	It bodes the abundance of rain, much hunger, illness and death.
5	Raudra.	From the east in Pûrvâshâḍhâ, Pûrvabhâdrapadâ, and Revatî.	With a sharp edge, surrounded by rays. Bronze-coloured. It occupies one-third of heaven.	It bodes the fighting of the kings with each other.
6	Calaketu.	West.	During the first time of its appearance it has a tail as long as a finger towards the south. Then it turns towards the north, till it becomes as long as to the south, the Great Bear and the Pole, then the Falling Eagle. Rising higher and higher it passes round to the south and disappears there.	It ruins the country from the tree Prayâga till Ujjayinî. It ruins the Middle Country, whilst the other regions fare differently. In some places there is pestilence, in others drought, in others war. It is visible between 10–12 months.

TABLE OF COMETS OF THE GREATEST HEIGHT IN THE ÆTHER.—*Continued.*

7	Śvetaketu.	South.	It appears at the beginning of night and is visible during seven days. Its tail extends over one-third of heaven. It is green and passes from the right side to the left.	When these two comets shine and lighten, they bode health and wealth. If the time of their appearance exceeds seven days, two-thirds of the affairs of men and of their lives are ruined. The sword is drawn, revolutions prevail, and there will be misfortune during ten years.
8	Ka.	West.	It appears in the first half of night, its flame is like scattered peas, and remains visible during seven days.	
9	Raśmiketu (?)	The Pleiades.	It has the colour of smoke.	It ruins all human affairs and creates numerous revolutions.
10	Dhruvaketu (?)	Appears between heaven and earth wherever it likes.	It has a big body, it has many sides (?) and colours, and is bright flashing.	It bodes health and peace.

TABLE OF COMETS OF MIDDLE HEIGHT IN THE SKY.

Their number.	Their names.	From what direction they appear.	Description.	Their prognostics.
1	Kumuda.	West.	Namesake of the lotus, which is compared with it. It remains one night, and its tail is directed towards the south.	It bodes lasting fertility and wealth for ten years.
2	Maṇiketu.	West.	It lasts only one quarter of a night. Its tail is straight, white, similar to the milk which spurts out of the breast when it is milked.	It bodes a great number of wild animals and perpetual fertility during four and a half months.
3	Jalaketu.	West.	Flashing. Its tail has a curve from the west side.	It bodes fertility and well-being of the subjects during nine months.
4	Bhavaketu.	East.	It has a tail like that of a lion towards the south.	It is visible only one night. It bodes perpetual fertility and well-being during as many *months* as its appearance last *muhûrtas*. If its colour becomes less bright, it bodes pestilence and death.

Page 317.

TABLE OF COMETS OF MIDDLE HEIGHT IN THE SKY.—*Continued.*

Their number.	Their names.	From what direction they appear.	Description.	Their prognostics.
5	Padmaketu.	South.	It is as white as the white lotus. It lasts one night.	It bodes fertility, joy, and happiness for seven years.
6	Âvarta.	West.	It appears at midnight, bright shining and light gray. Its tail extends from the left to the right.	It bodes wealth during as many months as its appearance lasts *muhûrtas.*
7	Samvarta.	West.	With a tail with a sharp edge. It has the colour of smoke or bronze. It extends over one-third of heaven, and appears during the *saṁdhi.*	The lunar station in which it appears becomes unlucky. It ruins as well that which it bodes, as the lunar station. It bodes the unsheathing of the weapons and the destruction of the kings. Its influence lasts as many years as its appearance lasts *muhûrtas.*

This is the doctrine of the Hindus regarding the comets and their presages. Page 318.

On meteorology.

Only few Hindus occupy themselves in the same way as physical scholars among the ancient Greeks did, with exact scientific researches on the comets and on the nature of the other phenomena of heaven (τὰ μετέωρα), for also in these things they are not able to rid themselves of the doctrines of their theologians. Thus the Matsya-Purâṇa says:—

"There are four rains and four mountains, and their basis is the water. The earth is placed on four elephants, standing in the four cardinal directions, which raise the water by their trunks to make the seeds grow. They sprinkle water in summer and snow in winter. The fog is the servant of the rain, raising itself up to it, and adorning the clouds with the black colour."

With regard to these four elephants the *Book of the Medicine of Elephants* says:—

"Some male elephants excel man in cunning. Therefore it is considered a bad omen if they stand at the head of a herd of them. They are called *manguniha* (?). Some of them develop only one tooth, others three and four; those which belong to the race of the elephants bearing the earth. Men do not oppose them; and if they fall into a trap, they are left to their fate."

The Vâyu-Purâṇa says:—

"The wind and the sun's ray raise the water from the ocean to the sun. If the water were to drop down from the sun, rain would be hot. Therefore the sun hands the water over to the moon, that it should drop down from it as cold water and refresh the world."

As regards the phenomena of the sky, they say, for instance, that the thunder is the roaring of *Airâvata*, *i.e.*, the riding-elephant of Indra the ruler, when it drinks from the pond Mânasa, rutting and roaring with a hoarse voice.

The rainbow (lit. bow of Ḳuzaḥ) is the bow of Indra, as our common people consider it as the bow of Rustam.

Conclusion. We think now that what we have related in this book will be sufficient for any one who wants to converse with the Hindus, and to discuss with them questions of religion, science, or literature, on the very basis of their own civilisation. Therefore we shall finish this treatise, which has already, both by its length and breadth, wearied the reader. We ask God to pardon us for every statement of ours which is not true. We ask Him to help us that we may adhere to that which yields Him satisfaction. We ask Him to lead us to a proper insight into the nature of that which is false and idle, that we may sift it so as to distinguish the chaff from the wheat. All good comes from Him, and it is He who is clement towards His slaves. Praise be to God, the Lord of the worlds, and His blessings be upon the prophet Muḥammad and his whole family!

(Annotations, pages 247–402, and Index, pages 403–431. Sachau's very detailed notes contain references to many of the Greek texts mentioned by Al Biruni as well as to the Indian works. There are also some attempts to clarify the mathematical calculations.)

DATE DUE